Wounded Wisdom

A Buddhist and Christian Response to Evil, Hurt and Harm

Wounded Wisdom

A Buddhist and Christian Response to Evil, Hurt and Harm

Ross Thompson

BOOKS

Winchester, UK
Washington, USA

First published by O-Books, 2011
O-Books is an imprint of John Hunt Publishing Ltd., Laurel House, Station Approach,
Alresford, Hants, SO24 9JH, UK
office1@o-books.net
www.o-books.com

For distributor details and how to order please visit the 'Ordering' section on our website.

ISBN: 978 1 84694 597 7

A CIP catalogue record for this book is available from the British Library.

Design: Stuart Davies

Printed in the UK by CPI Antony Rowe
Printed in the USA by Offset Paperback Mfrs, Inc

CONTENTS

CONTENTS

What we are today comes from our thoughts of yesterday, and our present thoughts build our life of tomorrow: our life is the creation of our mind. If one speaks or acts with a pure mind, joy follows one as one's own shadow... 'He insulted me, he hurt me, he defeated me, he robbed me.' Those who think not such thoughts will be free from hate. For hatred is not conquered by hate: hate is conquered by love. This is a law eternal.

Dhammapada 1.2–5.

The wolf shall live with the lamb,
the leopard shall lie down with the kid,
the calf and the lion and the fatling together,
and a little child shall lead them.
The cow and the bear shall graze,
their young shall lie down together;
and the lion shall eat straw like the ox.
The nursing child shall play over the hole of the asp,
and the weaned child shall put its hand on the adder's den.
They will not hurt or destroy
on all my holy mountain;
for the earth will be full of the knowledge of the Lord
as the waters cover the sea

Isaiah 11.6–9

Become that which you were before you were, but with the memory and understanding of what you have become.

Sufi Wish

I am sending you out like sheep into the midst of wolves; so be wise as serpents and innocent as doves.

Matthew 10.16

Introduction

The urge to write this book has emerged from my own search for better ways of responding to hurt than have been mine in the past. In midlife, through a mixture of bad experience and good counseling and meditation, I have become increasingly aware of many ways I am imprisoned by bad patterns learned in childhood. In my innocence, those were the best responses I could manage then, but they turned hurt into some form of harm, either to myself or to others or both. In my innocence, I sinned.

But this book is not about my sin and my innocence, but everyone's. A lot of everyone's life involves hurt and harm. And perhaps *the* main issue for everyone is how, as the hurt people we all are, not to be harmed and harm in turn. This is an urgent issue for a world that from the twentieth century onward has become increasingly embroiled in more and more conflicts that are regarded, by those who wage them, as battles of good against evil. Whether the 'good' is God or the Leader or Communism or Islam or Freedom or Justice, and wherever the ever fluid frontiers of the 'axis of evil' have been fixed, most such conflicts have been responses to perceived evil that have resulted in colossal actual harm. Though war has always been with our species, we have not always fought it on this basis, as we nearly always do now.

We are becoming aware, too, that the way we treat our environment represents, all too often, deep harm to the earth, of a kind that many are prepared to call evil. That too is a new way of understanding our relation to the world in which we live. At least, it is new for us in the West; I am told that many so-called primitive societies have long been careful not to harm the spirits of the animals and plants they need to use to survive. In this respect we are just beginning, perhaps, to catch up with them intellectually and spiritually.

Ecologically, we need to learn how to make our home on the earth without harming it, and ultimately harming and perhaps destroying the human species through destroying its home. (The human species, though 'tougher' than many of those fragile species that inhabit diminishing fringes of our planet, is certainly less tough than those many species that have endured for hundreds of times longer than we have: dragonflies, mosses, woodlice, bacteria…) Politically we are entering an unprecedented period when not just most nations, but probably most reasonably wealthy organizations that want them, will be able to have nuclear weapons and hence the possibility of doing whatever harm they desire to their fellow humans and the earth. So unless we can learn the art of what I call 'wounded wisdom' – the ability, in a world that has done us much hurt and considerable harm, of not harming, not even having an ego that is shaped by harm – we are doomed.

Innocence – Wounded and Wily

Though the huge ecological and political agendas just cited are there in the background of this book, the focus has to be on personal transformation. However hard we try, we cannot by force create a world where no hurt and harm happens. For the Buddha, suffering, *dukkha,* is the first elemental fact about the world; for Christians, harming – often called 'sin' – is our original and inevitable condition. But neither Gautama Buddha nor Jesus of Nazareth taught an ethic of resignation. They did not say that because suffering and harm are inevitable we should not try to overcome them; on the contrary, they are, because of their universality, the things we cannot avoid coming up against, in our world and in ourselves. But the overcoming is, for them both, full of paradox; both affirmed that we cannot overcome evil by force, harm by harm.

This book is about how we deal with hurt and harm in

ourselves without creating further harm for ourselves and others. There are other books already written and many waiting to be written that explore the overcoming of harm through social structures of justice. But that is not my focus in this book. If I touch on issues of justice, it is mainly in terms of looking at the personal quality of fairness – called *dikaiosyne* by the ancient Greeks and by St. Paul – that makes for justice in society.

In the days when I was a priest and took funerals, I was often dismayed when the main thing that was cited in favor of the deceased was that 'she never did anyone any harm.' I used to feel rather sad that there was no positive *good* that the person had done. In the same way, in my then Christian pride I looked down on Buddhist (and Hindu) *ahimsa* – not-harming – from the vantage point of a morally superior Christian ideal of love, which involved actively doing good. But bad things as well as good have been done in the name of 'love.' A dominant mother can tyrannize a child with her possessive loving attention. Children have been separated from aboriginal parents and locked away in orphanages, and mentally challenged adults confined to asylums, in the name of giving them love and care. We do need love, but love needs to be purified of all egocentric self-righteousness and self-investment, so as to become a love without hurt or harm. Conversely if we are truly free from the mechanisms in us that convert hurt to harm, we will not be passive non-entities that do neither harm nor good; we will be a liberated and liberating power for good. For the nature that has been side-tracked into the complex byways of self-defense and retaliation will come home to shine in its own divine light. Or so this book will argue.

The word 'wounded' in the title refers to the inevitable fact that we all carry wounds from the past. 'Wisdom' suggests that there are wise and foolish ways of responding to the fact. And the subtitle suggests that whether we are wise or foolish hinges on our response to the question of what should we do with evil, hurt and harm as I shall shortly define them. I try to show how evil, hurt and harm are things we can react to, negatively, or work with, creatively. Wisdom lies in working well with our wounds.

Hurt, Wounds, Harm and Evil

I have used world like 'hurt,' 'wound,' 'harm,' and 'evil' with a sense of progression that I have not explained. Basically in this book *hurt* means the bare pain, or any incidence of suffering, considered just as an experience. A *wound* is the trace which that pain leaves in our bodies or minds or both. When the knife cuts our hand, we have no choice as to whether it will bleed, whether it will need stitches, and so on – though of course we can influence the speed with which it heals by proper medical and psychological attention.

Harm denotes the damage done to us – as the unity of body and mind we are – by hurts and wounds. We all know that hurts and wounds do not necessarily harm us. The pain of the operation or the dental treatment may be what is needed to prevent harm. More subtly the painful wound of bereavement may be what is needed to open the way to new life beyond the loss; the wound of redundancy or dismissal or prison what is needed to write in our souls the way to a more fulfilling life; the pain of remorse part of the path to reconciliation; the pain of winter the only way to the sudden abundance of spring.

Yet time and again we see hurt only as harmful. And that is a self-fulfilling prophecy. If we experience pain as only and inevitably harmful, harm it will do, through blame and counter-attack, through the labyrinthine pathways of self-harm, or through the subtle loss of vitality and reality that arises from denial.

But a wound may be intended not to do us good – as with the dentist – but to do us harm. When hurts are inflicted solely to do harm and not good, we begin to want to speak of evil. A person who flies into a rage and says hurtful things to let off steam may be acting wrongly, or as Buddhists would say, unskillfully. But he is not evil in the same way as a man who deliberately plans the most hurtful things to say to or about a colleague in order to undermine their confidence in their work and lead to their dismissal. In the latter case something is going on, I would argue, that in kind though not in scale is in continuity with the planned horrors of genocide. It merits the term 'evil.'

There is another term that I do not refer to much, but might have – that is 'crime.' A crime is obviously an act that breaks the law. I do not have much to say about it, because though some harms and some evils are crimes, most are not. The perpetrators of genocide are often quick to point out that they are obeying the law. Though there is something much more 'evil' about the man who systematically derides his colleague, than about a hungry boy who steals a loaf of bread, the man is probably acting quite legally, while the boy is committing a crime. We are tempted to speak of genocide and the like as 'war crimes,' or 'crimes against humanity,' but there seems to me to be something very problematic about the idea of a crime done in obedience to the laws of the state that normally defines what is criminal or legal.

So for the most part I will leave the question of 'crime' out of the picture, and discuss such atrocities as 'evil' acts. Whether laws might or could or should make what is criminal coincide with what is evil is a huge matter for debate. For myself, I think the question of law is largely separate from the question of evil, and is largely concerned with dealing with harm. A society that outlawed 'ordinary' evil like that of the man who derides his colleague would have to outlaw so much else that it would create more evil rather than less, since it would restrict people in harmful ways as well as good. We shall come back to consider the way in which zeal for total safety can be very dangerous, the quest to eliminate evil can be a kind of evil, and the hunger for absolute purity can contaminate us.

But the question of how we should deal politically and legally with evil is not my main focus; it is touched on a little in Chapter 9, but only after we have learned enough from ordinary questions of harm to apply what we have learned to the special case of crime. This book is not about what *they* (the police, the politicians, the judges and so forth) should do about harm and evil, but about what *we* – you and I – can do.

So most of this book concerns very ordinary experience. There can be nobody who has not experienced hurt and harm, and blame, shame and the tendency to disclaim bad things; or who has not laughed, or sensed the tragedy of life, or felt remorse, or forgiveness or the need of it, or known at least some times of meditative stillness and beauty. These are the experiences at the core of the book. But at times, especially when exploring 'evil,' I have felt the need to look at extreme cases like child abuse and the Nazi Holocaust, even though thankfully I have no personal experience of these things. Some may find this disturbing, but a great many people have been abused in some way, or know someone who has abused or been abused. And a great many people in the world have experienced something like the Holocaust, and all of us know that atrocities are a recurrent aspect of human life on earth, much as we would wish otherwise. We all have to deal with such things, and it has felt important not to push such matters beyond the pale of language and thought, but to treat them in continuity with the much smaller, but manifest 'evils' of our day to day existence.

Outline

The book falls into two halves, a negative half and a slightly longer positive one. The first examines negative ways of dealing with hurt, harm and evil. Chapters 1–3 look at ways in which we turn hurt and wounds into harm to others and ourselves, by the mechanisms of blame, shame and distancing or what I call disclaiming. These negative responses are often unconscious and automatic, a matter of emotion generating harmful ideas about others and ourselves. However, though blame, shame and disclaimer are toxic, they are easily confused with positive qualities: a sense of responsibility, the process of remorse, and the need for detachment. Chapters 4 and 5 explore how harm in turn can become what we call 'evil.' Chapter 4 looks at notions of evil as something real, existing somehow 'out there,' while Chapter 5 looks at notions of evil as some kind of delusion or distortion of reality, which is basically good in itself. The latter, I shall argue, provides the better basis for a creative response.

The resources for a better response are the subject of Part 2. The Introduction to this part examines Jesus' teachings about 'becoming as children' and 'wily innocence,' notions which I argue to be crucial to any wise response. Chapter 6 looks at the traditions of tragedy and comedy as approaches to the universal human condition – traditions that come to us primarily from classical Greece, though tragic and comic sensibilities are probably universally human. Between them they inculcate a notion of responsibility without blaming. Chapter 7 examines the interpersonal processes of remorse and forgiveness, about which Christian faith has much to say, though again, of course, these processes are universal. The other-centered process of remorse is sharply distinguished from the self-centered, self-conscious feelings of guilt and shame. Chapter 8 turns to the interior search for ways of responding well to experience, including experience of hurt; here the Buddhist arts of mindfulness and meditation will prove central. Again, the liberating detachment that focused mindfulness induces is sharply contrasted with the absent-minded unawareness that goes with disclaiming our part in hurt and harm. Chapter 9 asks the question whether we should hope for a state beyond 'evil' and harm, and beyond even the memory of hurt. After exploring how we heal from physical wounds, the chapter questions the rationale that leads us to build systems of retributive punishment, and argues for and illustrates cases of an alternative 'healing' approach to justice. This chapter ends with the hope that all harm will one day be 'water under the bridge.' Finally Chapter 10 draws the threads together into a Buddhist Christian 'Ninefold Way' related closely to the Buddhist Eightfold Way, the eight Beatitudes of Jesus, and the nine fruits of the Spirit described by St. Paul. The book ends by affirming that, come what may in terms of society and suffering, a wise and wily innocence is possible in the here and now.

Each chapter is introduced by a poem of my own which will be referred to at some point, and concludes with a summary of the argument.

The Buddhist Christian Approach

The book is unrepentantly eclectic in its use of resources. Pagan Greek, Christian and Buddhist traditions jostle alongside each other as I try to piece together a valid way with harm. Some readers may be led to wonder what I am. Am I a Buddhist sheep in Christian wolf's clothing, perhaps, a fundamentally Buddhist mindset playing fast and loose with Christian ideas?

I hope not. I believe that it is possible to hold a position with integrity that is both Buddhist and Christian, enabling a kind of 'trialogue' of mutual questioning between the two traditions, and between both of them and contemporary understandings of life. I have argued the case for this in my previous book, *Buddhist Christianity* (2010), where I also explain why such an approach has become personally inevitable for me as in my struggle with hurts, harms and evils of my own. I have only two comments to add to that now.

The first is to echo Don Cupitt's suggestion that

> we need to become more Buddhist in outlook... Our religion will be a collection of personal religious skills and habits,

> which we will acquire by criticizing our values, by training our attention and our feelings, and by learning how to live our own transient lives. (2010, p. 24)

Religion's main benefit to humanity is surely to inculcate good habits and skills, enabling us to re-evaluate the values by which we live, to train our attention and feelings and so live better lives. The theology I try to practice is 'practical theology' which sees doctrinal traditions as a resource for theological reflection to achieve these goals. Buddhism has always known that doctrines and dogmas exist only as fingers pointing to the 'moon' of the practices by which we become enlightened. We should not worship the finger but what it points to. So this book looks at Buddhism and Christianity – along with other more pagan traditions of comedy and tragedy – in order to reflect on our experience of bad responses to evil, hurt and harm, and in their light find our way toward better practice.

We should not get too worried by the obviously big differences between the Buddhist and Christian 'fingers,' if the practice they point to is relatively similar. This brings me to my second additional comment. Suppose we were to develop two different scientific theories about the nature of matter. The axioms, the models, the equations of each are completely different and resist translation into the terms of the other. They look like rivals, except that they all make the same predictions, and the experiments that prove the one prove the other too. We would have to look for a deep likeness, a further analogy that contained both. This is how it seems to be between Christianity and Buddhism. The conceptual frameworks, the starting points, the goals, the techniques seem entirely different, but in practice the ethical outcomes seem similar, and what counts as a good life for one is remarkably similar to what counts in the other. And this not because all religions have the same ethics. They don't. But there is a core approach that seems to me to unite

Buddhism and Christianity in particular among the world faiths, which has to do with the way we are recommended to respond to hurt, harm and evil. (That is not to say that Buddhism and Christianity have always been better than those of other faiths at following those recommendations; Christian crusades and Buddhist warrior-monks suggest the contrary!)

Now in science there are cases where apparent differences have been successfully traced back to a unifying theory. In Quantum Physics, for example, we can describe fundamental reality in terms of particle and wave. But the mathematical expression of the theory holds both aspects seamlessly together such that quantum theory commits us to both descriptions at once. Though we cannot imagine how they fit together, at a conceptual mathematical level they do. My hunch is that Buddhism and Christianity have a deep underlying kinship of the same kind. We could even speculate that Buddhism has a rather 'wavelike' approach that focuses on spiritual movement and denies anything solid and continuous, while Christianity has inherited from the Greeks a more focused, as it were 'particle-like' way of describing things. We can see things from a Buddhist or a Christian perspective, but not both at once; but 'reality' – whatever it is – must be such that both perspectives are valid, and this invites further attempts to describe it.

Be that as it may, I am convinced that both faiths have led me to deep truth and life which I cannot deny. I also believe that coherence matters for any faith that has a message, any faith that invites us to *metanoia* or renewal of understanding and intent – as both Buddhism and Christianity clearly do. That means I am committed to trying to build a coherent way of affirming both Buddhism and Christianity. In the absence of any spiritual equivalent of the mathematics that underlies Quantum Physics, I may be bound to fail, or at best succeed only partially. But I can but try.

In *Buddhist Christianity* I tried to make a beginning of this task. But this book has a different agenda. It looks first at what is deeply problematic in the way we normally respond to hurt, harm and evil, and then looks at Buddhism and Christianity, among other traditions, for a better way. Building a coherent Buddhist Christianity is not the task of this book. All the same, if Buddhism and Christianity can come together and offer mutually illuminating approaches to this problem – if Buddhism and Christianity between them can help us in this practical way better than each can on its own – then it will obviously suggest that Buddhist Christianity is worth looking at.

Acknowledgements

I must thank those who commented critically, helpfully and encouragingly on the early essay that was the seed from which this book grew: especially James Alison, and colleagues at two 'work in progress' sessions at the British and Irish Association for Practical Theology. I am also grateful to friends at the Buddhist inspired Centre for World Peace on Holy Island, Arran, for providing space and teaching for the practices of meditation that have clarified and undergirded much of the aim of this book. And to John Hunt and Trevor Greenfield at O-Books for taking this book on and helping it through to completion.

As noted, my writing of *Buddhist Christianity* has been important in establishing the basis for this one, and I have yet to put in print my thanks to those who read, commented on and commended that book, including Gavin D'Costa, Paul Knitter, Rose Drew, Perry Schmidt-Leukel, Ruben Habito and Caroline Brazier. Reading for this book has been necessarily wide-ranging, and authors who have written good books I should have read, but which have not made it into my bibliography, must forgive me. But there are certain authors who stand out as decisive influences on this book, notably James Alison, Walter Wink, Angela West, Donald Kalsched, Miroslav Volf, Carla Van Raay and Thich Nhat Hanh.

I owe thanks to Beth Stoddart (now Wright) for Figure 1; and above all to Judith, my wife, who has carefully read draughts of this book and suggested many improvements, and borne with the many times when my focus was drawn into the writing, and far from many urgent practicalities…

Ross Thompson, August 2010

www.holydust.org; rosskathompson@aol.com

Part I

Hurt, Harm and Evil: How Do They Arise?

Faced with hurt, we can go on the attack and blame someone, we can internalize it into some kind of self-harm, or we can deny its existence or its importance to us. All three ways avoid facing the hurt simply as hurt. The hurt becomes the harm *you* did, or the unpleasant kind of thing *I* deserve, or *their* problem (not mine). The hurt is shifted into second, first or third person perspective. It ceases to be a mere hurt that passes, and becomes something more serious, a something that 'belongs' to someone, a reality in its own right that is liable to persist: not just a hurt, or even just a wound, but a harm. The three ways are interdependent: if I blame you, I want you to feel ashamed, and I disclaim responsibility myself.

In the Gospel Passion narratives we see all three kinds of response. Caiaphas and the high priests pour huge blame on Jesus as a threat to their religious system. He becomes the scapegoat for the sins of all: as Caiaphas is described as saying, it is 'expedient for one man to die on behalf of the people' (John 18.14). In the suicide of Judas following his betrayal of Jesus, and in the tears of Peter following his disowning of him, we encounter deep shame, purer perhaps in Judas' case where the desire for the earth to swallow him up becomes literal. In Pilate's washing of his hands, and also Peter's disowning, we find typical disclaimer: this crucifixion... this man... is nothing to do with me.

In Jesus' own response to his suffering we see none of these responses. Jesus does not deride or accuse his persecutors. (Though the Gospels have been argued to show an increasingly accusatory tone against 'the Jews' for allegedly wanting Jesus crucified, significantly none of this blame is placed on Jesus' lips at this most crucial juncture.) But nor does he recoil in shame. And he does not (except possibly in John's Gospel) withdraw to a point of glorious invulnerability above his sufferings; on the contrary Matthew and Mark emphasize his despair: 'My God, why have you forsaken me?' On the whole, Jesus seems to receive hurt just as hurt, without either denying it or transmuting it into somebody's harm. Chapter 8 will explore this kind of response further.

The first three chapters will explore how hurt becomes somebody's harm, through blame, shame and disclaimer respectively. Chapters 4 and 5 will look at the further step, whereby some people's harm becomes in our perceptions a more global and menacing and perhaps impersonal evil. These chapters will examine how we think of and feel and experience hurt and harm, and why we are led to speak of evil. Chapter 4 will look at the ways of saying these things really are part of 'how it is' in this world of ours – or to put it crudely and chauvinistically, 'life's a bitch.' Chapter 5 will look at different ways of seeing evil as what we make of a world that is fundamentally all good, though not all painless; or according to another familiar phrase, 'life is what you make it'.

Chapter 1

'You Hurt Me': Blame

Bitter, so bitter: the brother or sister's gift,
shining more bright in a parent's pleased eye
than your own. One so like you
but better, were better never
born.
            So do him now out of that bright
being that only shadows yours. Easier said
than done for one not used
to making lethal the twist of knife
through flesh so same and like
as to sicken.
            Then hide! Your own life
now makes its home in shadow just the same. Easier said
than done in a world so fresh
to man slaughter, that blood's untamed
cry can still clutch your bloody heart.
            I never did it sir,
never!
No one ever
did it now in a world grown
suddenly so sullen and shadowful.

Cain (based on Genesis 4.1–16)

Childhood's Pattern

He started it.

It was her fault.

He hurt me first

Don't blame me.

I never did it.

Who cannot remember saying such things, over and again, as a child? Or who cannot recall the vehement anger with which children make such assertions. This is not always because they believe they are true, more a matter of the absolute importance of deflecting blame from themselves. The Bible describes this kind of deflection amusingly in the story of Adam and Eve, where Adam blames Eve for tempting him to eat the forbidden fruit, and Eve blames the snake (Gen. 3.8–13). It is apparent too in the story of Cain and his murder of his brother Abel (the basis of my poem just quoted), though here this is achieved by disclaimer – 'Am I my brother's keeper?' (4.9) – rather than shifting blame to someone else.

No doubt children learn such responses from adults ever zealous to find out who should be reprimanded when things go wrong. But learn it children do, with a vengeance! From the anarchic playfulness of early childhood, at sometime around age 5 or 6 (according to the researches of Lawrence Kohlberg (1984)) children seem to enter a rigid and unforgiving moral universe, where rules are absolute and immutable, and apology and forgiveness very hard to countenance. Probably many of us remember – as children and later as parents – the hard struggle of a child to admit blame and say sorry, and the equally hard struggle to forgive another child who has hurt him, even if accidentally.

Of course adults are probably essentially no different, just more subtle in the important art of blaming and deflecting blame. Someone told me of a case where someone who had been burned when sipping a cup of coffee too soon succeeded in getting compensation from the café, because it had failed to warn him that the coffee might be hot! (This may be apocryphal, but it rings uncomfortably true...) Even packets of peanuts now carry a warning that 'the contents may contain nuts' lest the company be blamed for the results of a nut allergy – so much has blame and the fear of blame come to rule our world! Many have commented on the way our 'culture of blame' has made many fearful of doing anything bold that might be criticized (e.g. Pearn, 1998; Centner, 2008). Yet accountability to one another, so emphasized in our society, is clearly not something we should simply abandon. This chapter will explore whether we can have the positive features of accountability without the intimidating rule of blame.

Turning Hurt into Harm

When we are hurt, it is natural to want to know why – to explain the hurt. Knowing why we hurt can turn hurt to healing. My head hurts in the morning because I drank too much last night – so there is a way to ensure my head does not hurt like that in future mornings. I have these hurts because of such and such a disease. Thus diagnosed, I can explore what might heal me.

But very often I want to go a step further than diagnosis or explanation. It is this further step that leads from explanation to blame. My head hurts – I think – because my friend encouraged me to drink too much. I have this hurt because the doctor diagnosed my disease wrongly. Then I get rightfully or wrongfully angry. When I say, 'I blame you,' I am not just saying, 'I think you helped cause my hurt.' I am seeing my hurt as a harm, a violation done to me by you. You and I become, at least in the context of this alleged harm, enemies, opposed forces. The hurt becomes an issue between us. It may just be a passing issue, or it may loom larger and become something for which I require an apology before friendship or good relations are restored. I may require from the doctor – and in our time am increasingly likely to require – some kind of compensation for the mistake. If this does not happen the other may become someone I speak badly of, whose reputation I am determined to undermine. The friendship may end because I come to see my friend as a reckless guy who undermines my moral restraint. He has not just caused my head to hurt; he has caused me harm, he is harmful, he is a bad sort of person. So it is that through blame a hurt can affect – and perhaps infect – our whole perception.

Blame in this sense is an additional hurt I have to bear, over and above the original hurt. It is a specific hurt turned into a much wider harm – harm to myself, certainly, and to my relationship with the other, as anger turns to bitterness, and often harm to another as I exact retribution on the one I blame.

In this way, blame doubles our distress. If we cling to our blame, we get stuck in being the victim, and as theologian Miroslav Volf notes (2008, p. 11), the abuser triumphs twice. Volf describes how, while he felt vengeful and angry about the Yugoslavian officer who had savagely interrogated him, the officer as it were stayed in the living room of his soul. He continued to dominate his every thought and feeling. His first victory had taken place when by his superior power, cunning and ruthlessness he made his victim confused and helpless in his hands. But while the victim's rage continued, the officer continued to inhabit and control his mind, winning a second victory, more protracted than the first. (Sometimes that second victory makes us more angry still, entering a vicious circle of self-reinforcing bitterness; we get bitter about being bitter.)

We are all too familiar with the cycles of retribution in which people blame others for their hurts, and do them retaliatory harm. Those others then seek to 'get their own back' or else blame and harm other people in turn. In many societies vendetta is a solemn duty, and it is often escalatory, demanding fivefold or tenfold harm in return for a harm received. Sometimes this chain reaction runs down the social hierarchy: proverbially, the boss blames and punishes the man who works for him. He finds something to blame his secretary for. She goes home and rows with her husband. He takes it out on his child. The child kicks the cat. And so on.

This vengeance may not be very specific, singling out the people who actually caused and received the hurt. Harm to any of 'one's own kind' – one's kin, one's tribe, one's nation – is felt as harm to oneself, to be repaid by harm to any one of the 'other' kinship group, or tribe, or nation. Blame has a leaky, infectious character, so different from the precise analysis of specifics required in proper explanation and accountability. Where accountability traces ills – naively perhaps – to individual agents, blame attaches more readily to groups and kinds of people. It divides society dangerously into a good 'us' and a wicked 'them.' Blame is of course not the sole cause of social division and oppression and global violence, but it is surely a major catalyst. So this chapter will look at why blame is such a compelling force, and perhaps the most obvious of the ways in which hurt is turned to harm.

At the same time, few would deny that society needs to hold people to account for their deeds. Suing the council for the pavement stone I trip up on may be extreme, but the council ought not to get away with spending none of my taxes on the safety of the pavement. The first part of what follows will look at what makes for good accountability, but will also see the limits of this notion because causes are generally more complex than discussions of accountability can allow for. The chapter will then look at why we are so keen not just on explaining but on blaming, the sinister lengths to which blame has gone in some societies, and its dangerously growing ascendancy at our present historical moment. It will trace the underlying causes of our desire to blame, and ask whether it would be possible to retain what is positive about personal accountability in a world view that did not contain blame.

Accountability and Its Limits

The extraordinary attraction of the 'whodunit' genre of novels and films shows how much we relish the process of finding out who is to blame for a crime. A person is found dead on their bedroom floor with a knife in their neck. It is reasonable – but also compelling – to want to find out who is to blame. Usually in this genre there are obvious suspects who immediately get arrested and questioned or otherwise enter a cloud of suspicion. But the detective hero discovers subtleties in the picture that point elsewhere; a number of others enter the field of suspicion, and we try to work out for ourselves who is the 'real' culprit. Finally – usually against all our intuitions – this culprit is exposed, and at the climactic moment confesses or is arrested or commits suicide – in one way or another satisfying our deep need to see those who are truly to blame humiliated and punished.

In the face of large scale hurt we often say angrily, 'Someone's got to pay for this!' It is very important for society that some people get punished – sometimes, one feels, more important than that the right people get called to account. Disasters like train crashes or tsunamis are often followed by enquiries to find who is to blame; or in the case of natural disasters, who through their negligence caused more life to be lost, more suffering incurred, than otherwise might have been. We want, rightly, things to go better next time, and if we know who or what is to blame, we know who or what to change. So we are always inventing new procedures to make the world safer. Again, this is all to the good, up to a point, but Chapter 3 will argue that this process has gone to dangerous limits. And the isolation of blamable individuals often involves a crude simplification, an impoverishment of the complexity of the world we live in.

The Web of Causes

Imagine this example. A man is driving along at 29 miles an hour (just under the speed limit) on a wet and windy night at about midnight. Unknown to him, a parked car is leaking oil onto the road. Another car is parked on the zigzag lines near a pedestrian crossing in the center of town, where the lights have failed. A boy of nine rushes out onto the crossing. The man sees him too late, screeches on the brakes, skids on the oil and hits the boy. The boy survives, but will never walk again.

We could describe this justly as a terrible accident, meaning something caused by an unfortunate coincidence of many factors. But when we ask who is to blame, we need to single out one of these factors, a human one whom we can punish, or at least from whom recompense can be demanded. Who should this be? The man, perhaps? Though he was under the speed limit, perhaps he should have allowed for the bad weather conditions and been even slower. Perhaps he was not as alert as he should have been. The boy? Though it was a crossing, perhaps he should have seen the lights were not working and been more careful. His parents? What were they doing letting him out so late at night? The man who let his petrol leak? The man who parked on the lines obscuring the edge of the crossing? The maintenance team for neglecting the crossing lights?

The example is fictional, though there must be many factual cases quite like it, in which the need for legal clarity about responsibility and blame is in tension with the complexity of causes actually involved.

But let us take a very different, factual and political controversy that has dominated the world for several years now, and will no doubt continue to be debated for many years to come. The Iraqis have suffered huge hugely in the recent wars and the instability that followed them. Some 100,000 individuals are estimated to have been killed, including hundreds of Western soldiers. Who is to blame?

At the time of writing Tony Blair and the other ministers in the Labour Government that decided to go to war have given their testimony to an enquiry, with varying degrees of impenitence. Are they to blame, along with George Bush, for the decisions that led to war? Of course, in a sense they are because without those decisions the war would not have taken place. But if others had been in government would the decisions have been different? Certainly the Conservatives at the time were even more belligerent, and it could be argued that the politicians were only figureheads for a tide of public opinion that wanted security and retaliation after the attack on the Twin Towers in New York by Al Qaeda. The tide of public opinion has since changed and left the leaders rather stranded. So would it be fairer to pin the blame on the American and English people? Or on Bin Laden and Al Qaeda, who made them justly incensed? Or Saddam Hussein for brutally perpetuating the domination of Shiites and Kurds by the Sunni minority, laying in genocide against his own people the foundations of the bitter strife that ensued after his fall? But was the regime of Saddam Hussein himself in a sense the consequence of Western colonialism, which had patched together a state out of disparate peoples, and created deep resentments in a Muslim population humiliated by the imperialism of Christian nations?

Once we begin to think in terms of this vast web of interacting causes, it can come to seem irrelevant to ask which particular strand of the web caught the fly. We encounter the complexity of the whole causal sweep of history, in which the very need to blame and retaliate seems to generate a complexity of interacting factors for which no individual is to blame.

Should we then see the calamity in Iraq as a kind of inevitable human disaster – rather like the Tsunami, but sweeping humans and their decisions into its web of causes? Or as an epic conflict precipitated by the decisions of good and evil individuals? And if the former, what are we to say about individual accountability? Are trials for war crimes and enquiries into responsibility for war – not to mention trials for crimes in general – fundamentally misconceived? Should we be trying to isolate bits of web that catch particular flies? Or should we be looking for the spider who wove the web – which is, perhaps, the very tendency to blame and to define the wicked and blamable other? Should we focus on painstaking complex explanation, and cast the baby of accountability out with the bath water of blame?

Explaining and Blaming

In Greek the words 'blame' and 'cause' are the same: *aition*. Science arose in Greece as the search for the ultimate cause of the universe, in the sense of who or what is to blame for it. It is significant that science arose in the very culture that also produced tragedy. At the heart of many Greek tragedies, as the French philosopher René Girard has pointed out (2005), is a fierce argument as to which of the characters is to blame. With a comparable obsession, Greek scientists were determined to find out which of the cosmic 'players' (earth, air, fire, water, atoms, gods, or their more subtle modern variants) was 'responsible' for the way the world is.

A fragment from one of the earliest of these philosophers, Anaximander (c610BC–c546BC) describes the world as a continuing cycle of retribution. Each thing comes into being and ceases to be 'according to necessity; for they pay penalty and retribution to each other for their injustice according to the ordering of time,' (Kirk, 1983, p. 118). Later another philosopher, Heraclitus (c535BCE–475BCE) famously declared that the 'sun will not overstep his measures; otherwise the Furies, ministers of Justice, will find him out,' (p. 201). So for Heraclitus, the causality that keeps the sun in its course is a matter of justice. A similar connection underlies the Hebrew Psalm 19, in which the Law of the Lord both causes the sun to run its course and governs human morality.

But of course we have since come to draw a big distinction

between scientific explanation and issues of justice and blame. If we are looking for an explanation of the boy's death – say at a post-mortem – all the factors just listed will need mention. But a judge assessing a claim will need to find one person to pay out. In fact the idea of an accident in which neither party is to blame is ruled out, at least in British law: *someone's* got to pay!

Moreover a journalist wanting an article to catch the eye is almost certain to home in on one of the many causes. *'Wealthy demon driver cripples young innocent...'* or *'Council's carelessness leaves boy unable to walk...'* or *'Single parent neglect has horrific results for son'* will win the day by keying into readers' favorite agendas as to who is to blame for everything (the rich... government...the immoral underclass...). Read any newspaper and you will be able to discern the favored narratives of blame-worthiness which that paper both courts and sustains. *'Boy crippled owing to various contributory factors'* would be more accurate, but would not sell the paper...

The Persistence of the Demons

We are an age that prides itself on its scientific approach, yet in many ways our legal system and our newspapers have more influence than science. Abstractly perhaps we acknowledge that science reveals a world disenchanted of its blameworthy demons and its exalted gods, a world of complex continuous impersonal webs of causal processes operating both between people and deep within the recesses of their psyches. We no longer blame witches or angry gods for our crop failures. But the world we believe in still includes blameworthy 'demons' in the form of individuals who must be named and shamed – be they invasive government officials, bankers with big bonuses or the drug dealers of the 'underclass'; be they the proponents of irreligious permissiveness or Dawkins' dark religious 'meme' (significantly personalized) terrorizing us all out of rational humanity.

This fact became very clear in the terrible example that

emerged at the time of writing: the brutal torture and near murder of two young boys by two brothers aged 10 and 11 in Yorkshire. This provoked a shocked response reminiscent of that which arose from the murder of James Bulger in 1993. The papers varied as to what degree of blame attached to the two 'devil brothers' (as some papers named them), their abusive and neglectful parents, and social workers who had failed to intervene after warning signs regarding the brothers and their family. A report which detailed a complex array of contributory factors was only published in outline form, and one controversy raged over whether the full report should be publicly available, as well as whether the two brothers should be named. The mother of James Bulger (whose murderers were named and became targets of public anger) urged that without this naming and shaming, justice could not properly be done. Some urged the need for careful causal analysis, which required an openness which only confidentiality could ensure. Others urged that the priority was to call the right people to public account. Yet others questioned whether it is appropriate to blame individuals too young to fit the normal criteria for responsible behavior. The underlying issue, as ever, was whether what was needed was cool, comprehensive explanation or hot, focused blame.

In another case, two ten year old boys were found guilty of trying to rape an eight year old girl and put on the sex offenders' register. They had been playing a game – which many will remember from their own childhood – of 'show me yours and I'll show you mine.' At the trial, the girl said she was lying when she said she had been raped. Columnist Philip Johnston in the *Daily Telegraph* (24 May 2010) asked if there was 'any other country in the world where the prepubescent fumblings of children would result in a rape trial?' The main 'abuse' here would seem to be an abuse of all three children by the legal system that forced them to stand trial, and may leave the boys marked as 'sex offenders' for life. How would any of us fare if our explorations as children were made the indicator of how 'safe' we would be in adult life?

Clearly for some reason our culture is regressing from the kind of enlightened, accurate, multifaceted explanation that science offers. We actually prefer a world that has demons in it. And when children fall short of the ideal of innocence we like to impose on them, we find it especially hard not to see them as wholly evil instead.

Science in the Service of Blame

But perhaps the worst cases of mass blame in history have actually been aided by a false kind of science, a false kind of explanation that, instead of restraining blame, allows it to seep more widely and pervasively. This is perhaps why the twentieth century turned out to be the worst of all times in terms of sheer numbers deliberately slaughtered because they were held to be to blame. Time and time again, false science combined with the need to find scapegoats. Instead of tracing causes to responsible individuals, a crude travesty of science determined that whole races, classes or faith groups needed to be persecuted and eliminated to make society safe and sound. Jews and other racial or religious minorities, and kulaks and other classes, have been 'scientifically' analyzed as being enemies of society, and hence as outcasts that need not be treated with humanity. Typically – in the way Chapter 3 will explore some more – after the revolution, the politically correct 'science' tells us that all should be well. But hurt continues in the form of unemployment, famine, discontent... So the science tells us to go on looking for causes we can change. *Someone* must be to blame.

A false science then provides a way in which ills can be accounted for by casting the net more widely, and the law turns from the business of justice to the business of finding culprits. The purpose of interrogations and trials is often not to find the truth but to extract a confession, and so define a scapegoat. In this scenario, at Stalin's treason trials, as the Slovenian Marxist Slavoj Žižek, has pointed out (2008), even arguing a case for the defense was a proof of blameworthiness; for the truly loyal person would not go against the will of the people and the party. The very protestation of innocence was an offense, blameworthy in itself.

From the scientific imperative of explanation ('we must understand who and what caused this') and the legal imperative of justice ('the person responsible must pay for this') we have moved to the often heard but deadly imperative '*someone* (or *some* group) must pay for this.' The need to blame outruns the need to explain and the need to account.

And these tendencies are of course not absent from our democratic societies. Particularly terrible crimes like mass murder, terrorism and sadistic rape can provoke a collective anger that is in itself a quite natural emotional response. But the anger quickly turns to a need to blame that outruns the requirements of justice. People are locked away in prisons like Guantanamo Bay without adequate evidence because they might be terrorists. Children are put on the sex offenders register because they just might grow up to be rapists.

Why Blame Cheers Us

What is it that makes us continue to prefer blame to explanation; or, worse, to put explanation in the service of our need to blame? Why when we ask why some terrible thing happened do we tend to leap at one 'culprit' (or a closely related group of culprits) and blame him or her or them for it all. Why, when we ask why someone died and find that so and so killed then, does the buck stop with that person? Why do the further questions, why he killed, what made him a killer, seem to some to confuse rather than clarify the chain of accountability?

Fundamentally it is perhaps because it cheers us to blame other people, for three fairly straightforward reasons, and one more deep and complex reason. It boosts our self-confidence to believe we can always locate and identify discrete sources of hurt. Secondly, it is easier to act in a world with such discrete causes, and the idea gives us more sense of our own freedom and responsibility, as well as a means of control of others by legal process. And thirdly, it is aesthetically pleasing too. It makes for better reading in the papers, with the drama of the search for the criminal, the trial, and the climactic joy of conviction. It is not surprising that sometimes, when actual evidence is not foolproof, we use our imaginations to fill the gap.

But maybe the pleasing idea that hurt can ultimately be traced to personal causes is not ultimately true. Maybe it gives hurt too human a face. Maybe our sense of self and of justice depends more on our feeling for drama and our sense of self-importance than it depends on our sense of reality. Maybe grief, or a more diffuse cosmic rage, is often a more rational response to hurt than specific blame. Maybe truth lies more on the side of sorrow than retribution. Maybe there is a darker side to our need to blame – a reason lurking in the ancient depths of our human condition.

The Scapegoat

The French literary theorist René Girard argues that there is indeed such a dark side. Arguing from an immensely broad swathe of world culture, he contends that society has a need to construct blameworthy scapegoats in order to discharge the potential violence that arises from our acquisitive desires. Desire, he argues, begins with imitation. I desire the glass of orange drink because I see my sister desiring and drinking it. What comes to matter to me is not so much having the orange juice itself, as ensuring that my sister does not have more of it than me. (I remember, when as a child I poured the orange juice on a 'you pour, I choose' basis, how carefully I lined up the juice with my eye to ensure the glass she would choose would be *exactly* equal to mine. The fact that mother had lots more orange juice available if we wanted it was beside the point!)

So our desires tend to lead us into conflict for the same things. Society threatens to disintegrate into violent competition for the things deemed desirable within it. The societies that have survived are those that have come up with the solution, and the solution is always essentially the same: to agree on a scapegoat, a victim whom we can all unite in blaming for our lack of the things we desire. The victim deflects our violence from one another and enables us to live in peace.

The scapegoat may be a formalized and ritualized victim, a sacrifice – originally human, but in more sophisticated societies an animal like a lamb or goat – which is either cast out (like the original Biblical 'scapegoat' in Leviticus 20) or slaughtered in an act of redemptive violence. When the sacrificial system collapses because people cease to believe in the efficacy of sacred violence, ordinary mundane violence threatens to break out. In due course a secular form of judicial violence comes to replace the older sacred violence. The offering of scapegoats is replaced by the punishment of offenders. But the judicial process retains a sacred order, and like the sacrificial king-victims of old, the murderer going to his execution is both reviled and treated with awe, as by his death he pays the price for sin, and restores society to peace. Conversely the 'stars' and politicians we elect and treat with awe at one moment are inevitably soon dethroned by the press and excoriated for the faults perceived to be evident in them, though those faults are common enough in society at large. Finally, we tend to deny that these acts of redemptive violence are violent. We do not see punishment as a harming of the criminal that is justified in our eyes, but as a separate category, 'punishment,' that is somehow distinct from harm.

We can see the stages whereby mimetic rivalry leads to violence and its denial in the story of Cain as rendered in the poem that opened this chapter. First Cain imitates his brother in his desire to please God with an offering. But his offering is rejected by God while Abel's is accepted. This leads to painful rivalry and envy; in the poem Cain is cast in the shadow by the glory of his brother, and can only emerge into the light again by 'sacrificing' this brother, which he does. But God hears the blood of Abel crying out for vengeance. Instead of a pleasing sacrifice atoning for sin, it is a death requiring further sacrifice. The Bible seems to be laying bare the cycle whereby rivalry leads to cycles of never-ending violence. But the blame for the death is denied by Cain. The world becomes heavy with the shadow of violence and its denial; we all feel contaminated by violence and strive to avoid the contamination by pinning it on someone else. But in this case God limits the expiation Cain himself must pay; the mark on his forehead simultaneously protects him from death, and marks him out as an outcast, cast out from society to wander the earth as the original scapegoat was sent out to wander in the desert for the people's sins.

Is Girard's theory far-fetched? Do these ancient texts about rivalry and envy, blame and sacrifice have as much relevance to us today as Girard claims? Probably Girard does claim too much, when he tries to makes his theory account for almost everything about civilization from the first days until now! But I also know from my own experience – who does not – what powerful and crippling feelings envy and blame can be; and yet how difficult it is to avoid them. The common sense, rational view that the hurt in the world has a multiple complex of causes, some mutable, others not, seems incredibly hard to realize emotionally or sustain in the heart. The real causes of hurt are as subtle and airy as a spider's web, but emotionally they come to generate a blame we are always, in that significant term, trying to 'shift' – like a heavy liquid gravitating towards the lowest level, then shifting as we tilt our account of reality. What rings true for me in Girard's account is the way it explains this irrational transfer of impersonal hurt onto blamable people, and the ultimately blamable people we call 'evil'.

A Buckless Universe?

As scientifically minded, enlightened people, surely we should want to pursue the explanation of hurt further than 'evil' people, and ask what made those 'evil' people do the harm they did. If we took this approach, we would encounter a chain of cause and effect reaching backward into deep past time. We would uncover a universe where the buck does not stop, or at least, not anywhere we can identify or do much about. The buck for every wrong would be a great swathe of the whole unhappy interlinked self-perpetuating web of sin and crime.

In certain cultures this is precisely what explanation ends up with. Buddhists speak of 'bad karma from beginningless time.' The cosmos swarms with chains of hurtful causality; we are mere cogs in the never-ending 'wheel of samsara' that the universe is. The brothers tortured the boys because they themselves had been traumatized by parents who in turn were doubtless wounded victims of their past, in a wheel of causation that will continue to drag them and those around them down. Mahayana Buddhism speaks of 'dependent co-arising.' There is no single ultimate cause of why things are as they are. Things just cause each other; they are all interdependent. That means Buddhists are (in principle at least) free from having to blame any being when things go wrong.

Western Christians have traditionally seen us all as burdened by a dark inheritance of 'original sin' which makes us do the wrong thing even when we clearly perceive the right. 'Evil' in these scenarios is not the action of exceptional 'monsters' outside the ranks of normal decent humanity, but something that holds us all in its inescapable grip, though in some cases more tightly and terribly than others.

Such views can sound fatalist. But neither Buddhists nor

Christians are fatalists; neither faith denies a place for personal responsibility. Neither allows us to say when we are called to account, 'Sorry, but that's just my bad karma (or original sin) coming out!' For both traditions, accepting what has caused us and constrained us to be as we are is the precondition of genuine freedom and realistic responsibility. Later chapters will clarify how this is possible.

But for now we can make a tentative suggestion in the light of this chapter: that personal responsibility is an important though limited idea, but blame is dangerous to others and ourselves. When we blame someone we do more than judge that they are on balance the main cause of a case of harm. We think of the buck as stopping with them, rather than passing through them. We allow the intensity of the harm to distort our image of them so that we come to see them as mysteriously creating evil out of nothing. Consequently we begin to see them as evil in themselves. Dark mythologies come into play, of the kind that Chapter 4 will discuss, and these myths bring in their train emotions of hatred and thirst for punishment and vengeance. We begin to scapegoat the person in the way Girard describes, transferring to them our frustration at the hurt in our own life and in the universe, and seeking through their punishment a kind of relief from hurt that is not possible.

We do not need all that. Blame fails to deliver on its promises, and only doubles our distress. We need, instead, a way of allotting responsibility clearly and scientifically but lightly and provisionally, within the context of the obscure, unchosen mainsprings of our actions. And what can enable that to happen? The tragicomic perspective that Buddhism and Christianity share, as explored in Chapter 6.

Summary

1. From early childhood we learn the habit of blaming others and avoiding blame ourselves.

2. Blame sees what would otherwise just hurt as something deliberately intended to harm us or others. This adds to the pain.
3. It is important to call people to account for the hurt they cause, so they can learn to be more responsible and we can help ensure the hurt is not repeated.
4. However, in reality most hurt has a complex web of causes. The scientific attempt to explain events may have its origin in a search for blame, but involves a much more careful process than the singling out of individuals and groups for blame.
5. And sometimes a pseudo-scientific approach has combined with a desire to hold other, 'different' people to account, leading to terrible persecution of blamed minorities.
6. Blaming others pleases us because it offers simple, intellectually undemanding solutions; it relieves us of shame, guilt and the need for self-examination, and it sees the world in terms of a story of good versus evil, which is full of satisfying drama.
7. But the need to blame – as distinct from the demand for explanation and accountability – is ultimately escapist, pathological and perpetuating of harm. As Girard has shown, all blaming invokes a deep rooted impulse to scapegoat minorities.
8. As well as turning – in our hearts and minds – hurts felt into harm done to us, blame can turn harm into evil, harm done by agents who want to harm. By encouraging retaliation and strife, hurt is thereby perpetuated.
9. It is possible to hold people responsible without the impulse to blame. Buddhism and Christianity both refer to a complex web of suffering and harm in which we are all enmeshed, without denying personal responsibility.

Chapter 2

'I Hurt Myself': Shame

There lurks the blackest bile
            snaking through the arterial flow.
I think of hell:
            a scream, that things should not be so
but always will.

How would it feel
            to be fingered and felt in such a way
that the real
tasted no longer good at all
            but impossible to sick away?

The Bible says the body is a shrine.
            But a sanctuary defaced
is walled off like a tomb, where eyes
relish putrid stuff and the tongue writhes
            like a maggot in a world of pus.

Over this, delicacy and joy
            form just a brittle crust.
Underneath, the alloy
            has gone awry, can only rust,
            deprived of fundamental trust.

What can rectify original loss?
            A Christ, a mother not ashamed
of malformation, and the bloody task
of mopping up the vomit of abuse,

holding firm the convulsing frame
of a child made well and new.
Abuse

It is almost impossible not to blame someone. Often we blame another and perpetuate cycles of outward violence. But the alternative seems to be to blame ourselves, and set up cycles of inward violence equally beyond the reach of our rational control. This is the alternative this chapter considers. If the previous chapter showed us how often we turn hurt into harm and violence by seeking to blame and scapegoat individuals and groups, this chapter is about how often we allow ourselves to be a scapegoat, and or scapegoat ourselves, accepting a blame and shame that numbs us and does deep damage. The poem attempts to convey an extreme case of this: the way abuse can traumatically corrupt a child's whole sense of self and reality.

If the hurt we internalize is bearable, it manifests as a consciousness of general badness or unworthiness at the heart of our identity – the kind of thing we call shame. But we shall see that beyond a certain threshold hurt can be unbearable and repressed into the unconscious. It becomes 'trauma': a word that means 'wound' but refers especially to a wound that will not heal. As with a piece of shrapnel embedded in the body, healing takes place around it. Scar tissue – half-dead tissue that lacks the flexibility of living flesh – is created as a barrier between the alien matter and the body. An equivalent of scar tissue likewise protects the mind from a psychic wound that cannot be borne, supposedly protecting the self but actually inflicting more damage. The mind heals around the trauma, fixing it as part of its own identity, in ways that we shall explore. Hurt becomes harm to the self, and often, through half-dead, fixated behavior, harm to others too.

This chapter will begin by exploring shame of different kinds, distinguishing shame from other somewhat more positive emotions like guilt and remorse. It will then move via 'chronic' shame to the traumatization that affects the victims of child abuse and other assaults on the body and soul. These are phenomena that many of us will thankfully think remote from our own situation, but the chapter will then move on to argue that our whole society is in some senses governed by chronic shame and a kind of traumatic division against ourselves. Religion and law tend to focus on morality, responsibility and blame, but at best leave shame and trauma untouched, and at worst, draw on those feelings and intensify them in a vicious circle. The chapter ends with some suggestions about how we might be liberated from this circle, arguing that while blame may represent a first step towards 'detoxifying' ourselves of shame and trauma, it remains – as the previous chapter showed – fundamentally delusory. To shift from scapegoating ourselves to blaming another may represent progress if we are indeed innocent. But deep healing requires a radical forgiveness of ourselves and others in one and the same breath: an almost impossible move beyond the scapegoat altogether.

The Phenomenon of Shame

Shame seems to be a strong and universal human experience, and it comes as a surprise how little philosophers, ethicists, psychologists and theologians have focused on it until rather recently. It is not, to my knowledge, mentioned among Buddhists as the major cause of human suffering that it is, and Christian theology and Western literary tradition have focused much more on sin, guilt and repentance than on shame and its healing – a matter to which this chapter will return. But in recent times there has been growing interest in this very basic human reaction.

In an already classic study (2000) theologian Stephen Pattison sums up a wealth of this recent research and discussion, noting several aspects of shame (p. 71ff). These include a sense of being uncontrollably exposed, seen by others in a humiliating light, and turned into an object of judgmental gaze. This experience involves a heightened and distressing self-consciousness, rather than awareness of specific actions, or concern for others one may have harmed. The world and one's relation to it, and one's ability to communicate, are jeopardized, and the shamed person feels isolated and set apart from 'normal' society, paralyzed, despairing, dirty, contaminated, and unlovable in himself, altogether lacking in attractiveness or grace – 'disgraced' in fact. He will want to hide from public view: in a revealing phrase, he 'wishes the ground would swallow him up.' Physical reactions may underline this desire: he may turn his eyes 'sheepishly' away from the gaze of the accusing others, hanging his head and hunching his shoulders, and moving his hands to cover his face or his 'private' parts. Conversely he may blush, becoming brighter in hue and so expressing outwardly the increased visibility he feels. He may laugh nervously – a reaction of mysterious origins, discussed further in Chapter 6 – or paradoxically, he may start trembling or burst into tears. All of these reactions involve an increased sense of unwelcome bodiliness and the desire to cover what is felt as nakedness and exposure. The Indo-European root of the word 'shame' is *kam* or *kem* – to cover. The shamed person 'loses face' and becomes a mere body, a 'non-person' or '*persona non grata*.' In extreme cases, morally codified in some cultures, he may commit suicide.

As another theologian Paul Goodliff points out (2005), the classic Biblical story of shame is the fall of Adam and Eve in Genesis 2–3. After their sin of eating the forbidden fruit, they become ashamed of their bodies and sew fig leaves together to hide them. When they hear God's voice calling them, they hide. Goodliff comments on the fresco by Tomasso Masaccio, painted c1427, depicting Adam and Eve expelled from paradise by God.

Crouched head, fingers covering the eyes, palms covering

> the cheeks, elbows tight to the body: shame covers its expression behind a mask so that the face becomes hidden. (p. 90)

There is something very primitive about such reactions. When animals contest for dominance, the dominant animal will often expand its bodily profile by standing tall or sideways on and swaying, while the submissive animal will diminish its profile, lowering itself toward the ground, cowering, contracting and slithering away. But this animal reaction comes to us in a way that is distinctively human

> Shame strikes deepest into the heart of man [and woman]. While terror and distress hurt, they are wounds inflicted from outside which penetrate the smooth surface of the ego; but shame is felt as an inner torment, a sickness of the soul.
> (S. Tomkins, cited in Goodliff, p. 26)

So this very feeling of being 'too bodily, too much on the outside, too exposed to others' comes to us from deep inside. It will be a while in this chapter before we understand these paradoxes of shame.

In a sense, shame is always the same. All of the reactions Pattison cites seem to be present or on the verge of being present in any instance of shame. When slightly embarrassed by saying the wrong thing at a party, I may not actually blush, but I may feel the color coming to my cheeks. I may not burst into tears, or snigger, but I may feel a slight inner tremble. Everyone may not turn to look at me, but I may furtively look around to make sure they are not, and feel myself cowering inside even if I manage to look cool and unperturbed.

But of course shame will vary in intensity and in duration. My embarrassment will soon pass, though embarrassments have a habit – unlike feelings of fear and guilt over matters since resolved, but like anger perhaps – of making us undergo the reaction all over again at the sheer memory of their original cause. But though I may cringe whenever I remember my remark, the embarrassment is unlikely to destroy totally my sense of self-worth! Not so with what Pattison describes as chronic shame. Repeated experiences of shaming, especially in childhood, may lead to a total and chronic loss of self-esteem that no amount of later vindication can touch. As the poem describes, delicacy and joy can only be experienced as a brittle crust overlaying a person who feels himself to be inherently disgusting. The result may be repetitive manic bouts of actually disgusting behavior, or deep depression, or both. Here shame merges into the traumatized condition described shortly.

Shame, Guilt and Remorse

Our shame goes with others' disgust. When we feel shame we feel that others are disgusted or repelled by us, and when people are disgusted with us we feel ashamed, whether or not we deserve it. In J.M. Coetzee's novel *Disgrace* (1999) the main character is a lecturer who sleeps with his pupil. In his eyes the relationship is reciprocal, but on one occasion he does put pressure on the girl to have sex when she does not really want it. He is subsequently accused of rape, dismissed from his post, harangued by the press and shunned by former colleagues. Though he remains impenitent, he experiences all the feelings we have associated with shame. The disgust creates the shame without the mediation of guilt.

The distinction between shame and guilt is vital for writers like Pattison and Goodliff, and indeed for this book. It was probably the classicist E.R. Dodds who first drew the distinction between the shame based viewpoint of the early Greek tragedies, where actions that bring shame are punished by fate even where there is – as in Aeschylus' Oedipus – no guilty intent to do wrong; and the guilt-based ethos of Euripides, where it is evil intent and guilty actions that bring down wrath upon the doer. Since then much – perhaps too much – has been made of the distinction between shame based cultures, where what matters is the esteem of others, and guilt based ones, where what matters is that one's own intention be squared with one's inner conscience. Many detect a gradual shift towards a 'culture of narcissism,' obsessed with maintaining image and avoiding humiliation, in which celebrities typically go through the older kind of Greek tragic cycle where *hubris* – fame and esteem – is followed by scandal and shame.

Goodliff distinguishes the two responses in this way:

> Guilt is concerned with what I have done wrong, and its cure is reparation and forgiveness. If by my actions I am guilty of harming someone, I might feel the wretchedness of guilt, but I can do something about it, and that involves disclosure. Shame is more stubborn, and concerns who I am, not what I have done. Shame is not cured by disclosure or by confession, for it craves concealment, hiddennness and flight. (p. 6–7)

He also remarks (p. 4) that 'shame is a "sticky" emotion, and spreads like syrup... The disgrace... sticks to [the wrongdoer], his wife, his children, his church, and to a lesser degree, to his profession. It is different to guilt... for it is felt by the innocent.' That is why families often sever links with disgraced members. In some societies the victim of rape, though she did not intend the violation, may become a cause of shame that can only be cured – in extreme cases – by her death in an 'honor murder'.

Shame may outlast the process of guilt, confession and punishment. The 'hero' of Joseph Conrad's *Lord Jim* (1994) jumps ship in a storm with the captain and other comrades, abandoning the passengers to likely death. They are saved, and Lord Jim confesses before a tribunal and is punished with dismissal. Though his guilt is atoned for, his feelings of shame continue to underwrite his life. He goes to remote regions where his name is unknown, and a deep obscurity overlays his character like a mist. Finally he accepts death at the hands of a Malay chieftain as retribution for a crime that was not his.

But at this point we need to introduce a third term, alongside guilt and shame, namely remorse. Two examples from my own life may clarify this.

When I was about six, I was doing a rare good deed – sweeping the kitchen floor with a broom. Unfortunately the broom had a hook in the end by which it used to hang up in the cupboard. And unknown to me, my sister was creeping up behind me. The hook caught her in the eye, and she screamed. My mother managed at last to take it out, and took my sister to hospital. Soon she was fine again. But at the time I was convinced she would lose her sight. My mother saw clearly that I was not to blame, that this was an accident. And my sister was in too much distress to vent any energy in accusing me. There was no shame involved, and no guilt. But I felt terrible, because I loved my sister and felt I had done irreparable damage to her eye. In a word, I felt remorse, a feeling that had nothing to do with others' views of me, and nothing to do with my view of myself, but everything to do with my love for my sister and my sense of having harmed her.

Contrast this with a curious incident in my secondary school biology class. In the preceding week we had learned about the arthropods – creatures with segmented shells including crabs, spiders and insects. But in the meantime I had been reading about anthropoids – animals closely related to us human beings, like monkeys and chimpanzees. I was a bookish boy and words that read similarly seemed alike to me. So when the teacher asked the class what an arthropod was, I proudly put up my hand and replied that it was an animal closely related to a human being. The teacher was cross and dismissive, and the rest of the class may have sniggered a little to see one of the 'clever' boys brought down. But I was devastated. I had not done anything against my own moral standards, or to harm others: no guilt or remorse was involved. But I was excruciatingly shamed. To this day, though I can laugh when I tell the story, I still feel something of the desire I felt then for the ground to swallow me up!

We could summarize by saying that shame has to do with an 'extraverted self-consciousness,' in the sense of negative feelings about my image in others' eyes; guilt has to do with 'introverted self-consciousness,' that is, negative feelings about my failure to measure up to my own standards; while remorse is a matter of 'extraverted other-consciousness;' negative feelings about harm I think I have done to others. In Chapter 7 I shall argue that remorse is an important aspect of our sense of there being a reality and real people outside our own skin. Guilt, while an important response in some cases, is by contrast self-related rather than other-related, having the potential of becoming obsessive and over-judgmental of oneself and others. We shall see later how the Western and Christian emphasis on guilt and punishment has come to displace both the healing dynamic of remorse and recompense and the perverse dynamic of chronic shame and its difficult healing.

Shame, of course, is not always a 'bad thing.' It enables us to keep to appropriate social codes of conduct. It is what, for example, makes it psychologically *impossible* for me to go to church in the nude (there is no element of choice about this!) There are doubtless cases where – as our parents put it – we 'ought to be ashamed of ourselves.' Like many, I wish bankers and others like them felt more ashamed of the huge bonuses they get for being incompetent and made redundant; and that being hugely wealthier than your fellow citizen might feel as embarrassing as being hugely vaster than them in your waistline! The word 'shameless' is an apt criticism in these and many other cases.

But clearly my own example shows how often we become ashamed when we have done nothing shameful. Shame can make us self-obsessed about our image in a way that is totally out of step with any reality. As noted, shame can become chronic, leading to insuperable self-hatred. And the feeling of shame can become so unbearable that it is repressed out of conscious view, dividing the self against itself, in the manner now explored.

The Traumatic Split

People in whom chronic shame is repressed often come to exhibit compulsive or addictive kinds of behavior that is forever supposedly being reformed and forever sailing close to the winds of destruction. The behavior may involve alcohol, drug or pornography addiction, a tendency to wild and uncanny sexual or other behavior, inappropriate and adulterous liaisons, harassment or abuse. Or it may manifest in repeated bouts of depression or apathy. It is always self-destructive, and destructive of those close to the person, as well as – often – innocent others.

Why are conditions like this so irrationally and damagingly resistant to threats, therapy and kindness alike? For the Jungian psychotherapist Donald Kalsched, this resistance, and the question of how it might be overcome, was what first led him to write his pioneering work, *The Inner World of Trauma* (1996). He notes and explains the resistance in this way:

> I have had a number of individuals in analysis who, after an initial period of growth and improvement, reached a kind of plateau where they seemed to stagnate in therapy and, instead of getting better as a result of the treatment, seemed instead to get stuck in a 'repetition compulsion' of earlier behavior, which left them feeling defeated and hopeless... One part of them wanted to change and a stronger part

> *resisted* this change. They were divided within themselves... These patients were extremely bright, sensitive individuals who had suffered, on account of this very sensitivity, some acute or cumulative emotional trauma in early life. All of them had become prematurely self-sufficient in their childhoods, cutting off genuine relations with their parents during their developing years and caretaking themselves in a cocoon of fantasy instead. In psychotherapy they found it very difficult to relinquish their own self-care protection and allow themselves to depend on a real person. (p. 11–12)

Kalsched explains that the emotional trauma could, but need not, involve specific abuse; but it always involves

> ...unbearable psychic pain or anxiety... Trauma of this magnitude varies from the acute, shattering experiences of child abuse so prominent in the literature today to the more 'cumulative traumas' of unmet dependency-needs that mount up to devastating effect in some children's development... The distinguishing feature of such trauma is... 'disintegration anxiety,' an unnamable dread associated with the threatened dissolution of a coherent self. (p. 1)

The child builds a psychic line of defense to prevent the inner personal spirit from contact with a world that is experienced as lethal to it. This leads to what Kalsched calls an 'archetypal self-care system,' a 'dyad' in which part of the self becomes a precociously capable and adult 'guardian' or 'caretaker,' while the other becomes a vulnerable child who ceases to grow up, and is often dreamt as a little girl or an innocent animal. In clients where this has happened, psychotherapists have noted

> how utterly vulnerable, uninitiated, needy and infantile they are, on the one hand, and how haughty, inflated, arrogant,

> know-it-all and resistant they are on the other. This inflated inner defensive structure, like a 'king-baby' or a 'queen-baby,' represents the unholy marriage between the caretaking self and the infantile object. (p. 36)

The personality that results is marked by the inner repetition of cruelty, irrationality, deception and entrenchment. The inner caretaker both protects and cares for the inner child, and persecutes it with a ferocity that is far greater than that of any actual abuser. Hence Kalsched argues that we should avoid thinking of the caretaker as just the internalization of an original abuser. Moreover, the caretaker protects the inner child from the real world, so rational behavior adequate to the real world fails in crucial respects to be learned. People who are otherwise intelligent and sane behave in ways that can be disastrously irrational, compulsive and destructive, well beyond the fallout from the original trauma.

Incapable of normal patterns of adult intimacy, and shrouded by a deep shame imposed by the caretaker, the inner child often colludes with the caretaker in maintaining a veil of secrecy and deception. Yet what objectively speaking are lies are not experienced as such, since they protect the truth of the inner child. This makes the person deeply resistant to outside help; the caretaker is jealous of its role as the only helper the child can really trust. Though the caretaker heaps deep hurt and shame upon the child, no outward truth is allowed in to induce real remorse, change and growth.

The exception to this – I note – might appear to be sadomasochistic relationship. One explanation of masochism might be that the inner child manages to project the abusing caretaker onto another person, and conversely with sadism the caretaker projects the inner child onto another. The dualism between a tightly controlled disciplinarian puritan and a wild animal-child full of cravings that need to be tamed is lived out through two people rather than one. It is still a fantasy that is being lived out, full of repetitive ritual. On the other hand, because the fantasy dynamic takes place between two people who have to do ordinary things together (like eat supper and wash up) besides acting out fantasies, there may be a way forward here into a healing relationship. Certainly it is vital to distinguish cases in which the fantasy dyad is lived out within a broader consenting relationship, from those in which a 'caretaker' self imposes his sadism on another without consent.

Carla's Story

Kalsched bases his observations on a wide variety of traumatized experience, not just the victims of abuse as such. Nevertheless we have become lately much more aware of the widespread incidence of child abuse. From being a remote and seldom mentioned 'incest' that prevailed in morally dysfunctional families altogether 'other' than one's own, child abuse has come to seem alarmingly very close to us all, in our families, our neighborhoods, our churches. A variety of American sources (including Finkelhor, 1994 and Whealin, 2007) indicates that about 15% to 25% of women and 5% to 15% of men were sexually abused when they were children. (Many others were abused by violence or neglect.) Only 10% of these were abused by strangers, 30% being abused by close relatives (brothers topping the list, followed by fathers) and 60% by other acquaintances. It is perhaps because abuse has emerged as something closer to us than we had liked to think that we have felt all the more the need to demonize it as the epitome of evil, creating a stereotype of the predatory stranger that reverses the statistical picture.

In this context any book about responding to evil, hurt and harm will need to say something about how we should respond to child abuse. In the light of Kalsched's treatment of trauma and others' treatment of shame, we can see child abuse as, indeed, a terrible shaming action committed mainly by those who at one time have themselves been deeply shamed, a traumatizing of others by those who have been traumatized (though not necessarily by sexual abuse). To be sure, only a minority of abused people become abusers themselves, and that is a sign of great hope; but a great many bear the scars in terms of a greater predisposition to depression, crime, and difficulty in sexual relationships. Abuse must be reckoned as one of the largely hidden mechanisms by which hurt passes itself on from generation to generation. If we can say anything at all about how healing may come in such situations, we will have contributed a lot to the working out of better ways of responding to harm that partakes of the nature of evil.

There are a lot of books out there now that 'tell the story of abuse,' but Carla van Raay's *God's Callgirl* (2006) is one I have found compelling in its honesty, humor, realism, generosity and lack of self-dramatization. It brings to life the horrible nature of what we have rather abstractly called 'trauma' as it happened to a child from the age of three. When Carla's father abused her, she writes,

> he was telling me that he was nice, that he liked me, and also that I was the worst, the most sordid girl in the world. He told me this by his furtive actions, his compelling body. No words were ever spoken during our night-time encounters. Understanding all this was beyond me; there was no way I could work it out. My solution was to hide, and pretend that I did not have bad feelings. *Become invisible, Carla, hide who you really are.* This was difficult, because I felt I did not have a private self. (p. 47, her italics)

Theologian Alistair McFayden (2000, p. 73ff) has described four aspects of the evil of child abuse, and we see all four here. There is traumatic sexualization (Carla experiences her father's desire as a kind of bodily language she could not at that stage understand – 'there was no way I could work it out'). There is a total mismatch of power between Carla and her father. There is deep betrayal of trust by the father who was otherwise often kind and playful, and whom she continued in other respects to love. And there is a stigmatization that does not lie in anything her father said, but was implicit in what he did. Following a pattern that is very common in cases of child abuse, Carla was the 'different one' in her family, often the scapegoat for their troubles.

But we note two other factors. There is the chronic shame – a feeling of being a 'sordid' object in the eyes of her father – that would stay with her for much of her life. And there is the urge to 'hide who you really are' that goes with shame and leads (especially in the case of those too young to have formed a sense of a 'private self') to the persecutory dyad that Kalsched describes.

The effects of Carla's abuse lasted a lifetime. At the age of seven she relates how she saw a naked small girl and felt an overwhelming urge to maim the girl's genitals. She overcame the feeling, but felt her own shameful nature was confirmed. Only later would it be clear how she was not to blame – that such feelings had been written into her by her father. We are aware that the abused sometimes become abusers, but do not always realize how early in life this can happen.

As a teenager Carla became a nun, and entered a world that was deeply abusive in a different way; as the radically different one, she was stigmatized and punished by the leadership in many subtle ways. On leaving the convent she became a prostitute working in a massage parlor. This proved less abusive than the convent, offering a kind of warmth she never encountered there. But in the end Carla came to realize that it was not the way to sexual wholeness, a goal she sadly never achieved.

Hiding from Humanity

There are obvious connections to be made between Kalsched's

analysis of the traumatized self and Girard's unmasking of the anthropological mechanisms of stigmatization and blame, discussed in Chapter 1. Kalsched's inner caretaker safeguards the survival and unity of the psyche by means of stigmatizing an inner child, which remains as a place of irresponsible madness in an otherwise rational self. In the same way, the corporate representatives of society achieve its unity and apparent rationality at the price of mimetic violence against a sacrificial victim. When shamed we feel ourselves entering the place of the scapegoat, looked at by society's wider circle for what is contemptible and condemnable.

But even if we do not buy into Girard's whole theory, we are faced with a deep collective involvement in shame and trauma. Though only a (substantial) minority of us will have suffered sexual abuse as children, most of us will probably bear the memories of shame and trauma of some kind, as well as participating actively or vicariously in the shaming of others. Shame is common to humanity and distinctive of humanity – no animal so far as I know has the self-consciousness required to be vulnerable to shame, and perhaps the kind of consciousness that distinguishes the human species goes hand in hand with this vulnerability. Should we posit an 'original trauma' in which self-awareness arises, as in the Garden of Eden, inherited by all humanity? And is this trauma what is described (in some ways misleadingly) by Christian tradition as 'original sin'? I shall argue so.

Shame, as we have seen, involves an impulse to hide. In particular I suggest it involves a hiding of those parts of us that do not fit with society's image of what it means to be human. In shame we feel seen and judged because of, and in trauma we repress and persecute, those wild unsocialized animal features that do not cohere with the clean disembodied image we like to project about ourselves. But as the American philosopher and ethicist Martha Nussbaum has argued (2004) in doing so we tragically hide from our true humanity, and put on instead a sanitized mask of sociability. She suggests that we are all confused by our own deep shame about our bodily, animal and mortal nature, ashamed of our inability to be pure rational spirits. The result is what Pattison has termed 'ontological shame' – shame about our basic condition, as sexual, needy, often dirty self-conscious animals.

Societies define themselves in different ways, so though there is convergence in what societies define as immoral (murder, stealing, lying), there is far greater variety concerning what is shameful. In English society to belch at table is highly embarrassing, while in Arab countries not to do so brings shame upon the host. What can and cannot be eaten and how, the age of marriage, and the acceptability of homosexuality and polygamy vary immensely. But mostly what is shameful covers the same kinds of thing: mainly what we do at table, what we do in bed, and what we do in the toilet. It is when we are clearly animals (with nutritional, reproductive and excretory needs) acting in social or intimate personal contexts (table, bed, toilet) that the tension between the animal and the social arises most intensely, and the need to define limits and shame those who transgress them arises most intensely. It is the parts of our bodies most closely associated with the animal functions that arouse most shame (though in different settings, the most desire!) And though the content of the shameful varies, the feelings of embarrassment and disgust associated with shame remain universally the same.

The sociologist Mary Douglas (2002) has noted how many rituals serve to purify society of the danger of contamination. 'Contamination' here combines the sense of physical dirt and disease, moral 'impurity' and deviance from definitions of the 'normal.' We see precisely such a combination in the legal and sacrificial system of the Hebrews, and in many other societies. The need to keep our bodies clean, to expel and deal hygienically with excrement, and to avoid eating rotten or toxic food means that societies with strict purity codes concerning these things will have obvious survival value. At the same time the 'body politic' will tend to survive best if it has ways of dealing with those within or without its boundaries who are felt to contaminate or pollute it. Caste and class systems, education and assimilation programs, armies, police, surveillance, prisons, lunatic asylums, sex offenders' registers, refugee detention centers, religious purity laws, concentration camps and so forth are among the means nations have used to achieve this.

The cultural critic Morris Berman (1989) rather ambitiously sees the denial of our animal nature as key to the history of civilization itself. In our prehistoric state – still to be seen in many so-called primitive tribes – animals were seen as quasi-divine or as companions in a shared universe, and both ritual and practical survival engaged the whole mind-and-body unity. But agriculture and civilization involved our separation of domesticated – 'civilized' – animals from the wild, feared ones, and the development of hierarchies in which the 'lower' echelons, including slaves, worked with their bodies, while the 'upper' ones concerned themselves with the mental and spiritual – governing, making laws, and maintaining relationships with the gods, now typically seen not as one with the earth but as 'above.' Many feminists would add that this is the point at which the 'spiritual' male came to take a higher place than the female, who was inseparable from physical concerns like birth-giving, child-rearing, cooking and, typically, cleaning (the elimination of dirt). Berman sees the dominance of the lofty, spiritual, controlled and masculine over the messy, bodily, spontaneous and feminine as coming to repeated crisis – a point that many feminists have of course echoed.

Berman's analysis can be criticized at many points. Some of his examples of crisis – the 12th century persecution and elimination of the Cathars by the Catholic Church, and the Nazi

Holocaust – cannot credibly be seen as the persecution of feminine, embodied folk by puritan, hyper-spiritual elites. It was the Cathars who were the dualists, emphasizing the evil of material creation and the need to transcend it through ascetic spiritual practice, while the Catholics represented a more earthed, sacramental and institutionally incarnated religion. And in many ways the Jews represented an austere, transcendent monotheism as against the brutally earthy Nazi cult of blood, race and soil. Nevertheless it does seem true that something analogous to Kalsched's dyad – the spiritual persecutor versus the shameful messy child – has operated as a deep structure within many civilizations. Despite the fact that the greatest crimes like genocide and child abuse have no parallel elsewhere in the animal kingdom – and far from resulting from an overflow from bodily passion, clearly involve a huge amount of rational cunning and organization that is characteristically human – our bodies and our animal desires have become the scapegoat for all our troubles, 'sin' being equated with bodily drive and the 'bestial.'

So it could be argued that civilization itself rests on a violent dualistic split, both within society and within the self. And if such a split in the self is typically the result of early trauma, the social equivalent might also be the result of some primordial trauma. Girard suggests this is indeed the case. James Alison speculates further (1998) that at some stage in the past there must have been a 'fall' from the holistic existence of instinct-governed animals into a life governed by the imitative desire that makes us rival egos. This is the way he gives new meaning to the old idea of 'original sin' which is universal to humanity but which does not represent our real human nature. We are all divided against others; but this division also divides us against ourselves and our own spontaneous nature. We do not have to be that way.

Sigmund Freud put things differently, seeing humans as

fundamentally ruptured between a tyrannical superego – an accusing conscience, often projected as 'God the Father' – and an anarchic 'id' full of unrealizable desire. This certainly sounds like Kalsched's dyad. Hope lay for Freud in the ability of the ego – generated as it were by the friction between these two tyrannizing forces – to enact a compromise or truce between them. But Freud also pointed to myths of primordial sin in which the male children murdered their own abusive father, founding civilization on a guilty act that had to be buried in the unconscious.

These are big issues to which Chapters 4 and 5 will return when we consider different accounts of the nature and origin of 'evil' as a whole. For now I return to the specific, and ask whether the shame of original traumas can be healed in the life of chronically shamed and traumatized individuals, and whether the blame criticized in the last chapter may not have a positive role here.

The Healing of Shame and Trauma

Few societies deal well with the radically shamed and the behavior of the traumatized. We can now see why. If society itself depends on shaming and stigmatizing behavior that it defines as 'off limits,' it is unlikely even to want to integrate and heal such behavior. To stop shaming the shamed would be to abandon the ways in which a society defines itself. I shall look briefly at the way religion often deepens shame, and the futility of a 'name and shame' approach to the behavior of the chronically shamed. On the other hand I shall argue that anger and blame may be necessary first steps towards the healing of the abused, but that there are further steps to be taken if the self-protecting resistance of the abuser is to thaw into a healing, other-directed and realistic remorse.

1) Shaming the Shamed

It is for the greatness of your iniquity
that your skirts are lifted up,
and you are violated...
This is your lot,
the portion I have measured out to you, says the Lord,
because you have forgotten me
and trusted in lies.
I myself will lift up your skirts over your face,
and your shame will be seen. (Jer. 13.22b, 25–6)

This Old Testament passage shows us a God who punishes his people for their shameful behavior by shaming and abusing them still further. Israel is likened to a whore who has been exposed and violated by the surrounding nations, and God himself is now about to take his turn in lifting her skirts to expose her shaming parts. The idea of God as inducing shame and abuse runs throughout scripture (see Young, 2007) culminating in the burning alive of the whore of Babylon:

> They and the beast will hate the whore; they will make her desolate and naked; they will devour her flesh and burn her up with fire. For God has put it into their hearts to carry out his purpose. (Rev. 17.16b–17a)

If such themes are thankfully remote from the minds of most (though by no means all) of the faithful today, the idea of the all-seeing surveillance of God can still come across as all-shaming as much as all-loving.

But more subtly, the very idea of God may underpin the kind of shaming dualism between mind and body we have encountered. As Pattison argues, we have depicted God as wholly other, disembodied, pure and holy, entirely good, jealous for obedience, without desires and passions, all powerful and all-knowing, and punitive. God needs nothing from us and we deserve nothing from him. In all these ways God seems to represent the ideal 'caretaker' in Kalsched's sinister sense, demoting us to and perpetuating us in the status of the punished child: shameful for everything that makes us finite, bodily vulnerable and human. Certainly when Carla entered a monastic order to serve God, her shame was only intensified; it was when she rediscovered her body and her desirability as a woman that she found – albeit imperfectly – a degree of liberation.

To counter such tendencies, feminist theologian Marcella Althaus-Reid (2004) urges us to construct an 'indecent theology' that juxtaposes images of God with things we find shocking. Perhaps this only intensifies and deepens a tragicomic thrust that has always been there in the Christian story, which depicts God as a disgraced criminal obscenely suspended on an instrument of execution (see Chapter 6).

But it is not only religious people who feel an urge to heap more shame on the shamed. As Chapter 1 explored, our society increasingly demands that we name and shame 'deviants' of all kinds. Many argue, first, that our disgust at deviant behavior should be a criterion for what is criminal and needs to be punished; and secondly, that shame should form an integral part of the punishment itself.

Martha Nussbaum has argued very strongly (2004) against both points. Disgust – the sense that something is shameful – is not a good guide to law or morality, she contends, and shaming is never an appropriate punishment. The 'shameful' or 'disgusting' offender, she argues, is the one whom society has permitted, and who has then permitted himself, to exhibit animal, bodily, dirty and mortal aspects of ourselves we do not like to acknowledge. Typically society refers to its scapegoats in the language with which it refers to the subhuman – 'monster' or 'beast' – or even the inanimate – 'filthy,' 'dirty' or 'sordid.' By stigmatizing such an offender, society reinforces its exalted image of itself as rational, spiritual, pure and immortal, as against all that is wild, coarse, dirty and deadly. But Nussbaum argues very cogently that when judges and the press condemn actions as 'monstrous' and 'disgusting,' they are operating with ancient confusions. Until we overcome our revulsion, she argues, our proper moral outrage will remain fundamentally confused, and we will never be able to assess crimes for their genuine injustice and offense. Law and public policy, she argues, should focus on bringing people to account for specific deeds that have done identifiable harm; it should never seek to use disgust as a criteria for culpability, or use shame and humiliation as part of punishment.

2) Shame, Remorse and Repentance

But this brings us to the next point. We have already mentioned the differences between shame, guilt and remorse. When we try to apply the categories of guilt and remorse to cases of shame-based harmful behavior, the result will only increase the shame and the resulting harm. Calling people to responsibility, remorse, repentance and recompense for the harm they have done to others is central to the maintenance of a healthy, just society, Nussbaum argues, as it to the maintenance of a good and just family or workplace. But before people can begin to be responsible, we need to free them from our disgust and their own deep shame.

Psychiatrist James Gilligan has argued (2002) that shame is an emotion human beings cannot live with for long. Rather than feel shame, people who are continually exposed to shame and humiliation tend to tune out feelings altogether and lose the empathy and remorse that check our violent tendencies. It follows that punishments that increase shame will increase violence. If we want to prevent violence, we need to minimize the deep inequalities that cause shame in the first place.

To have a responsible self you need, obviously, to have a sense of self: a self capable of choosing good actions and shunning harm, a sense alive to the vulnerability of other selves and the possibility that one's actions may do them good or harm. But this sense of self is what chronic and traumatic shame distorts. Remorse cannot be felt from a place of shame.

Shame – the primitive sense that one is worthless – places more 'adult' questions of responsibility and remorse – whether one is doing good or harm – outside the frame. Shame seldom leads to repentance in the sense of actually making amends and resolving to behave differently. The shamed character lacks the inward strength for such a move, and the traumatized character lacks even the inner integrity. The conscious part of the self may resolve to change, but the wounded inner child or animal will sooner or later trip that resolve up. The shameful part of the soul is kept from sight and not integrated into the self in a way that would allow it to be rationally assessed in responsible decisions. It tends towards secrecy, and so acts against the acknowledgement of real responsibility. The disgraced person typically denies doing the shameful things, because the sub-self that is doing them is not integrated into the responsible person.

Conversely the person with chronic shame finds herself unable to claim real responsibility even for her good deeds. On one level the person may feel herself to be, and be treated by others as, an essentially competent and able professional with a small problem that is best not mentioned. However, at an unspoken level it feels as if she is 'really' regarded by those who know, and regards herself, as a deranged maniac masquerading as a competent human being. This is because unlike guilt, with its focus on what the person does, shame has a habit of making the shameful features define what one really is. However brilliantly she *does* her job, therefore, she still *is* unacceptable, and never quite makes it to be a proper person, because she is black, or lesbian, or just because she is 'that Jane' – however the institution or society to which she belongs defines the non-person. This sense of being a demon with a human face is reinforced by the defensive mythologies of both the individual's psyche and wider society. Individual and society collude in keeping the person in her scapegoat role.

It is not the case, of course, that we should absolve shameful 'deviants' (however society defines them) from all responsibility for their actions. The behavior of a pedophile may well spring from deep trauma – often abuse in his own childhood – and from a fantasy life he has never chosen. But he has chosen to act out those fantasies in a way that has caused real and lasting harm to another. McFayden argues (2000, p.139ff) that his core sin is what was traditionally called 'sloth,' a lazy acquiescence with his own destructive psychic flow, a failure to harness the energy needed to extract himself from the forces at work within him and to channel his desires to goals that are better or at least less hugely harmful. He needs somehow to break out from his inner circuit of shame toward a remorseful awareness of the harm he has caused by his action and its consequences. Some of the consequences may be unjust, or unanticipated and not bargained for; but in Buddhist terms these too need to be accepted as karmic results of what he chose to do.

But the way break out of the inner circuits does not begin either with naming and shaming, or with the call simply to 'be responsible.' Neither the storm of public outrage, nor genteel, patronizing platitudes about the need to repent help at all towards the necessary breakout from a personality built around its wounds. What may help may be on the one hand the hot, heartfelt and spontaneous rage and tears of the person abused, and a cool, undramatized, sober coming to terms with one's own reality.

3) Outrage and Blame

Most psychologists who have studied abuse and therapists who have dealt with its effect would affirm the very positive step forward that takes place when the survivor is able clearly to name and blame (and in some cases, first, even to remember) the abuser.

This is not universally the case. Some victims wish merely to forget the past and move on, setting as much psychic and physical distance as they can between themselves and those who abused them. For some – like Carla – reconciliation becomes a central agenda; but Carla felt, outside the abuse itself, cherished by her father, and this made reconciliation seem possible and desirable. There are those who forgive straight away and spontaneously, as in the case of the father who spontaneously forgave the Omagh bombers for killing his daughter. Even if we find forgiveness a much more difficult and painstaking and, in some cases, perhaps impossible process ourselves, we should not deride those who find it simple. Perhaps, after all, forgiveness is a matter of getting beyond our wounded complexity to something very simple and pristine.

But for yet others, the search to bring the perpetrator to justice becomes central. For such people, calls to be forgiving rather than full of rage are premature and potentially harmful. There are four reasons for this.

First, rage and blame at the perpetrator represents a move towards justice and indeed reality. The damaging self-blame that can lead survivors of holocaust and abuse to deep depression and even suicide is shifted to blame for the person who was in reality responsible. The guilt that may have attached to a kind of 'consent' in the case of the child who wanted intimacy and comfort; or the Holocaust survivor who survived, perhaps, because he colluded with the Nazi authorities in policing his fellow Jews, or because he stole bread from weaker victims who later died; such actions are revealed for what they truly were, the desperate struggle of the powerless, who are innocent by comparison with the calculating schemes of the powerful who deliberately engineered the need for such desperate choices. The blame begins to attach to the right person or people, those actually responsible for the whole situation. A deep morass of festering suffering and shame begins to transmute into appropriate rage.

Secondly, very often the victim encounters a wall of denial. The abuser often denies he has done wrong, or claims that the victim colluded; and this may be backed up by the family or the institution in which the abuse occurred. Notoriously this happened a great deal in the Roman Catholic Church, and the anger of many victims seems to me to be more directed against the denial or obscuring of wrong by the Church than against the abusing priest himself. And rightly so. Faced with such denial the abused person has two choices: to collude in the denial and internalize the shame as a supposed wicked slanderer; or to widen the anger by calling the institution itself to account.

So thirdly, when perpetrators are named and blamed, a shift takes place from the primitive and 'leaky' dimension of shame and disgust to the more rational realm of moral accountability. From being 'the blackest bile/ sneaking through the arterial flow,' an inchoate bitterness that can pervade the whole of reality, the darkness is given a focus in the choices of an identifiable individual or group. It is no longer an unthinkable monster that lurks within the darkest memories, but a nameable person 'out there' who can be hated. If he is to be truly loved, or at least forgiven, such a person must often be first hated. Hatred is for many doubtless the necessary first step forward from fear, the step that at least treats the other as a human person rather than a dreaded object.

And fourthly, unlike institutional derision and cold legal process, the actual rage and grief of the victim is what can awaken the abuser to the reality that there is another human consciousness out there, which he has harmed. This may not happen; like the wrath and the legal process, the tears and rage may make the abuser cringe more tightly inside his familiar protective shell. But it may be the first dawn of a new reality: a pain outside the self, grasped in the pain of remorse.

Though this section focuses on intense instances of abuse, the same four points could be made about less intense but long-term cases in which a person or group is put in a place of oppression and shame. When women, for example, stop feeling ashamed of their womanhood, or in need a man to impart a sense of value, and begin to assert their value in their own right, this is often accompanied by a feeling of rage. Suddenly a life lived in the shadow of men looks like a life half lost, full of potential never realized. Firstly, anger and even hatred of men in general, or a partner in particular, represents a step forward into reality, as a woman's full human nature is at last fully grasped. Secondly, the anger may impart energy needed to combat denial by institutions that have normalized patriarchy. Thirdly, a vague, debilitating lack of self-esteem gives way to feelings that are more focused and enabling. And fourthly there is a chance that rage may wake some men up to their unconscious complicity in values that, once they are aware of them, they no longer wish to live by.

4) From Shame and Blame to a Healing Remorse

So the move from shame and self-loathing to blaming the individual abuser can be a real step forward. It is a move forward in healing and a move forward in one's understanding of reality. But it does not take people all the way to complete healing; for rage and anger are a form of ongoing inner harm, and not only when the perpetrator is beyond the range of justice. And it does not supply us with the whole truth. As Bishop Joseph Butler argued long ago (1987, p. 137):

> anger may be considered as another false medium of viewing things, which always represents characters and actions much

> worse than they really are... Thus in cases of offense and enmity, the whole character and behavior is considered with an eye to that particular part which has offended us, and the whole man appears monstrous, without any thing right or human in him: whereas the resentment should surely at least be confined to that particular part of the behavior which gave offense: since the other parts of a man's life and character stand just the same as they did before.

In particular, anger does not yet see the victimhood of the victimizer. To see the abuse as the work of an accountable wrongdoer is to see it more truly than to see it as just what the abused deserved. But as noted in the previous chapter, blame, though often necessary, is always superficial. To get at the truth, we need to go deeper, in the way explored at the end of Chapter 1: to explain and understand in terms of the long-term chains of abuse that go from father to son and daughter, from abuser to abused. Perhaps we need to take on board the emphasis of the indigenous Canadian Hollow Water community (of which more in Chapter 9), who in their struggle to overcome endemic child abuse and other crime returned to their elders' insistence that harm can only be understood and dealt with by looking back and forward for seven generations.

To see the abuser as abused, or at least imprisoned, but still responsible for his collusion with the forces that impel him, is to see truly. That way, surely, lies the path to seeing abuse rightly, and being eventually delivered from it. And it is also the way whereby the abuser may begin to find the pain of remorse more bearable than the pain he has locked inside himself for so long and disowned: knowing that the journey of remorse and recompense, though it is his alone to tread, is undertaken in a kind of 'chain gang' in which he is bound by cause and effect to the rest of humanity. As Chapter 7 will develop further, through coming to see the one he has harmed as a vulnerable human being like himself, he can begin to return from his self-imposed isolation to the human race.

The same points apply, once again, to the more general cases of oppression. The feminist who is enraged with men has grasped important truth about her value in her own right. But she still sees men in a partial light. To move on, she needs to see that patriarchy is not the invention of individual men. Rather it is an ideology that oppresses men also, often crippling their emotional response and leading them into combative pathways versus other men, in which whole rich tracts of the personality have to be repressed and denied in the interests of preserving a male image. It is as wounded and diminished himself that the male has needed to wound and diminish women, and find in women a way of giving some value to his own insecure ego. Ultimately what will change a man is not further angry attacks on his ego, but a feisty compassion that can open the way to remorse and change.

But how is this possible? How can the hurts that have harmed us for so very long recede to being once again just hurts we have received in the course of life, and grown through? How can remorse help us break out of our abusiveness when, as Rowan Williams has noted, remorse is one of our *Lost Icons*, (2000, p. 95ff), less and less available in the cultural mainstream where the ideal is never to admit wrong, never to lose face? These matters are at the heart of what I hope this book can help us resolve.

Summary

1. We can turn hurt to harm by externalizing it and blaming others, but alternatively we can internalize it in two main ways: as shame, and as trauma.
2. In shame our wounds make us feel like a social wound or contaminant. Various kinds of shame can be distinguished, from embarrassment about specific acts – which

enables us to change – to chronic shame, which makes us feel bad about being ourselves, and undermines change.

3. Whereas remorse focuses on harm done to another and the need to repair it, chronic shame focuses on ourselves as somehow inherently harmful and toxic. Though guilt can be distinguished from shame, it can either be chronic and negative in the same way as shame, or a creative pain closer to what we call remorse.
4. Chronic shame follows the perverse logic of traumatization: wounds cannot heal because we have written our identity around them, creating an internal scapegoat and persecutor. Child abuse represents an extreme case of such trauma and its effects.
5. But there is a sense in which we all contain a dualistic split. Our ethics are often rooted in shame and a hiding from our own humanity and animality, priding ourselves on our independence and responsibility while actually manifesting repetitive and damaging responses.
6. The chronically shamed and traumatized are not helped to change by further shame, or by shaming understandings of God, or by the call to responsibility and repentance.
7. Blame of the true, external abuser can represent a step forward towards truth, and so can help abuser and abused alike. But what is ultimately needed is a remorse that shifts the abuser from his own inner circuit of trauma, enabling him to see the traumatized other in her own reality. Later chapters will explore this further.

Chapter 3

'I Avoid Hurt': Disclaim

Sorry I was not
there. The limbs
You pinned with the steel of sins and
Sorrows, and head you crowned in shame,
are not.

            If there is now a body to hurt more,
It is somewhere else beyond the land
Of the clenched fist and teeth that spit
The rage of the dead.

            Left only is the creamy curl
Of bands fit for the birthing of one who drinks
Now at a greater water, deep in abundance
those hands, so hungry, and mouths, so tight
Cannot milk,
            moving elsewhere....

He is not Here (Mark 16.6)

One of my clearest early memories will doubtless strike a familiar chord with many men and some women. At the age of about six, I fell in the school playground and grazed both my knees quite badly, so they bled. Immediately I tried to stand up and walk on as if nothing had happened. Though I trembled, I did not let any tears out, because I had learned as all boys do that boys do not cry – only 'sissies' do.

Since then it has become hard for me to access any painful emotion. I have put on a brave and happy face that says all is well with the world, and in the words of the Beatles song I loved, there is 'nothing to get hung about: strawberry fields forever!' Of course, life still dealt me blows from time to time. I still got hurt. But I did not feel it. Instead of a natural reaction of body and mind in harmony, I pushed all hurt out of consciousness, and the hurt became a harm that operated at an unconscious bodily level, like the physical trembling after that first fall, even whole the conscious Ross went on smiling at the world. More recently, I have had to learn all over again how to feel.

We have seen how hurt can become harmful when we project it outward onto others in anger and blame, and when we internalize it into ourselves in the self-scapegoating of shame. But there is a third and more subtle way in which hurt can become harmful, which we began to touch on when we noted that trauma can be so bad that we deny it and force it into the unconscious. We can simply move away from hurt and ignore it or pretend it has nothing to do with us.

This is the movement of Pilate washing his hands of the death of Jesus, declaring that (despite the fact that it was he who pronounced the death penalty) the death of Jesus was nothing to do with him. This is the movement of the priests who in the parable of Jesus (Luke 10.29–37) walked past the wounded man on the other side; it was of course the robbers who caused the suffering and possible death, nothing to do with them... It is the response of firm's public relations officers who, while regretting the accident that has crippled their employee for life, point out that all proper health and safety measures were in his place, and the accident was nothing to do with them... It is the response of the other parent who turns a blind eye to the son or daughter's abuse, as if it were nothing to do with them... or the concentration camp official who was 'only obeying orders,' following all the correct procedures, and that the unfortunate suffering and death of the inmates was nothing to do with him...

Thankfully, abuse, torture and killing do not come naturally to most of us. Yet an immense amount of it happens. In a family, there may be one abuser, but several who turn a blind eye. In a genocide or ethnic cleansing probably only tens or hundreds are actively involved in the planning, and tens or hundreds of thousands involved as troops actively committed to the action, but the numbers inhabiting the territories being 'cleansed' will amount to tens or hundreds of millions. Well armed as the first two categories may be, they are not sufficient simply to intimidate or force the population at large to collude unwillingly in the atrocity. So if atrocities continue, a large share of the cause must be the ability of nearly all people to turn a blind eye, or say that it is nothing to do with them, or simply to ask too few questions and be too easily convinced by the propaganda that says it that it is all for the best.

This lazy denial or cynical dissociation of ourselves from the wrongs around us and even within us is a strange kind of sin, since it involves no action and is largely beyond accountability and the law. But it is a necessary though not sufficient cause of the way hurts can spread and grow into large scale harm. That is to say, though people at large do not willingly cause the harm to happen, and other causes like leadership propaganda are involved, without their inaction it would not happen.

This chapter will explore five ways in which we avoid hurt as something that need not impinge on us.

- We can simply tune out, so far as we can, the experience or knowledge of hurt.
- If we cannot avoid knowing it, we can deny its reality, or at least its reality for us, and seek a mystical kind of invulnerability.
- If we cannot deny the reality of pain, we can normalize hurt or justify it as really for the best, a blessing in disguise.
- If we cannot justify hurt, we can consign it to the past, and

try to create a future that is safe from hurt and harm.

- And if that seems difficult or practically impossible, we can deny our share in responsibility for it, saying the harm has nothing to do with us; it must be caused by others, without whom a harm-free utopia would prevail.

I shall argue that many of these strategies for avoiding or disclaiming hurt are necessary in certain contexts. Were we to face all the evil of the world in one go, we would probably be traumatized into insanity; just as we do need sometimes to hold people responsible for their acts, and sometimes shame is appropriate to our behavior, so we often need to filter suffering out to make it manageable. But all the strategies have a tendency actually to turn hurt into something more harmful than it needs to be. I shall end the chapter by suggesting we need to develop what I shall call a 'global mindfulness': a deeper way of owning, without shame or guilt, our connection to the hurt of the world which we all receive from and contribute to.

Tuning Hurt Out

Daily in the media we confront earthquakes, famines, terrorist attacks, and horrific cases of cruelty. For our sanity we have to find ways of dissociating from this, setting a distance between it and our emotional life. An element of 'disclaim' – regarding this hurt as 'nothing to do with me' – is unavoidable if we are to remain sane, and the trick is to know when our disengagement is itself becoming pathological, allowing many processes of hurt and harm to go on existing when they need not.

We have a number of ways of setting a psychic distance between ourselves and world pain. One is simply geographical – much of the suffering takes place in far-off parts of the world, or in ghettos and so-called 'sink estates' in our own land, where the privileged would never dare to go. When I took up a post as priest in an old estate in Bristol with huge deprivation and drugs problems; though I had lived in Bristol for nearly 20 years it was the first time I had been to that place. No big roads went through it; it was off the map except for the media interest it often aroused. Many now live in 'gated communities,' living in privileged ghettos sealed off from poverty and crime.

Another way of distancing suffering has to do with newsworthiness and the effectiveness of propaganda machines. We hear a great deal about certain wars, including those our own nations are involved in – Iraq, Afghanistan – and those where there are large or influential lobbies within our nation making the case for one side or both – as in the conflict between Jews and Palestinians. But other wars that have caused immensely greater suffering and death – like that in the Congo which has involved an estimated 5.4 million deaths, gang rape on a massive scale, and genocide against the pygmy people – are largely ignored, partly because their sheer duration makes them cease to be newsworthy, and partly because they involve only people from a continent that seems remote and unconnected to us. It would be an instructive exercise to plot a map of the world for which distance from us was not determined by miles but by the number of press releases over the past decade. A kind of social geography would doubtless emerge in which the Middle East is near at hand, but Africa mainly remote. (Though oddly the farthest part, the south, is relatively close!)

Another way of distancing is institutional. The sufferings of old age, severe illness, mental ill-health and death are not matters we often encounter on our streets because they are dealt with in special institutions – nursing homes, hospitals, funeral parlors. The facts of life that sent the Buddha on his journey to enlightenment – the suffering of birth, sickness, old age and death – can easily be avoided, at least until they affect our close relatives and friends, whereupon we often feel a curious shame and need to hide ourselves away from public view.

Yet another is linguistic. No country I am aware of has a

budget for 'attack' or 'invasion' – it is always described as 'defense' even when this involves military occupation and war in far-off lands. Stalin 'liquidated' his enemies, which sounds like a delicate chemical process! When Americans bombed villages in Vietnam, it was often described as 'liberating' the village. Such language enables people to cause terrible suffering and death that they would not tolerate if they had to do it face to face and describe it simply as 'killing the villagers.' In the same way in abortion we never 'kill the embryonic human in the womb'; much more abstractly we 'terminate the pregnancy.' (I am not one of those who believe that abortion is absolutely always wrong; but I think we would debate the matter with more integrity if we asked when it is right to kill embryos in the womb. In the same way the matter of war is discussed with integrity only when it is asked when it is right to mobilize armed forces to kill people systematically on a huge scale.)

Another distancing mechanism is chauvinism of some kind – racist, sexist, 'speciesist' or whatever. Those who suffer are not really like us; in some way it does not hurt them like it would hurt us, sensitive creatures that we are. Battery farmed hens may suffer greatly, but we think of them as being only birds, barely sentient and without experience of anything better. Slavery is regrettable; but in the minds of the slave owners, most slaves are big tough African types; they are thought of (though of course not explicitly described) as not being human in the full sense of the word. There have been huge Iraqi and Afghan casualties in our recent wars, but it is the British and American ones who really seem to matter, if our news bulletins are anything to go by.

Of course it is a positive feature of globalized communication that we know much more about war and other suffering in far-off places than we ever used to. We see much more of the pain of war graphically presented on our screens, and the impossibility of censoring the internet – though it has regrettable consequences in the easy availability of extremist and pornographic sites – does mean that we can see conflicts from more than our own nation's point of view. It is inevitable that we have to censor some of this suffering in our own minds. But we need to be aware when a more systematic and biased kind of censoring begins to operate that effectively dehumanizes parts of the human race, and implies – without it ever being stated – that some people's sufferings do not matter as much as others. When that happens, it becomes easy for forms of violence to perpetuate that would outrage us if they took place in our own mental 'backyard'.

Mystical Invulnerability

However, if we become more fully aware of the suffering all over the world, and refuse to tune it out, we may well become tempted to minimize it by another more mystical route, by denying the essential reality of what we experience. The retreat from the real world into an inner world, where suffering can either be avoided in painless bliss or transmuted to joy, seems to be characteristic of many kinds of religion, though the religious are not the only people for whom it is possible.

I described above the beginnings of this process in my own case. Of course, I knew that my knees were hurt and bleeding, but I insisted to myself that this did not matter, that it was not a fact that left any mark on me. It is no accident that in adolescence I turned from my robust and realistic atheism to a fairly introverted kind of religion, in the first instance Buddhism, which gave me a way of rising above suffering. This book will draw mainly on Buddhism and Christianity for their rich wisdom in offering positive ways of responding to hurt. But it needs first to be acknowledged that both faiths have often been used to encourage very negative reactions, and done so in two characteristic patterns.

The previous chapter noted how religions can intensify our shame and disgust in the face of hurt and vulnerability. In this way they increase the attractiveness of withdrawal, escape or dissociation from the world of hurt. Many kinds of religion advocate a flight from the material world towards union with ultimate reality, beyond what the prayer at compline calls the 'changes and chances of this fleeting world.' Though it is present in mystical and Gnostic understandings of Christianity and even Islam and Judaism, this escapist flight seems to be especially encouraged in decadent understandings of the Eastern religions – Hinduism, Buddhism and maybe Taoism.

Typically the body is seen as the reason why we often hurt. We have seen that this is only partly true. Perhaps hurt, being a sensation, has to start in the body, but what only hurts the body may harm the soul. And even bodily pleasures, according to many religions, may harm the soul if indulged with wrong intent, or if they create an addiction or dependency. Nonetheless the avoiding of hurt quickly accelerates (as noted) into the avoiding of the body or even of material reality itself, or the declaration (in Plato and in the Hindu Vedanta, for example) that the material world is fundamentally illusory and what is real is the soul or spirit, which finds bliss in release (*moksha*) from that world.

It is this flight from pain that I express in this chapter's opening poem, which imagines Christ as entering by his resurrection a place where he is 'safe from harm.' But there is surely too something rich and positive about a 'greater water, deep in abundance' from which the tight mouths of the violent cannot drink. I had in mind here the 'hungry ghosts' who inhabit one of the 'hells' of Buddhist mythology. This is a place full of delightful foods, but the mouths of the ghosts are too small to enable them to fill their big hollow craving bellies! The image suggests that salvation does not come through escape from the world, but by opening ourselves more fully to it than our narrow world of tight envy and clenched violence normally allows us to.

An alternative to the escape beyond pain – found in some of

the ascetic extremes of Hinduism but also strands of Christianity and Shia Islam – is to consecrate pain as being itself the way to bliss. If the escape from hurt represents a manic aspect of religion, this alternative suggests something more like the religious equivalent of masochism. In the strange alchemy of masochism, bodily feelings of shame and pain are linked with sexual pleasure. Masochism, perhaps, is the ultimate optimism, the supreme way of saying that however bad things get, we can triumph – even in our orgasmic bodies. The unfortunate corollary is that in both masochistic sex and masochistic religion, ecstasy is harnessed to an inner dynamic of the mind, rather than an intimacy with the other or with God that might transcend subjugation and punishment.

The escapist and masochistic strands are present in all religions, but exist alongside other strands. The problem with them is that they make hurt either fearful or desirable, something either to escape from or to indulge in. Suffering becomes so large in the consciousness – so menacing or attractive in itself – that the response is either to minimize it or become obsessed with it. Suffering cannot settle down alongside happiness to become a natural part of our life in the world and our intimacy with others or with God.

If I had not felt the wound in my knees to be so humiliating, I might have been able to feel the pain for a while. That might have led me to weep, and to be comforted by someone close to me, and then to smile and carry on with life unencumbered.

It's All for the Best

If we cannot avoid the experience of hurt, and cannot deny that the hurt really affects us, we can still deny that there is any harm in the hurt. We can give the hurt a bright future that makes up for the present pain. As the lines in the well-known song in *Godspell* puts it, '*someone's* got to be oppressed... Yes, it's all for the best!'

In this strategy, suffering is accepted as a necessary part of a process leading to an ultimate good. People including children work away in 'sweatshops' in many countries to produce the cheap goods we use, but this is seen as part of the 'economic development' that will bring them and us greater prosperity in the long term. In the ultimate balancing of accounts this 'deficit' can be written off. Though there are horrors, they are inevitable and God, being loving, must have made what the 18th century philosopher Gottfried Leibniz called 'the best of all possible worlds.' The word 'eudemonistic' has been coined to refer to views that make little of hurt and harm because of a blind or reasoned optimism. (The word actually refers to the 'good demon' or 'good luck' of the Greeks.)

But many would question the whole notion that hurts can be somehow traded off against future good things, so as to make suffering 'for the best.' Dostoyevsky's character Ivan Karamazov, in *The Brothers Karamazov,* dramatically brought this home when he declared that he did not think a whole perfect future utopia justified the tears of a single innocent child. This may be overstated. It would surely be right to have one's child inoculated against diphtheria, for example, even if the injection brought tears to the child's eyes, because the pain could be traded off favorably against the possibility of a terrible disease. But in this case we know as a medical fact that hurting the child now is the necessary price to pay for a greater future good for that same child. What must be called into question is the idea that if there is a hurt, it *must be* for the future good, even if we do not know what that good is; that every cloud *must have* a silver lining. That trivializes the hurt.

The trivialization is parodied in a well-known scene from the Monty Python film *The Life of Brian*. Here Brian, dying on the cross, starts to smile and sing a jolly song beginning, 'Look on the bright side of life!' In time all the others crucified with him begin to sing along and even, so far as they can from their crucified positions, jerk their limbs and heads as if to dance. To see all hurt and suffering as having a 'bright side' is, in the end, to view them as lightweight. It will tend to suggest that, because things will sort themselves out without our intervention, we do not need to seek justice or the alleviation of pain. Both Buddhism and Christianity have at times seemed to think along these lines, but the authentic forms of both faiths take their very starting point from the 'dark side of life': the immensity of suffering in Buddhism, the prevalence of sin and death in Christianity.

The Dangers of Absolute Safety

At first sight it seems much better to take hurt totally seriously, but engage with it in the belief that all hurt can be banished, and the world can be made free from risk. Of course it is one of the good characteristics of our modern world – with its medicines and therapies and political idealism – that we seek to deal with hurt and to limit it as far as we can. But by imagining we can construct a world where harm won't exist and nobody will get hurt any more I suggest that we have come to an unprecedented idolization of safety that is actually quite counterproductive and dangerous.

From D.P. Strachan (1989) onwards, the hygiene hypothesis has become widely accepted. According to this, our modern obsession with total cleanliness can leave children underexposed and under-immune to diseases that did not trouble them so much in the past. This can stand as a parable. As humans, we need a little risk, a little dirt, a little danger, so that we acquire what it takes to identify and negotiate big risks when they come our way.

There is obviously nothing wrong with wanting to protect people from risk. Parents who did not want to protect their children would quite rightly be suspect. But of late the government itself has begun to take a parental role towards all its subjects, as if its chief role were to ensure that nobody ever comes to grief. It has become what Michael Portillo famously called a 'nanny state,' with an unprecedented amount of legislation designed for 'health and safety' and the like. In itself this is all quite laudable, but as Mary Midgley points out, 'safety is a means to other ends, not an end in itself... That is why, when we see a need for it, we can make an effort to overcome fear.' (1984, p. 43) This effort is what we call courage, the virtue that makes people put their own and even others' safety at risk in the interests of higher ideals like freedom and justice.

But what has happened lately reverses this, turning safety into the goal to which freedom and justice are sacrificed. This represents an idolization of safety, turning what should be a means into an end: a kind of collectively imposed cowardice.

We seem all too ready to accept loss of liberty – detention without trial for terrorist suspects being one major controversial example – in order to feel a bit safer, a bit less likely to be hurt or to die. In reality the danger of dying through terrorist activity remains extremely minimal compared, for example, with the danger of dying from cancer or a road accident. But nobody countenances the possibility of imprisoning or torturing *potentially* dangerous drivers, whereas such things have been advocated and employed against potential terrorists. Terrorism – partly because of the way terrorists themselves deliberately cultivate fear and hatred by the savagery of their crimes, but doubtless also because terrorists tend to belong to religious or racial minorities, and so attract the scapegoating mechanisms we have discussed – has become seen as an enormous danger, an evil threatening the sacred safety of society itself.

In such a context, nobody asks what the purpose of safety is, or what balance of safety or risk is best for the flourishing of human beings. In the workplace, Sidney Dekker (2007) argues from his experience of nursing, air traffic control and professional aviation, that a just culture will protect people's honest and inadvertent mistakes from being seen as culpable. But that may make people less wary of making dangerous mistakes. On the other hand a society that polices all possible risks and, when things go wrong, hunts out who to blame and even criminalize, will inhibit everyone from creative innovations, because not all innovations can be tested in advance for all possible risks. There is a balance to be struck between safety and justice. But in our increasing concern for safety, we may be failing to register how unevenly the balance is tipping.

Now every good parent (at least, if not corrupted by the prevailing idolization of safety) knows that mollycoddling – running round making sure that children never do any activities in which they could possibly get hurt – is as damaging to a child as negligent exposure to danger. I remember as a child of ten or so being free to roam widely round our town with my sister and various friends. One place we loved was the woods that bordered on the recreation ground. The slopes were steep and we knew all the places where you could skid down through tracks between the branches. The place had its dangers in the form of sharp thorn bushes. But we came equipped with skills and intuitions our parents had helped instill, like looking after each other, and being wary of strangers, *especially* unusually friendly ones. And we learned new skills through negotiating the risks together.

Such play would be far more difficult these days. Parents who allowed such freedoms and risks might be thought negligent. But is our 'safer' world better – or even actually safer? Educationalist Heather Eliott has argued (2010, p. 12) that 'a combination of the media and legislation regarding children's welfare is making us increasingly wary of how we as adults respond to children, especially other people's children.' She relates an experiment by Esther Rantzen, co-founder of Childline, in which child actors pretended to be in difficult situations in public places. Out of 5,000 people only *two* stopped to help. Is that safe?

There are limits to how far legislation can make things safe, in this and other areas. A CRB disclosure is a very fallible guide, since people who have never harmed a child, but have been accused of doing so, will be barred from children's work, while people who have, but have not so far been accused, will be allowed. More might be achieved by two things. On the one hand, under current legislation a child who reports abuse may trigger an invasive investigation, in the course of which he will be interrogated and his evidence legalistically probed, with results outside his control. We need to create an environment where children can discern signs of danger, feel assured that they themselves need not be ashamed of anything degrading that is done to them, and rest confident that any worries they voice will be dealt with respectfully and carefully. And we need to reverse a sinister trend in our culture noted by Rowan Williams towards the premature sexualization of children. Speaking of children's talent competitions, Williams notes how 'the stereotypes of predatory male and seductive female are happily exploited and thought to be rather touching in children of six to eight years old,' (2000, p. 25). If children are led to present themselves in such ways, it can only increase their vulnerability.

And on the other, we need to do the utmost to strengthen the resolve of those who acknowledge a sexual attraction to children, but are determined not to harm them. A welcome development in this respect are the Circles of Support and Accountability, pioneered by the Mennonites in Canada and now widely available, not least through the churches. These circles have effected a remarkable 70% reduction in the rate of re-offense. But they are only available for ex-offenders, who have an established malign habit to undo. One might expect even more success those who have never harmed children, but acknowledge a temptation to do so though they are determined not to. However, in his courageous talk, *The Sin that Dare not Speak its Name* (Greenbelt, 2010), John Bell from the Iona Community noted that to do so is to meet with a very unpredictable response. Sometimes confession of an inclination is confused with confession of an offense, which legally has to be reported in the interest of those being abused. Bell anonymously cited two cases where support was found and the person succeeded in avoiding any acts of harm, and one where a person did not find support and went on to harm.

I have dwelt on the matter of child protection, not only because it is so important to get matters right, but because it focuses very sharply on the three issues of blame, shame and denial with which this first part of the book is concerned. In this area there is a particularly acute need – both for children at risk of harm and for adults with a potential to harm – to lift matters out of the wall of silence within which they have been contained since time immemorial, into confidential places of openness and accountability, governed by the preventive and healing justice discussed in Chapter 9. Only if that can happen can we seriously hope to shed a transforming light on the obscure tendencies that make for child abuse, and make it a thing of the past. That may be a utopian hope, but I hope it is not naive.

The Dark Side of Utopia

If hurt persists, and it seems impossible to rid the world of harm, then we can still dissociate ourselves from it if we can find others to blame, and present ourselves or our people as innocent victims incapable of harm.

Characteristic of modernity is a jettisoning of the ancient view that suffering is an inevitable part of life. The Buddha affirmed this view as the first Noble Truth. Suffering is one of the three marks of existence (along with impermanence and the lack of any abiding soul). Western Christianity affirms original sin: we are all prepared to cause suffering as we pursue what we crave. But to cut a very long story short, in the 'Enlightenment' in the 18th century – the century of the American and French revolutions – such doctrines began to be overturned in favor of an 'original innocence' or 'original blessing.' This was epitomized in Jean Jacques Rousseau's declaration that humankind is 'born free, but everywhere he is in chains.' Suffering was no longer regarded as our natural state, but as something we could change, by throwing off the chains of oppression. Utopia was just round the corner; we would be there now... if it weren't for *x*.

The downside of this claiming of original innocence was that someone, or some group, had to be this ***x***. No longer was the cause of suffering located – as it is in Buddhism and Christianity in their different ways – in each and every one of us. Someone, or some group, had to be challenged to change, to abdicate their oppressive hold on humanity; and if they could not change they had to be destroyed for the common good. So the centuries of revolution – the 18th, 19th and 20th centuries, and continuing in the 21st[t] – unleashed an astounding mix of hope and progress, and hatred and terror. As the literary critic Terry Eagleton remarks (2010, p. 123), 'the more tediously angelic our official regimes grow, the more they give birth to a mindless nihilism.' In the name of restoring innocence, the guilty had to be hunted down and unmasked. Not everyone could be innocent; so a fierce competition began to assert one's own group's innocence and others' guilt.

The feminist Angela West (1996) joined in the occupation of Greenham Common in protest against cruise missiles. There she experienced the competition for innocence as a sinister factor that undermined the feminism of her comrades. She writes of the high hopes of a new world in which women were liberated from their victim status to a new innocence.

To be present in the early days was to experience something

> in the nature of a baptism. We were immersed in the waters of a feminism that proclaimed us henceforth free from the sins that the patriarchal world had ascribed to us, and released us into a liberated perception of reality, where we would learn to trust those closest to us (other sisters) and to distrust those who had taught us to blame and distrust ourselves and other women (i.e. mainly men). (p. 50)

However, reality did not always live up to these high ideals, and

> when feelings and desires do not measure up to the self's ideal, then there is always the problem of what to do about them. For feminists, guilt itself is a feeling they are not supposed to feel, for we are supposed to have been liberated from that too. There is of course a time-honored way of dealing with inconvenient guilt, and with desire that disturbs but which cannot be fully admitted. It involves the ejection of our violence and that which we are forbidden to feel on to the Other, the one who can be safely cast out from the bonds and bounds of the community. (p. 53)

Camp life broke into rival factions, ceremoniously 'walking out' from meetings, or expelling others for their betrayal of true feminism. This sectarian history is reminiscent of earlier movements that have promised a new beginning through liberation from an oppressive world, like Christianity and Marxism.

Angela West writes about societies – for example socialist and feminist ones – that are explicitly based on the 'innocence' of liberated innocents, but much of what she argues applies to society more widely now that it has come to see itself as being delivered from the guilty Christianity of past generations to a new, liberated innocence.

> Purity is what the new movement seeks to preserve at all

> costs — because its purity is its power. Yet it is an endeavor by its very nature impossible to achieve — for purity of this nature cannot be preserved in the human community at large. And so purity has to be formalized, institutionalized, to be no longer the result of virtue or grace, but of reason/ rationality — a rationale. The threats to internal purity which arise through conflict and fallibility in a normal human community have to be displaced on to outsiders — those terribly necessary outsiders. Whether by means of show trials or scapegoats, power has to dress itself in a cloak of radical purity. (p. 76)

Since West wrote these words, many strands of feminine and left wing thought have lost something of the presumption of innocence she described, becoming perhaps more mature, sober and perplexed. Yet at the same time the puritan legalism and obsession with politically correct procedure and policy, which West saw epitomized in those radical movements, have become more general and normal. Sometimes we seem to spend more time giving account of our work than actually doing it. As in a Kafkaesque nightmare, we have become the age of the 'form,' able to do nothing of significance without inscribing ink on paper. There is now a 'me' that is scattered abroad on many different parchments and computer systems, each representing something for which I may be called to account, or else enabling some other person to avoid being called to account by me. Sometimes this 'paper self' seems to be eclipsing the 'me' of flesh and blood.

Gillian Rose (according to Shanks, 2008) has argued that in our society people compete not so often to be powerful and 'win' (though that does happen) but to acquire the status of victim, of being the oppressed, the underdog. Of course – as noted at the end of the previous chapter – often it is correct and important to affirm one's victimhood, and trace the blame to its real cause in an oppressor or abuser. But we cannot all be victims, and none of us victimizers. Clearly victim status has acquired an attractiveness that goes beyond its credibility.

Why has it become so attractive to be the victim in our society? Probably because of the way the victim is presumed innocent; the ills of society have 'nothing to do with him'; not he, but some other is to blame. Being the victim is another way of disclaiming our share in hurting and harming, and distancing ourselves from a complexly corrupt world. Innocent victimhood has an almost religious purity. It is as if the deep hold of the crucified Jesus on the Western imagination has combined with the need of a 'post-Christian' age to affirm original innocence, to create the assumption that the victim must always be holy and right.

Certainly Jesus himself tended to associate with the underclass, the victims. But it seems to me what he did was something subtly different from our sanctification of the victim. There is no evidence to suggest that he exalted some kind of nobility in the prostitutes, tax collectors, lepers and other outcasts with whom he associated, that made them 'worthy' of his love. Nor do we see him urging his disciples self-sacrificially to lay aside their natural revulsion and embrace such lowly and disgusting people! For they were themselves chosen from the same ranks of people: Jesus urged them to befriend them as the 'undeserving poor,' because they themselves were 'undeserving poor.' Jesus does not invite us to love the marginalized because they are holy and innocent. Rather, as the best translation of Jesus' rendition of the commandment goes, we are to 'love them as [people like] ourselves.'

In modern times there has been a radical pushing back of the boundaries of what behavior is seen as acceptable. But what has not been affirmed in this move is the fact that even the people who do things we should never come to regard as acceptable – thugs, drug barons, child abusers, terrorists, the moral equivalent of the prostitutes and tax collecting collaborators of Jesus' day, people who are far from innocent – are accepted as people made in God's image and welcomed into God's Kingdom. That may still be as much a scandal to us today as it was for the authorities in Jesus' time; it seems to undermine any idea of law and order. Whether it actually does will be explored in later chapters.

Our modern idolization of the victim – if this is not too strong a word – reverses the kind of acceptance offered by Jesus. Instead of resting in a fundamental equality and solidarity in our flawed state, we see a purity in the victim that we want to imitate, and that leads us to compete, because obviously, as noted, not everyone can be innocent of the flaws in our society. Instead of claiming our share in the world's ills as the only sound basis for our transformation, this kind of view leads us to a panicky disclaiming of responsibility, because if we don't promptly disclaim the mud and fling it elsewhere, others will ensure that it clings to us. That leaves us with the harmful alternatives explored in the first two chapters: we either have to blame, or incur shame.

Towards a Global Mindfulness

In the ways described so far we are able, often, to shrug off great suffering as somehow not there, or unimportant, or beneficial, or eradicable, or at least nothing to do with us. But how *should* we respond to hurt? If we own the suffering and our complicity in a lot of it, will that not just make us feel guilty and ashamed, and so add to the pain?

Often there genuinely is no causal connection between our personal actions and people's suffering. In cases like the tsunami, earthquakes, and atrocities by vicious regimes, surely a deep sorrow is appropriate. And in the cases that involve deliberate human action, anger will be appropriate too. But it would be completely inappropriate to feel guilt, since I am not responsible for these things at all.

But what about the many cases where there is a definite causal link? The sweatshops will continue whether or not I personally buy their products, but they could not exist without the trade in which I participate. Hens will not stop being battery farmed just because I buy free range, but if I buy battery farmed hens and eggs I participate in the causing of their suffering. Internet pornography is not my personal fault, but if I use it I collude in the exploitation it involves.

To say such phenomena are 'nothing to do with me' would clearly involve a pathological kind of disclaimer of the pain I do not personally cause, but do participate in causing. On the other hand it seems to me inappropriate to ascribe the same blame to sharing in causing as we do to being personally responsible. If someone dies as a result of the conditions in a sweatshop, it would clearly be inappropriate to put everyone who bought the products on trial for manslaughter. Nor should we put all users of pornography on trial as rapists, or (animal rights activists notwithstanding) put all the consumers of battery farmed chicken on trial for cruelty to the birds.

Nevertheless in cases where crimes like rape and murder are witnessed by people who stand by and do nothing to help, there has been a serious debate about whether such people are partly responsible and should be prosecuted. What degree of collusion in an act makes a person partly responsible for it? Are those who witness a rape and egg the rapist on more responsible than those who disapprove but do nothing? They are colluding more; but on the other hand those who are clear the act is wrong surely have more responsibility to do something about it. Are the priest and Levite who walked past the wounded man in Jesus' parable (Luke 10.29–37) to be considered guilty of his assault? French law criminalizes such behavior, but British law does not. The concepts of 'collusion' and 'participation' in an act, and the degrees of accountability for the act they involve, require careful ethical scrutiny. But then, once criteria are worked out, should the same criteria not be applied to those who witness great injustices in the media, and could take some action against the injustice, but do nothing? That includes me, often.

In the West we have inherited from Greece and from Judaism and Christianity an ethic that focuses on intention – on what we want to happen and directly cause to happen. Few people intend things like genocide and atrocity (though of course they cannot happen without some people doing so). So we can feel, in a world full of suffering, relatively free from sin. Buddhist and Hindu ethics, by contrast, draw on the notion of karma: the idea that we are the cause of a lot of suffering without intending it, and we are responsible and will ultimately suffer for all the suffering we cause, whether it results from our intentional activity or from our inactivity or ignorance. Ultimately in these perspectives it is ignorance (*avidya*, literally 'lack of vision'), not intention, that underlies suffering, and we are responsible for our degree of ignorance or enlightenment.

Such considerations have not always led Buddhists to take action to alleviate suffering; but the resources are there, and there is a growing movement of 'engaged Buddhism' that gets involved in political issues, but from a different perspective from the classic Western concern to hold individuals to account for injustice. It is not that we should feel personally guilty for the sufferings others cause, but there is a kind of awareness which, if lacking, shows a moral deficiency. If we are right to feel at all sorry or angry about an instance of suffering, then if we have participated in causing it that anger or sorrow ought in part to be directed against ourselves.

We do not really have a word or a concept for the kind of feeling that is appropriate here – something between grief and remorse, weaker than guilt and self-blame, but stronger and more penitent than simple sorrow and anger, and strong enough to motivate appropriate change. I shall call it a 'global mindfulness': a cultivated awareness of and openness to the joys and sufferings of the world and the web of causes that link me to them. Ordinary mindfulness in Buddhism is a cultivated non-judgmental awareness of the experiences, thoughts and feelings that go on in my mind, regarding them just as they occur without buying in to the concepts and narratives that I habitually connect with them. It is walking to the railway station while being fully aware of just the walking, without narratives like, 'I've just got to get that train.' Global mindfulness would be a cultivated non-judgmental awareness of the experiences, thoughts and feelings that go on in the world, opening our own minds to them as much as we can, and trying to see them in their own light and not according to the narratives our society has spun around them. But it is not yet clear that 'global mindfulness' names anything actually possible. Chapter 8 will explore mindfulness as such, and whether it is possible to extend mindfulness in this global way.

But if we are to get beyond our vacillations between crippling guilt and blame on the one hand, and the various forms of disclaimer on the other, we need to begin to develop something like this global mindfulness. It may be one way in which we can begin to motivate real change and real healing for a world in whose suffering we are all causally implicated in highly complex ways.

Summary

1. As well as seeing hurt as harm caused by external others whom we blame, and internalizing hurt as a harmful shame, we can deny the reality of hurt as it affects us, in which case it still harms us and others.
2. We can avoid experience or knowledge of hurt in various ways. This enables us to go on contributing to the hurt without knowing it.
3. We can know of hurt but deny it is real at all, or real for us.

The falsely 'mystical' religions that separate us from the world of pain and seek spiritual invulnerability, and those that masochistically glorify pain, allow or encourage real harm to continue.

4. We can know hurt is real but justify it as being for the best. This allows us to tolerate hurts and injustices when we do not need to.
5. We can know hurt is bad but believe we can abolish all risk of it. But the legislation that seeks to make us safe at all costs removes us from the life and growth associated with risk, and creates a society of wary suspicion in which we are more at risk than we were before.
6. We can see the difficulty of abolishing hurt but retain belief that utopia is still possible 'if only… those others were not involved…' But the consequent rage, blame and in some cases terror only increases hurt and harm.
7. We need to find a way of owning sorrow as something that belongs to us – in that we feel it, we cause it, and to some degree we need the risk of it – without being crippled by the burden of this owning, but rather enabled to effect change.

Chapter 4

Hurt Written in Stone: Evil as Real

In the beginning was the great sorrow. God traced
hesitant fingers over its intractable
womb.
            Then God said, let there be
bliss. And so there was, spirals of it dancing out
from the womb.
            The men did not like
to be made of sorrow, so chose to make it
for others instead. They made war and religions,
cunning and cruel. Yet sorrow would come
to its own: lovers and loners and fathers minded to dig
down to the rock of heart.
            Knowing what battles and barren obsession
did to their children, the women
were otherwise left bereft with the sorrow alone.

But the Word was made sorrow, nailed
to a tree full of it, where the women were left
to it.
            Still pregnant it is, cracking open
to spill its gifts of truth. And the power
to be its children, dancing, delivered.

Original Sorrow

Our response to hurt is rarely something we consciously choose. Nobody chooses whether to feel ashamed, or to flare up in anger against a 'culprit,' and when I denied the pain in my knees, it was not possible for me to do otherwise and say to myself,

'Come on, Ross, let's have a go at feeling the pain and crying for a change!' This is because the way we deal with hurt is interdependent on the narrative we have been taught to use in describing it. The narrative and the response form a mutually reinforcing circle that is very hard to break. I had learned (from parents? friends?) the narrative that big boys don't cry, and that made me determined that, as a big boy, I would be strong; and my success in stemming the tears confirmed the narrative: as a big boy now, I myself very rarely cry.

Behind each of the different responses to hurt described so far, we can see a kind of account that not only makes hurt harmful, but inserts it into a grand narrative of something much bigger than us and our individual hurts, something we tend to call 'evil.' With blame goes the story that evil resides in certain people. With shame goes a sense that something about me is evil and despicable. With the various kinds of disclaimer just discussed goes a variety of mythologies – mystical, pessimistic, optimistic, utopian – that include accounts of what evil is and how it should be dealt with. Each of these responses writes a way of responding to hurt in stone, making the response seem natural and inevitable and impossible to change.

This chapter and the next will explore these big, broad accounts of evil and how they can facilitate positive or negative ways of responding to hurt and harm. Often these big accounts are myths we have unconsciously swallowed and never questioned, like my idea that big boys don't cry. Bringing our own mythology of evil out into the open enables us to question whether it is really what we believe, and whether believing it has actually helped us or hindered us in our responses. Sometimes myths that have seemed like iron laws crumple to dust when questioned, like old parchment when exposed to air.

Much of these chapters will look at how we see evil in the global picture, but that is intimately connected with what makes us see individual acts or people as evil. This is the question with which I begin.

Individual Evil

> A rabbi in Lodz was forced to spit on a Torah scroll that was in the Holy Ark. In fear of his life he complied and desecrated that which is holy to him and his people. After a short while he had no more saliva, his mouth was dry. To the Nazi's question, why did he stop spitting, the rabbi replied that his mouth was dry. Then the son of the 'superior race' began to spit into the rabbi's mouth and the rabbi continued to spit on the Torah. (quoted in Gaita, 2004, p. 1)

This action by a Nazi officer is described in Chaim Kaplan's Warsaw diary (1999). To describe it as a wrongful act would fail to capture what makes us so angry, horrified and perhaps grief-stricken about it. There is something in this incident which we can only rightly call 'evil' and which puts to the test the conception of evil we have; which is why, harrowing as it is, I shall need to return to it.

Not every wrongdoing, and not every case of hurt or harm, calls for the language of evil. The milder language of suffering, badness, sin and wrongdoing is often sufficient. But many of the cases I have used in the previous three chapters invite description in terms of evil and wickedness. It would be grossly inadequate to say that the child abuser, or the perpetrators of genocide, or the boys who tortured other children almost to the point of death were just behaving badly or making the wrong decision.

So what are the factors in an action that call for the language of evil? I suggest four factors all need to be there.

The first is obviously *enormity* – a word which itself conveys either huge in quantity or horrifying in quality, or both. Though people might think it wrong to lose one's temper, or to make a tactless remark, or to tell less than the whole truth in order to save one's own reputation, we would not describe such acts as 'evil.' In the case of Kaplan's Nazi the quantity of actual physical hurt or harm is perhaps small, but the quality of the humiliation and degradation and probably mental harm is extreme, and the calculated causing of this is what we have to call evil.

The second factor – obvious in this case – is that the action is done with the *intent* of causing harm. An engineer who miscalculated and constructed a faulty dam, which subsequently broke and caused thousands of deaths through flooding, might be criminally negligent, but he is not evil. And despite the huge amount of maiming and loss of life they cause, only animists would call a tsunami or earthquake 'evil'; and they would do so because they saw these things as intentional agents rather than just natural phenomena. The being causing an evil act has to be conscious and consciously doing harm to the victim(s).

The third factor is in tension with this: a kind of *irrationality* that defies empathy. Although the agent is of the kind we would normally describe as responsible, we find it hard to understand the action in terms of rational and responsible agency. The harm seems to be done just for its own sake, for we cannot discern a higher end that might justify it in the mind of the agent. Of course the perpetrator may be ready with some kind of rationalization, but such rationalizations fail to qualify as reasons we can accept. The actions cannot be justified – or even condemned – in the normal language of accountability. When Harold Shipman – an intelligent, rational and ordinary-seeming doctor – caused the succession of at least 218 deaths of his elderly patients for no apparent reason, we cannot either empathize or understand. We feel a need to do more than call upon Shipman to explain his deeds; whatever explanation he offers we feel would be only a rationalization of what is an essentially unjustifiable evil. Likewise with Kaplan's Nazi. It is not only that we ourselves cannot justify these actions; we cannot see what reason might have justified them in the mind of the perpetrator.

So 'evil' does not just mean unjust or wrong. Some non-evil deeds may be more wrong, morally, than some we rightly call evil. Terrorist acts are a case in point. Though many regard them as evil, I do not think they always have the typical characteristics of evil. Though we cannot see terrorist actions as justified, we can see what might have justified them in the mistaken minds of the terrorists themselves. We may even be able to imagine the kind of circumstances that might make us commit similar acts. In David Mitchell's novel, *number9dream* (2001), the hero, Eiji Miyaki, is given and reads the diary of his uncle, who died as a Japanese kaiten pilot near the end of the Second World War. Kaitens were torpedoes that the pilot sat in and guided, so that when the ship was hit the pilot himself was destroyed along with his target. As we read of Eiji reading, we sympathize at least with what in his uncle he came to admire – a cool matter-of-fact heroism whereby he was able to lay down his life as part of an increasingly desperate war effort. We glimpse something of the mind of the suicide bomber: not an individual madman or monster, more a rational participant in a narrative or a situation that has gone mad and monstrous.

The same could be said of those who planned and carried out the atomic bombings of Hiroshima and Nagasaki. They were not evil monsters, merely rational strategists working in a monstrous situation of total warfare where rational and humane standards had been abandoned by all sides. The harm they caused was immeasurably greater than that caused by Sutcliffe or Shipman or Kaplan's Nazi; it was unjustifiable and wrong, but not the act of evil men.

By contrast, the vandal who doctors the brakes on a bike owned by someone he does not know and cannot have any grudge against, so that it will crash and maybe maim or kill the rider (an act I heard perpetrated in a parish where I once worked) is rightly called evil. Though the harm he does is much less than that caused by the terrorist and certainly by the bombing of Hiroshima, there is the characteristic gap in understanding why anyone should want to do such a thing.

But the actions of Shipman and the Nazi are not only unjustifiable, but inexplicable. So a fourth factor about evil actions is *inexplicability*. The action resists explanation. It does not represent the kind of thing we call mad rather than wicked. People grope around for the psychological, sociological or historical mechanisms that might explain, for example, the Holocaust. Hitler had a terrible upbringing, and the history of Germany had led to great humiliation and burning resentment. But other individuals have been equally harshly brought up, and other nations equally humiliated… and so on with all the factors that can be cited… and no holocaust has resulted. Evil crimes are much less original and more tediously alike and in a sense 'rational' in their effects than good or creative acts. As Hannah Arendt has pointed out (1994) in relation to Adolf Eichmann, who is often regarded as 'the architect of the Holocaust,' there is a 'banality' to evil acts. They are not the acts of madmen. Yet such acts have something unique about their origins that defy not only justification but also explanation. As a result, though we may well feel incensed or grief-stricken about evil deeds, the emotion that predominates is generally fear or horror. We sense a dangerous power at work, but do not know its limits.

When an explanation is found for what seems to be evil, we are less inclined to call it evil. When Peter Sutcliffe, who murdered 23 women in West Yorkshire in the late 1970s, claimed he was commanded by God to kill prostitutes, people were unconvinced. If this was indeed a case involving psychotic delusions of grandeur, Sutcliffe was mad rather than bad. But serial killing like his (and Shipman's) requires a rational ability to plot, plan and calculate that is rarely possible for the genuinely insane. Sutcliffe, we feel, might be just offering a rationalization, a way of understanding an impulse that is inexplicable to us and perhaps even to himself; in which case we would be more inclined to use the word 'evil.'

In one well-known case (reported in the BBC news on 21 October 2002) Russell Swerdlow and Jeffrey Burns of the University of Virginia reported that when they removed a brain tumor from a patient, he stopped engaging in compulsive sexual behavior, including child abuse. In such cases pity may prevail over horror, and having explained such a person's behavior, though in no way would we want to justify it, we will be less inclined to deem it or the doer of it 'evil.'

Once again, we note the crucial difference between the scientific matter of explanation and the ethical question of justification. Often right-wing people resist trying to explain why harms are done (in medical, psychological or sociological terms) because they think explaining an act will justify it. Conversely left wingers sometimes do seem to think that if we explain why actions are done, we exonerate the agent. I will long remember the leader of the gang who had been caught throwing stones at my vicarage window saying 'Sorry – it's just the way we're brought up round here!' Chapter 1 argued for trying to explain why actions are done, not as a way of avoiding accountability, but as a way of making accountability more precise. Only when we know what causal influences are at work do we really know where free choice lies.

When a harmful action defies both justification and explanation, it seems to me appropriate to call it evil. But doing so only names a revulsion combined with a gap in our comprehension, unless we have a broader theory of what evil is.

In most of the cases cited, we would readily extend the term 'evil' from the deed to the doer. In the case of merely wrong or bad deeds we do not automatically label the doer 'bad' and find it quite easy to think of a 'good' person doing bad or wrong things from time to time, and vice versa. It is easy to understand how a person who is in general very responsible can sometimes act irresponsibly – for example, through sudden overpowering emotion, or not having all the right information, or misevaluating the information he does have. But because 'evil' acts are those we cannot readily interpret as the responsible acts of a human being like ourselves it becomes harder to identify the subject of the actions as fully human and not either a subhuman or a trans-human demon. We fill the gap in our understanding with some kind of account of global evil.

Global Evil?

So far I have looked mainly at what makes us want to call individual acts and perhaps individual people 'evil.' But when we speak of 'the problem of evil' we often have in mind the whole global story of pain and wrong. Could this be 'evil' according to the criteria proposed?

Certainly suffering and pain loom vast in the history of humanity, and indeed of life itself. Much of this is caused by conscious and rational beings intending it to happen, though it is hard to see such intentions as those of humane and rational beings. And the cause of all this is mysterious, buried deep in the very nature of human society and – some would argue – the cosmos itself. Vast chains of cause and effect – hurt and vengeance, abuse following abuse – sweep across the face of human history, leaving a deep scar that makes no fundamental sense. Many of the most astute spiritual guides are aware of this chain as it sweeps through and distorts their own mind. As noted near the end of Chapter 1, Buddhists call this 'bad karma from beginningless time' which each individual needs to confess, own and reverse in her own life.

In the absence of secular explanations of this global evil we are tempted to invoke the mythological and supernatural. This is not an entirely irrational step. If evil deeds bear the mark of conscious intention and yet lie outside the scope of normal human accountability and explicability, it makes some sense to invoke centers of superhuman consciousness. But it matters hugely which mythology we invoke. For our response to 'evil' will largely be shaped by what we believe it to be, and how it is to be responded to. And many of the mythologies, as we shall see, are extremely misleading, and make matters worse, intensifying what they seek to destroy or transform.

This chapter and the next will look at the range of these mythologies of evil. This is not an abstract attempt to solve 'the problem of evil' – trying to answer the theological-cum-philosophical problem of how the reality of evil is compatible with an all-powerful yet loving God. Our concern is more practical: to unearth the ideas that wittingly or unwittingly shape our practical responses to hurt and harm, for better or worse. So these chapters form a natural bridge between the negative reactions discussed in the first three chapters and the more positive pathways explored in Part 2.

We shall find confirmation for the suggestion that many of the different mythologies of evil look like the pathological responses to personal hurt, writ large. These ideologies give false credence to a negative form of response to hurt, and allow a pathology to rule our response in ways we need to be freed from. They represent a kind of writing of pathology in stone. But we shall begin to see, too, that there are other ways of looking at evil which are doubtless no less mythological, but more agile. These liberate more creative ways of responding to evil less conditioned by evil's own agenda, as it were: in the words of the poem making possible 'bliss, spirals of it, dancing out from the womb' of sorrow itself.

Good and Evil: Three Models

There are arguably three fundamentally different ways of looking at both personal and global 'evil.' The first is symmetrical. Both good and evil are real qualities actually there, either in the cosmos or the psyche or both. Some people, or some forces in the psyche, or some cosmic or supernatural or political powers exist which really are evil. These are locked in long-term or eternal conflict with equivalent forces or powers that are good. The second is asymmetrical. Good is real but 'evil' needs quotation marks. Good is absolute but evil is relative to good. 'Evil' exists in the mind, as a delusion or a fundamental alienation from reality, or in desires or actions which negate or resist reality, or as a marker for our inability to understand or explain. The third view is symmetrical again. Both 'good and 'evil' need quotation marks. Neither denotes any real power or quality 'out there.' Both are relative. This is perhaps the most widespread view today, at least among the philosophically sophisticated: good and evil are *both* in the mind, and there is no objective difference between the two.

Whatever the merits of the third view, it is not of much use for the purposes of this book. The reason for this is that it seems obvious that no good way of responding can emerge from seeing behavior like that of Kaplan's Nazi as simply questions of personal preference. I hope the terrible cases of evil I have cited make it obvious to the reader that the subjective view of good and evil – though it may have its place in abstract philosophical discussions – is of absolutely no use whatever when it comes to the issues this book is wrestling with. If all we can say of the Nazi's behavior is that we from our personal point of view find it distasteful, while others with different values may find it admirable, then we cannot respond well to the terrible harm that he is objectively perpetrating. For fear of inappropriate blame and shame, such views precipitate us into a massive disclaimer.

So I will not discuss the third view, which has been advocated and opposed in many books. Good critiques are found in Mary Midgley's *Wickedness* (1984) and elsewhere. The rest of this chapter will look at the symmetrical views of good and evil as equally real. And the next chapter will explore the view that 'evil' is not real in itself – not because it is subjective in the way it is for the third view, but because it is parasitic on the reality of the good.

Evil as...the Eternal Enemy

Theologian Walter Wink (1992, p. 13–17) sees the most prevalent understanding of good and evil as epitomized in the ancient Babylonian myth, in which the world itself is the result of a primordial conflict between the she-dragon Tiamat, epitome of all that is chaotic and dangerous, and her heroic son Marduk, who slays her and creates the world from the broken pieces of her body. Wink argues that our many myths and legends, our historical descriptions, our comic strips, films and dramas – and we might add, most computer games – are just reruns of this myth. In all of them a vulnerable hero overcomes evil forces that seem massively greater than he. (And usually, as in the original myth, it is 'he' not 'she'!)

The underlying vision here is cosmic dualism; the view that sees the universe as riven by a conflict between archetypal and more or less equal forces of good and evil. The vision became official in the Zoroastrian religion which originated in Persia in the 10th or 11th century BCE. But it has seeped into Judaism, turning it from a relatively simple monotheism to belief in arrays of angelic and demonic hosts fighting over humanity. From this apocalyptic Judaism it passed into Christianity, influencing the many 'little apocalypses' in the teachings of the Gospels and above all the great Apocalypse or Book of Revelation that closes the New Testament. It formed the basis of the Manichean faith, which Christianity officially rejected, but never fully exorcised. It pervades the rhetoric of Christian crusade and Islamic jihad alike. George Bush, Junior claimed to be defending the good democratic nations against the 'axis of evil' (Korea, Iran and Iraq). The Iranian leaders refer to the United States as 'the Great Satan' against which all methods of conflict are justified.

Wink probably exaggerates. It has been argued from a great

wealth of literature that there are at least seven basic plots capable of making a 'good read,' of which the great battle is only one (Booker, 2004). And while prevalent in the monotheistic cultures and their secular descendants in the West, it seems to me that the cosmic battle is not the main understanding of the Eastern faiths, for which evil, if not existence as such, is ultimately delusory. Nevertheless the hold this theme has on the imagination is undeniable; it is after all *exciting* to think of yourself as involved in a great cosmic battle, in which your smallest decisions take on cosmic significance as aiding either the good or the bad to win. It helps to be on the side of 'good,' but even 'evil' acquires a powerful luster.

But despite this dramatic attractiveness, the theme has at least three fatal flaws as an account of evil. The first is that whereas the idea of absolute good may be coherent – a perfectly good and beautiful and loving and honest and brave and wise and knowing and just and strong being is quite conceivable – it is very hard to imagine how all bad qualities could inhere in a single absolutely evil being. Just how long could a completely hating, repulsive, deceptive, cowardly, stupid, deluded, unjust and irresolute being last? Milton had to give his Satan quite a few virtues – courage, intelligence, organizational and leadership ability, including fairness to his followers, and a vision that inspired and motivated them – to make his evil pride workable. The notorious evil figures of the past, the Stalins and Hitlers, had much the same kinds of virtue. That course does not mitigate against the evil of what they did, but only makes all the more evil the deeds of those who had such power, ability and authority to do good.

What is involved here is not just a failure of imagination, which some genius may one day rectify by depicting in a convincing way a being who contains all the evil qualities and no good ones. Rather it is a logical tension. One of the vices, for example – traditionally called pride – consists in a totally egocentricity, an inability really to believe in and so attend to the needs of any being outside the self. Another vice – cowardice – could be defined a tendency to prioritize one's own safety over the common good when faced with dangers 'out there' threatening the self. Pride will lead a person to overestimate his own powers and fail to give credibility to the dangers, since they are outside the self; so a proud person is unlikely to be a coward, though he may be the opposite, foolhardy. Conversely cowardice will undermine pride by convincing a person that dangers outside are real and possibly stronger than the self. Pride and cowardice are in a logical tension with each other, if not outright contradiction. The same could be said of other qualities that might merit the term 'evil': the system of surveillance and knowledge required to exercise domination, versus dishonesty, self-deception and willful ignorance; an evil charisma capable of attracting others into a web of destructiveness, versus sheer stupidity or mean mindedness; a devious, pragmatic ability to change strategy, versus pig-headed inflexibility.

So on the mainstream Christian accounts there is a contradiction in the very idea of an entirely evil being: 'for Aquinas there is no such thing as a being that is bad,' (Eagleton, 2010, p. 125). On such views, to be a being is to be created and loved by God, to possess a certain inner coherence and unity, and to participate at least minimally in the goodness of being alive. A Mahayana Buddhist meanwhile would say that to be a sentient being is to have Buddha nature, to be on the path to enlightenment. So to be a being is to be good in significant ways, and that is incompatible with being nothing but evil.

So different kinds of evil are in logical tension, if not contradiction with one another and with being at all. With good qualities it is different: many virtues seem to work together. A humble person is likely to be honest because he acknowledges realities outside herself and does not distort them in her own interests, and conversely honesty and concern for truth will humble a person before the great wonders of the world. Love casts out fear and makes a person brave. Energy, patience and tolerance make it easier to find out the whole truth and become wise. It is easy to imagine a perfectly good being – humble and truthful, loving and brave, long-suffering and wise – and people have done so throughout history, giving this being names like 'God' or 'Christ' or 'Bodhisattva.' If there is a logical incoherence in such ideas it is not obvious. But there cannot be a consistently absolutely evil being. The theist who aims to be like God has a demanding but reasonable goal, but the Satanist who models himself on 'absolute evil' is deeply confused, to say the least. There is a fundamental asymmetry between good and evil which cosmic dualism fails to grasp, but which the monotheistic faiths, at least in their better moments, have.

So why has the idea of good and evil as competing realities had such a hold? Surely Girard has a large part of the answer here. The idea of the world as a struggle of good against evil allows us to name and shame the 'baddies.' In a dualist framework, the doers of evil acts are evil in themselves, either unwillingly possessed by evil or actively committed to abetting it. And the fact than none of these evil people openly declares himself to be on the side of evil only proves that he is; for entirely evil people are by definition dishonest. In other words, the good-versus-evil cosmology writes of our pathological desire to blame in stone. By encouraging angry and blaming reactions to hurt as something evil, this view actually makes people more likely to do the kinds of evil acts that enable others to see them in turn as evil, in a vicious circle. This is the second flaw in cosmic dualism: it is not only incoherent in itself, but vicious in its effects.

The third flaw in dualism is that its explanatory value is zero. It is very tempting to see Kaplan's Nazi as an evil man given over to the service of an evil ideology. As a description this may be true in its own terms, but it is no more than a description. It adds nothing to the understanding or the possible overcoming of such evil in the future. If when asked why someone did something evil we just say 'because they are evil,' or 'because the devil made them,' we add nothing to our possibilities either of wisdom or compassion; we merely add one more spin to the vicious cycle of blame.

...Flesh versus Spirit

In the cases so far considered, the conflict is seen as being between different peoples. Thus St. John's Gospel speaks of the conflict between 'children of light' and the 'children of darkness.' But Christianity and Islam offer a subtler and more humane variant, whereby the line of demarcation between good and evil cuts through each individual, so that the place of jihad or holy war is primarily within each of us. Sometimes the fathers and mothers of the Christian ascetic tradition describe themselves as doing battle with demons outside them; but this external language often seems to be a figure for an inner spiritual war against the *logismoi,* the obsessive thoughts and evil suggestions that arise from 'the devil within'.

Cosmic dualism offers two ways of seeing the war between good and evil as taking place within each of us. Both ways fasten onto the contrast between humanity or culture or civilization on the one hand, and animality or nature or savagery on the other, and link this contrast with that between good and evil. But they do so in opposite ways. On the first variant, we inherit from the animals, or share with the animals because of our embodied nature, savage desires and instincts. Our only hope lies in being subjected to the laws and values of human civilization, which help us to curb and bridle this wild and primitive evil and bring it under the control of the good, reasoning self, and on theistic views, of God.

There are many suggestions of this kind of inner conflict in

Plato with his mind-body dualism, and Aristotle's definition of humankind as the 'rational animal' sums up the genus or nature we share with animals and the rationality that differentiates us. But St. Paul turned this ontological tension into a moral war: 'I see in my members another law at war with the law of my mind, making me captive to the law of sin that dwells in my members,' (Rom. 7.23; compare 1 Peter 2.11). It was this spiritual war that the desert tradition developed, in a manner that came to inform many of the ascetic, monastic and puritan forms of Christianity. Sin was regarded by the Greek fathers as a case of *catastrophe,* literally an 'overturning' or 'takeover' in which, instead of ruling our passions with our minds, our minds were ruled by our animal passions.

Meanwhile Satan came to be depicted, not as a fallen angel, but in the now familiar way as a rapacious semi-animal with horns, forked tail and cloven hoof. The same ferocious bestiality can be seen – subtle enough to be haunting rather than caricaturing – on the faces of Christ's tormentors in Hieronymus Bosch's *Christ Mocked* (c1495). The war between rational mind and wild animality is depicted in many a novel, not least Golding's *Lord of the Flies* (2002), which sees children left on a desert island, without adult civilizing influences, degenerating into a wild and cruel paganism. It is the view that accords with empires – whether Roman, Spanish or British – enabling them to see themselves as the bringers of civilization to savage pagans who are not far removed from animals.

A flesh-versus-spirit dualism has positive features. It suggests the battleground between good and evil runs within each of us, making it much harder to scapegoat and blame individuals for what goes wrong. What may result instead, though, is shame about our 'animal nature' which we are always having to clothe in an appearance of rationality. The deep shame described in Chapter 2 and the flesh-versus-spirit understanding are likely to reinforce one another.

On a flesh-versus-spirit view behavior like that of Kaplan's Nazi would represent the resurgence of a primitive bestiality. But to describe it in this way is to demean the beasts. In truth only human beings can behave with the deliberate vileness we call evil. Nor is it plausible to see a highly civilized nation like Germany simply giving up on its culture and reverting to savagery. In fact many of those who committed atrocity had a high regard for music and culture. So the next section considers whether the explanation of evil lies in the dynamics of civilization itself.

...The System versus Nature

The dualistic conflict between good and evil makes good drama, as noted, and features in a great many novels, films, computer games and so forth. The forces of evil always seem heavily armored, and disciplined by a harsh fear of their leaders. The hero or (more rarely) heroine is by contrast good, brave and vulnerable. He seems outnumbered by the dark forces, and we are led genuinely to fear he will be overcome; his task seems impossible. But in the end he prevails.

But I detect a shift in the kinds of dualism these stories present. When I was young there was a lot of classic 'flesh-versus-spirit' dualism about. The villains were 'wild and primitive' American Indians, or dissolute villains, often German, Russian, Mexican or otherwise 'alien,' while the hero was generally a self-controlled, taciturn, white Anglo-Saxon male. But with the likes of *Bonnie and Clyde* (1967) and *Butch Cassidy and the Sundance Kid* (1969) we see something very different. The heroes could now be villains, outwitting vastly superior grey forces of law and order. The enemy were often machines, like the Daleks in *Doctor Who* (1963 onward), conformingly alike, or even, as in *The Matrix* (1999), a computer program that ran and even produced society as a kind of virtual reality. The heroes and heroines (more heroines about now) were often eccentric individualists, misfits following their own gut cunning rather than conform. Some of them were comic antiheroes: Charlie Chaplin and Mr. Bean alike wending their naïve way through society, outraging conformist society and forever getting into fixes by their foolishness, but also triumphing through a kind of cunning that was paradoxically consistent with it. The heroic stories had shifted to what I shall call a 'system-versus-nature' model (which perhaps the comic antiheroes had always represented).

On the cusp, poised between the two models, stands Herman Melville's much earlier story of *Moby Dick* (1851). On the face of it this ought to be a classic 'flesh-versus-spirit' story in which the wild monster of the deep is slain by the noble hero: a story in the lineage of Gilgamesh and Tiamat, St. George and the Dragon, and Beowulf and Grendel. But the snow-white sperm whale, Moby Dick, is portrayed as a being of awesome innocence – 'a gentle joyousness – a mighty mildness of repose,' whereas Captain Ahab, who leads the mission to kill the whale, is a dark and obsessive character. What should have been an epic battle story becomes a tragedy in which the defects of Ahab work themselves out to effect his own doom and that of his comrades. This is more than just the good old plot spoilt by the willfulness typical of modern authors (as Christopher Booker suggests – 2004, p. 358–65). The old narrative of wild chaotic nature subdued by heroic 'man' is giving way to the Romantic narrative that has increasingly prevailed since: innocent nature is threatened by humankind, whose lust for domination will in the end prove tragically self-destructive.

Where had this new plot come from? Side by side with the view that nature and 'primitive' people are savages needing to be civilized, there has long existed a vision of the 'noble savage' and a view of nature as somehow pure and virginal until defiled by human exploitation. Along with the old Christian baptismal rejection of 'the devil' and 'the flesh' went a defiance of 'the world.' The Greek word here is *kosmos*, meaning order, both cosmic order and political order, but with suggestions of the 'cosmetic': gaudy make-up papering over the unsightly cracks, superficial order imposed on reality.

So when Satan tempts Jesus, it is implied in Matthew 4.9 and explicitly stated in Luke 4.6 that Satan has the power to bestow on him all political authority. St. Paul seems ambiguous in this respect, seeming to contradict the Romans passage just quoted when he writes

> Our struggle is not against enemies of blood and flesh, but against the rulers, against the authorities, against the cosmic powers of this present darkness, against the spiritual forces of evil in the heavenly places. (Eph. 6.12)

When with Constantine Christianity acquired the task of morally policing the state, such passages became rather an embarrassment. Christians could not afford to be seen as waging a war against authority and power; better to see the enemy as the uncivilized and bestial, as in the views just described. But when in modern times the Constantinian settlement began to be shaken by revolution, and secularism gained momentum, the terms of the dualism were reversed once again. Some came to see Christendom as the oppressor, because it poured unnecessary guilt upon instincts and feelings that were wild but pure. We noted how Rousseau urged us to throw off our chains and regain our original innocence.

Meanwhile the poet William Blake declaimed against the dark satanic mills, Newtonian rationalism and the Puritanism of the Church, opposing to them the innocence of desire.

> All Bibles or sacred codes have been the causes of the following Errors:
>
> 1. That Man has two real existing principles: Viz: a Body & a Soul.
> 2. That Energy, call'd Evil, is alone from the Body; & that Reason, call'd Good, is alone from the Soul.
> 3. That God will torment Man in Eternity for following his Energies.
>
> But the following Contraries to these are True:
>
> 1. Man has no Body distinct from his Soul; for that call'd Body is a portion of Soul discern'd by the five Senses, the chief inlets of Soul in this age.
> 2. Energy is the only life, and is from the Body; and Reason is the bound or outward circumference of Energy.
> 3. Energy is Eternal Delight.
>
> (from *The Marriage of Heaven and Hell*, in 1971, p. 149)

The three points rejected form a neat summary of spirit-versus-flesh dualism. Blake argues for the contrary three points: the rejection of dualism (though not in a materialist way: the body is the sensory aspect of the soul); the affirmation of the bodily energies, which reason 'bounds' and shapes in a positive not a repressive way; and the identification of this bodily energy with 'eternal delight' rather than eternal punishment. In his *Songs of Innocence and Experience* (1970) Blake explores the positive aspects of childlike innocence, often menaced by experience, but in the end capable of attaining an 'innocence in experience.'

However, as noted in Chapter 3, this utopian vision came to have its dark side. When Blake wrote, the industrial revolution was beginning to bring the 'dirty' exploitative face of Western civilization closer to hand than it had once been out in the colonies. Some in modern times saw Utopia just round the corner, coming to us through a combination of scientific progress, mass education and technocratic regulation. But Romantics like Blake saw 'progress' of this kind as 'Satanic'; his heirs, the student revolutionaries of the 1960s, derided it as 'the system,' while many eco-feminists of the '70s and '80s despised it as patriarchal rationalism. In these movements Utopia was sought, contrariwise, in a lifestyle in which aggressive technocratic thought was replaced by peaceful love and sentiment. So the characteristic dualism of modern times was born, in which 'evil' political systems and scientific rationality stand opposed to 'good' nature and spontaneous feeling.

In many ways I am a child of the '60s. I do think that – and shall explore later how – childlike innocence has a redeeming power in the face of evil. But just as classic good-versus-evil dualism underwrites our tendency to blame others as evil, and the 'flesh-versus-spirit' dualism can generate deep shame about our own physicality, the 'system-versus-nature' view encourages us to think of ourselves as innately innocent in the face of corrupt systems, so that we readily disclaim our personal part in suffering and evil. We think of ourselves as victims of an evil system, ignoring the fact that any 'system' must be made up of the likes of us.

...Overcoming the Barriers

The two kinds of dualism just considered seem to be opposed. But remarkably they are combined in the philosopher Adam Morton's 'barrier' theory of evil. Morton defines an act as evil 'when it results from a strategy or learned procedure which allows that person's deliberations over the choice of actions not to be inhibited by barriers against considering harming or humiliating others that ought to have been in place.' (2004, p. 56) In other words, he argues – and quite convincingly from many specific cases – that we all have barriers against doing deliberate harm to others, but certain people learn to transgress those barriers. They do so because they find it is to their advantage, or because their culture encourages it, or sometimes just through the sheer excitement of overthrowing inhibitions.

Morton's view is subtle. On the one hand, he is saying that we have natural tendencies to harm which we normally learn to inhibit; and that is in line with a spirit-flesh dualism. On the other hand he believes that evil comes about through a 'strategy or learned procedure' of going against our inhibitions. We have to be 'educated' or to train ourselves in order to become like Kaplan's Nazi. And that looks like the system teaching us to go against nature. All in all, in Morton's view, evil arises out of a collusion between our rationality and animal instinct in overcoming our natural barriers against harming. Two seemingly opposed kinds of dualism are combined. However, this account takes us beyond any straightforward notion of a dualistic battle between good and evil, towards the idea of evil as a matter of human choice and effort – the kind of view considered in the next chapter.

...The Way The World Is

It is possible to combine these same two kinds of dualism in a much more negative way, in which both sides of the battle are dark, and we are left as a speck of potential light caught between the upper and the nether darkness. For we may be pessimistic about both our animal nature and our political systems. In this case we move beyond dualism to a more monistically gloomy view. We see ourselves as sparks of isolated goodness trapped in a uniformly evil natural and political world.

The Christian Gnostics saw things in this way. They believed that to get beyond evil we have to get beyond being itself. They saw the world as created by an evil being, whom we might regard as an inversion of Marduk. If the Babylonian hero had created the world by splitting the dark mother into pieces, for the Gnostics an evil being had created the world by splitting up the primordial goodness, dispersing the fragments into isolated souls. Our true home lay in the primordial goodness of the true God, utterly beyond the created order.

Orthodox Christianity set its face against the Gnostics, who faded from mainstream history, to resurface again in many heterodox movements. Among them were the Cathars of southern France, who were persecuted out of existence in the thirteenth century. But many today implicitly or explicitly adopt their world-denying pessimism, with or without the hopeful spark in the soul.

In the nineteenth century the Buddhist-influenced German philosopher Arthur Schopenhauer wrote of

> The terrible side of life. The unspeakable pain, the wretchedness and misery of mankind, the triumph of wickedness, the scornful mastery of chance, and the irretrievable fall of the just and innocent... and here is to be found a significant hint as to the nature of the world and existence. (1969, 1:252–3)

Schopenhauer sought liberation from the will to live that binds us to this world. And for many, modern science undermines the romantic view of an innocent nature and shown us instead 'nature red in tooth and claw,' either indifferent or hostile to human moral aspirations. 'Life's a bitch' and to find goodness we have to turn from the world and look within.

Such views are strangely attractive to many in the way they enable us to hold together an idealistic vision of the good and a tough illusion-free realism about the world. 'Realistically' in this world the likes of Kaplan's Nazi will triumph over the rabbi, but 'idealistically' the rabbi – assuming he stays faithful – is in touch with a truth that goes deeper than the world. In this poignant spirit, the Holocaust survivor Elie Wiesel describes in his harrowing classic *Night* (2008, p. 107) how in the concentration camp a teenage boy Juliek managed to find a violin, which he played in the night as the men lay piled on top of one another, dying.

> He played a fragment from Beethoven's concerto. I had never heard sounds so pure. In the silence.
>
> How had he managed to free himself? To draw his body from under me without my being aware of it?
>
> It was pitch dark. I could hear only the violin, and it was as though Juliek's soul were the bow. He was playing his life. The whole of his life was gliding on the strings – his lost hopes, his charred past, his extinguished future. He played as he would never play again...
>
> I do not know how long he played. I was overcome by sleep. When I awoke, in the daylight, I could see Juliek, opposite me, slumped over, dead. Near him lay his violin, smashed, trampled, a strange overwhelming little corpse.

The music of Beethoven points to that world of beauty and civilization that the Nazis were systematically destroying. In the broken violin that destruction has its pathetic icon. Yet the music went on, on to the end, even in the camp. The destruction had not and could not destroy it.

The music reaches deep to the heart of a beauty that just exists, exists with a reality that shows up the terrible nightmare of the camp for what it is. Of course on one level the camp was as real as the music; indeed if power is reality it is more real, since the camp overcame the music and destroyed the violin and the player. But if beauty and integration with the rest of reality is real, then the music was the more real, and the camp a dream whose systematic, mad alienation from reality had sometime to come to an end. The music is like a lodestar pointing to the true north of what the Jewish philosopher Emmanuel Levinas has called 'good beyond being,' revealing how inverted the values of the camp were and how death-bound its direction. One can almost feel the camp keeling away into nightmare under the serene stasis of the music. Nothing in the camp could touch the reality of the music – everything in the music triumphs over the madness of the camp – except in time, when the music ends, and in the physical world, where it is crushed to pieces with Juliek's violin.

Such a vision can be compellingly attractive. But ultimately it seems to me to lead to the mystical invulnerability described in Chapter 3, which is a way of disclaiming our belonging to the world of suffering and placing ourselves beyond all harm. If we believe in this vision we may care about the music but let it lead us away from the world where men lie dying. We may nurse the divine spark of the soul but only by cupping our hands around it to protect it from the chill winds of reality. And also we will ignore the way the world, tough and improvident as it often is, is shot through with poetry; how this world of samsara, full of suffering and decay, is as the Mahayana Buddhists affirm one with Nirvana; the way this messy earthly world is, as the parables of Jesus evoke, full of the Kingdom of Heaven. Even the notes of the music and the violin are, after all, parts of the material world.

Against the Gnostics, then, we need to affirm that life is not *just* a bitch; or if it is, it is a beautiful bitch! And the beauty does not come to us from a remote point of simple purity beyond the world; it ever arises out of the world and subsides back into it also, in complex ways. So liberation is not about escape, but about staying where we are and finding what beauty we can in the here and now. Lament is always appropriate, but so is celebration. What music is not either one or the other, or both?

Yin and Yang

In this light it is possible to see good and evil as cosmic forces that are in conflict or tension, but intermingled and emerging out of one another, ultimately interdependent. This is what the well-known yin-and-yang symbol suggests. Light and dark, intertwined, complete a circle. In the center of the light part, a blob of darkness emerges, and in the middle of the dark, conversely, light.

Yin and yang are not strictly good and evil. The Taoist and Confucian cultures that were the setting of the original symbol were deeply concerned about ethical behavior, but remarkably free from the battle of good and evil that is so familiar in the West. In this context yang – symbolized by the light – represents the active, heavenly, creative, masculine principle, while yin represents the receptive, earthly, nurturing, feminine principle. That said, the symbol is readily adapted, and often used to provide a vision of good and evil that is subtle and perceptive.

We have already noted how evil often rests on good qualities like courage and leadership, and later we will take up the suggestion that evil is always parasitic on good. The yin-yang symbol suggests more: that at the heart of what is good, evil is always likely to emerge. We need to be vigilant whenever we establish a monastery or a Utopia for the pure, for it is precisely there that the conditions for evil to emerge are ripe. And we must be especially wary of those who are holy and preach the good life, because (witness the fall of many a revered charismatic preacher) pride, self-deception and hypocrisy lie in wait. Conversely – and consistently with a perspective based on the practice of Jesus – it is to the outcast and the 'evil' that we must go if we want to see the emergence of good, the tough wisdom, compassion and courage that can flower in the harshest of conditions.

In this perspective we do not deny the evil of what Kaplan's Nazi did – rather in a way we define, clarify and enhance our sense of it – when we look to the good: the good that probably was his once, before he was corrupted by fascist ideas of where the good lies, and the good that might yet be his again, if revulsion at his own deed led to real remorse. We gain a greater hold on the beauty and meaning of works of art if we are clear about evils from which they have emerged, evils which may in some cases be their precondition. In *The Circus Animals' Desertion*, the poet W.B. Yeats described the great images of his poetry as emerging from 'the foul rag and bone shop of the heart.' Conversely we need to be clear too about the evils that are always near at hand where true goodness is present. The barrier between the real goodness that empowers, and the pretence of goodness that overpowers, is wafer thin.

All this suggests that the yin-yang model may aid us toward a nimble and perceptive response to evil that takes us beyond blame, shame and disclaim. There remains one big problem with it, which is the perfect radial symmetry of the symbol. In it, yin and yang belong together and make the whole through their equal balance; neither is ultimately preferable. If we relate this model to good and evil, it could lead either to a disclaiming of the horrific and destructive nature of evil, or a resigned acceptance of evil as necessary along with the good. But such moves would ignore the fundamental asymmetry we noted between the qualities that are good, which reinforce one another, and those that are evil, which are ultimately contradictory of one another and of the very idea of being. What we need, perhaps, is a way of reconciling the subtle Eastern wisdom presented in the yin-yang model, with the more challengingly prophetic Christian asymmetry explored in the next chapter, which identifies the good with what is creative and real, and evil with destruction and delusion.

Order and Chaos

One interpretation of yin and yang would take this asymmetry on board. Two trends in the universe are too evident to deny. One is that it us running down towards ever increasing 'entropy' – a technical term for disorder, randomness, and chaos. The Second Law of Thermodynamics predicts that the cosmos will end in a terribly monotonous, cold and shadowy formlessness. On the other hand, there is also quite obviously an evolutionary trend towards ever greater richness and complexity. Quite how these opposing trends could be compatible is a deep question that need not concern us in detail; the broad answer is that the incredible complexity we see on a local scale is paid for by increased entropy on a wider scale. For example, life in all its complexity is fuelled by the burning up of the sun's fuel.

Such a view might suggest a cosmic dualism, in which entropy is 'evil' and order 'good.' But that interpretation would lead to a sad dualism in which 'evil' will score the final victory over 'good.' Such dualism inspires a familiar modern kind of stoic heroism, dominated by 'reason's grief' (Harris, 2006 – see *Tragicomedy and Truth* in Chapter 6). According to this, we do battle against 'evil' knowing we will lose, but affirming that 'good' commands our loyalty all the same, and we must hold out for it as long as we possibly can, however bleak the prospect.

However, the identification of good with order is questionable, given what we know about life. It seems that life flourishes neither in situations of great entropy (clouds are not alive) nor in situations of rigid order (crystals are not alive) but in situations where order and chaos interact to produce new forms. Environmental catastrophes seem to be what is responsible for the great evolutionary leaps forward: for example, the extinction of the dinosaurs, probably because of catastrophe induced by meteorite impact, enabled the evolutionary diversification of the mammals. Chaos seems to have the effect of reshuffling the cards to enable new patterns to emerge: 'good' emerges out of 'evil.' Conversely fixed and inadaptable order tends to decay into chaos: 'evil' emerges out of too much 'good.' For a popular account of this, see James Gleick's *Chaos* (1988).

Here we see how a yin-yang kind of dualism seems to hold between order and chaos, with life emerging out of the interflow between the two. This does not mean the two are symmetrical; chaos and order are not co-equal qualities, since in common thought chaos is only definable as the lack of order (though in information theory, I believe, the reverse may be the case). An order-and-chaos yin-yang model therefore need not lead to a resigned acceptance. On the contrary the model suggests that, if we wish to promote life and goodness, then in situations of relative anarchy we will need to be builders of order; but conversely, in situations of massive, rigid and oppressive order we may be called to be revolutionaries, creating the life-giving element of chaos. In this way we will become 'nimble' in our use of the old fixed dualisms.

But in this model good and evil have disappeared as fixed, qualities. They both emerge in and through the interaction of order and chaos. When the interaction goes harmoniously or well, there is 'good': when it goes badly or discordantly, there is 'evil.' Good and evil have disappeared as nouns and reappeared as adverbs. This anticipates the idea, discussed in the next chapter, that evil is insubstantial, but real in its processes or effects.

Summary

1. Whenever we think of evil as some kind of thing – a being or a force – out there in the real world, we underwrite one or other pathological way of responding to hurt.
2. When evil is seen as the great Enemy, a 'Devil' co-eternal with good or God, then that Enemy acts as kind of cosmic scapegoat, taking the blame for all we find painful and hurtful. But inevitably we see that enemy as possessing and driving groups of people we need to fight and overcome. Hurt becomes a cause for battle and war.
3. When evil is seen as the enemy lurking in 'the flesh' we are

precipitated into a spiritual war against our own bodily drives. The latter become shameful, disgusting and menacing.

4. When, on the contrary, evil is identified with the system ranged against us innocent individuals, it becomes all too easy to disclaim my own part in harm and to blame oppressive or reactionary others.
5. The Gnostic alternative for which all the world – flesh and spirit, politics and the ordinary individual – is inherently evil, likewise involves a massive disclaimer of my own part in hurt, since I belong to the elite of those seeking release from the world as such.
6. The yin-yang model seems to offer a much more optimistic and subtle picture of the place of good and bad in the universe. But by making good and bad co-equal and inter-penetrating aspects of the cosmos, it can lead us to ignore the asymmetry between them, downplaying the sense in which good is to be preferred. That means another kind of disclaimer, a minimizing of evil.
7. However, if yin and yang are seen as images of order and chaos, these criticisms may be overcome. But then evil and perhaps good are best understood not as nouns but as adverbs.

Chapter 5

Hurt Spun Out of Nothing: Evil as Negation

That evil spins its own tangle
Of darkness within your breast.

You look for it – dark eyes delving down
Consuming threads – you lose yourself,

Eclipsed. But now the swan-arched bend
Of your bewildered neck casts on your stream

Of death – unnoticed –
The unwoven crescent image you may not reach.

Moonlit Swan, Falmer Pond

The previous chapter explored views which see evil as a kind of reality or power symmetrical with the good. This one looks at views that see only the good as real, and evil as an absence, denial, distortion, destruction or other kind of negation of reality. Do these suggest better ways of responding to hurt and harm?

Once again I distinguish these views from the view that evil and good are subjective matters of taste or preference. Though in the outlooks discussed in this chapter there is nothing that really exists which we could justly call 'evil,' when we describe actions and events as 'evil' we are not simply voicing an aversion. We can respond to such acts and events in more or less appropriate ways, and this appropriateness is a real and substantial issue, not just a matter of personal preference. I shall not discuss the view that Kaplan's Nazi was merely doing something some people might find distasteful, but others quite admirable. There were doubtless fellow Nazis who would have found it commendable, but they should not be given the philosophical solace of a fashionable relativism. They were, quite simply, wrong, and all reasonable people know that.

Evil as Absence of Good

> Life's but a walking shadow, a poor player
> That struts and frets his hour upon the stage
> And then is heard no more: it is a tale
> Told by an idiot, full of sound and fury,
> Signifying nothing.
> (Shakespeare, *Macbeth*, Act 5, scene 5)

This is how Macbeth, after his ruthless rise to power and now confronting his downfall, sees life: as a poor play hammed by bad actors, full of superficial drama, but without any ultimate meaning. Though sometimes presented as an example of Shakespeare's own nihilism, Shakespeare's character is expressing rather the nihilism that becomes inevitable to those who have committed themselves to evil actions. Such actions can be full of terror and dramatic intensity, but cannot enlighten us, cannot create or express any meaning. In that sense evil is 'unreal.' To communicate, to open minds to reality, to live in response to the world that is really there – these are forms of goodness. To deceive, to be deluded, to deny what is there, to destroy it – these are the patterns of evil.

So for Plato, our highest good lay in the contemplative vision of the form of the Good. But evil had no form; there was nothing in it we could contemplate or understand. In the first book of Genesis the phrase is repeated, 'God saw *all* that he had made, that it was good.' It followed that there was nothing that was created bad or evil. So Jewish, Christian and Platonic Greek thought converged on the idea that evil could only be a *privatio boni*, a privation of good, good gone wrong.

The idea became explicit in St. Augustine:

> The Almighty God, who, as even the heathen acknowledge, has supreme power over all things, being himself supremely good, would never permit the existence of anything evil among his works, if he were not so omnipotent and good that he can bring good even out of evil. For what is that which we call evil but the absence of good? In the bodies of animals, disease and wounds mean nothing but the absence of health... for the wound or disease is not a substance, but a defect in the fleshly substance... Just in the same way, what are called vices in the soul are nothing but privations of natural good. And when they are cured... in the healthy soul, they cannot exist anywhere else.
> (*Enchiridion*, Ch. 11)

Augustine here offers two kinds of reason why evil is only a privation of good: the Judeo-Christian idea that an all good Creator could not have created irredeemable, substantial evil, and the idea (deriving from Aristotle) that evils, like diseases and wounds, are defects, insubstantial in themselves and unable to exist except as the defects of something good.

According to Aristotle, all beings arise from the struggle of matter to 'flourish' in form and pattern. Though we may not share Aristotle's science in detail, we all have the basic idea of a 'perfect lily' in which we see what a lily really is, as opposed to a deformed or diseased specimen that has failed to realize its genetic potential and does not show us what a lily should look like. In this context, evil is what prevents the flower from flourishing. For the flower, disease or drought or genetic deformation would count as 'evil.' But to know what counts as 'evil' we need to know what kind of 'good' we are considering: in this case we are considering the good of the lily, but in ethical contexts we are usually looking either at the flourishing of human beings or that of creation as a whole. So, for St. Thomas Aquinas, following Aristotle,

> the more a thing succeeds in realizing its true nature, the more it can be said to be good. The perfection of a thing, he argues, depends on the extent to which it has achieved actuality. Things are good if they flourish in the way appropriate to them. The more a thing thrives in its own peculiar way, the finer it is. So for Aquinas there is no such thing as a being which is bad.... Aquinas regards evil not as something existent, but as a kind of deficiency of being. Evil for him is lack, negation, defectiveness, deprivation. It is a kind of malfunctioning, a flaw at the heart of being... an incapacity for an abundance of life. (Eagleton, 2010 p. 124–5)

So for Aquinas, goodness and beauty are the first mystery, evil the second and derivative one. Evil acts are, like creation itself, a mystery spun 'out of nothing.' Both creation and evil transcend explanation and understanding, for nothing 'justifies' them (c.f. Eagleton, p. 65). Both are *sui generis*. But the mystery of evil is parasitic upon the mystery of creation because it is an undoing of what is done in creation, an unmaking of what is made. Evil represents a defacing of the beautiful face of reality.

Good as Privation of Evil?

Before we move on, however, a big question needs to be answered, which is that often things seem to be the opposite way round. Goodness and virtue often involve the overcoming or at least some kind of response to already existing evil, hurt or threat. Courage is a response to dangerous and threatening things, compassion and endurance are responses to suffering, justice a way of adjudicating fairly in a world where people harm and oppress each other. If God is to have all the virtues then it would seem that God actually needs a created world that includes suffering to do so; or else needs to become an incarnate human being so as to struggle with evil in the way we do. Otherwise we humans would have kinds of goodness – like the virtues just cited – that surpass those of God. This would contradict the traditional understanding of creation and incarnation as free acts of an already perfect God. Some theologians have consequently embraced a suffering God; if God cannot suffer, we may have virtues that God may not.

But it seems to me there is a confusion here which relates to that noted at the end of Chapter 4, between evil and chaos. Neither the danger which courage confronts, nor the suffering that compassion feels for, nor the unevenness of fortune that justice challenges *need* to be understood (though they can be) as 'evil' in themselves. It is surely better to see such things as forms of disorder that our impulse to order needs to engage with, so as to create good. It is possible to conceive of a perfect being in whom order and chaos are eternally present, forever bringing forth good and never evil. Such a being could be called perfectly brave, compassionate and just. Perhaps this is one of the many things the Christian doctrine of the Trinity tells us: that in God the order represented by the Father is forever engaging with the chaotic energy or spontaneity of the Spirit to give birth to the Word who is perfect goodness and being. (There is more on these themes at the end of this chapter.)

Evil, by contrast, names a detraction from this boundless ever-creative process. Unlike goodness, evil has its limits, because it can only deface the good that is already there. And the defacing can only be caused by a being who is there, one who is real, and who is in Christian terms part of God's good creation. So evil acts always go against the grain of who the doer really is, usually by a surrender of the freedom of the whole person to the operation of a repetitive mechanism of one part, or by a freezing of the broad and complex vision to some simplistic ideology, or generally by what Augustine describes as 'the inclination of what has more being for what has less being,' (cited in Eagleton, 2010, p. 126).

Sin is therefore is far from 'original,' having no creative power of its own.

> We need to examine skeptically the idea that sin is very sexy and exciting. The fact is that sin, whether original or personal, is really very boring, deadly boring in fact. Sin is about compulsive repetition, about never being able to do a new thing or reach a new place. (West. p. 109)

As mentioned, most computer games draw on the 'good versus evil' model, but there are interesting exceptions. A game I recently played, called *Dragon Age,* was for the most part a typical struggle of good-looking heroes and heroines against nasty-looking demons, but it had a part, called 'The Fade,' in which the hero could get trapped and separated from his companions. The Fade was claustrophobic and confusing, because doorways kept leading you back into the same set of rooms; there was no way out. And when at last you came upon your companions, they refused to help you because they were lost in their own dreams or nightmares. One character believed he was back at home with his family and all was well with the world – classic denial. Another was trapped with her mother in childhood battles full of blame and shame. In the end, as you moved round and round in this repetitive world without an outside, you yourself began to doubt whether you were lost in your own nightmare. This seemed to me much more what 'evil' is like than dragons you could slay – 'compulsive repetition...never being able to...reach a new place.'

Of course, the precise sense in which evil can be said to be unreal needs very careful defining, because famine, disease, and the concentration camps are very real indeed to those who experience them. They were and are real in their devastating effects, in precisely the power they exert over those who suffer from them. But evils are unreal in the sense that they reveal nothing; they have no deeper meaning. The landscape outside my window is real because it reveals the presence of countless realities, each growing in its own integral way, all interacting as a coherent ecological-cum-agricultural whole. But the Holocaust, for example, manifests no such coherent inscape; it is nothing but a disconnected and incoherent tissue of horrors, like a nightmare.

This is why such horrors resist our attempts to describe them, whether in art or in historical narrative. Art tries to express, and history to describe, an underlying meaning. Through them we try to make sense of the pain that seemed so senseless. We seek for *The Heart of Darkness* (1902) which Joseph Conrad's hero found successively in the physical darkness of the Congo jungle, the moral darkness of the Europeans' brutal exploitation of indigenous people, and finally the metaphysical darkness of his own soul. We even gain – if we are honest – a kind of satisfaction from the twinges of fascination, awe and horror, as we contemplate an evil so massive, so finely orchestrated and all-encompassing as the Nazi Holocaust. Such an awe is of course just what the perpetrators of the crimes sought in serving the primordial mythologies of fascism: mythologies of a fearless, unscrupulous, cunning and amoral heroism more ancient than the Judeo-Christian ethos of love and justice.

But at the heart of this Nazi bombast and neo-pagan bluster, as Hannah Arendt has so convincingly shown (1994), lies mere banality. We are left with the almost unbelievable pettiness, shallowness and – in a sense – ordinariness of men like Hitler (the nice man who loved animals and flowers), Eichmann (according to Arendt, a banal, unimaginative bureaucrat who was 'only obeying orders,' and lacked the breadth of mind to grasp the full consequence of his dutiful obedience). Likewise Stalin (set alongside the formidable Lenin and Trotsky) shows such a very ordinary, even kindly face... just right for a grandfather... The tales of fascism and Stalinism are alike, 'full of sound and fury, signifying nothing.' After the three successive layers of the 'onion' of Conrad's novel have been peeled away, there is nothing left to discover. The darkness has no heart.

So in the accounts of the Holocaust, it is the senselessness of it all that strikes one as well as the barbarism. As one victim recorded by Wiesel asked, 'Why didn't they just shoot us?' The concentration camps cost the Nazis a huge diversion of strategic effort and person-power that was desperately needed to defend the *Reich*. The benefit to the *Reich* of the labor camps was minimal, the cost immense. Even in the face of the advancing armies, when it would have been simpler to abandon the prisoners to starve in the winter cold, or shoot them, the prisoners were systematically evacuated to other camps so that the machinery of torture and slow, systematic extermination could continue. Immense resources of science and rational organization were devoted to the maintenance of this deeply irrational process. It all reads like one crazy nightmare in which all hold, not just on humanity, but on cold rational strategy, indeed on reality as such, was lost.

How Does Evil Happen?

Now if evil is in this way a terrible defacing or distortion or betrayal of good, we desperately need to know where this betrayal takes place. Where and how does the plenitude of being, all that is good, give way to what is manifestly not good? I shall discuss five main understandings.

In two understandings, the betrayal takes place in the mind, in what we falsely believe. Evil is delusion. I shall look at Buddhism, which (like Hinduism) sees illusion (*avidya*) as the source of all suffering and all of what we call evil. And I shall look, secondly, at the approach of modern scientific secularism, for which evil is a primitive concept that simply disappears when we can understand and explain what goes on in term of the laws of nature and the mind.

In the other three understandings, the betrayal takes place in the will, in choice. A choice is made against reality itself. Evil on this account has more than mental reality – as suggested above, it is real in its effects, in the power it wields – but that power is only destructive of reality; it cannot create any new reality or truth. On one account the choice is human, mythically symbolized in the choice made in the Garden of Eden. So we shall look, thirdly, at Augustine's account of 'original sin' as a chain of evil consequences stemming from a primordial choice. On another account, considered fourth, the choice is again a human one but in a sense a positive step anticipated by God. In the myth, God chose to put something forbidden in the garden, creating a precarious free choice to obey or disobey. And on a third view, the choice is unashamedly traced back to God. In creating the world, God chose some things to become real and rejected others to be nothing. Evil is a kind of shadow side of God's act of creation. So Section 5 will trace the different ways in which 'evil' may be seen as integral to the purpose and even the story of God.

Finally the chapter will offer a model of my own that combines the strengths in all these understandings.

1. Delusion

Alongside Juliek's violin, one of the most haunting passages in Wiesel's *Night* is his description of his father's smile in the concentration camp where he and others about him are freezing in the snow, many already dead.

> He sat up and looked round him, bewildered, stupefied — a bereaved stare. He stared all round him in a circle as though

> he had suddenly to draw up an inventory of his universe, to find out exactly where he was, in what place, and why. Then he smiled.
>
> I shall always remember that smile. From which world did it come?
>
> The snow continued to fall in thick flakes over the corpses. (2008, p. 102)

We cannot know what lay behind that smile, though the thought of it as a historical smile that once happened in the midst of the Holocaust is striking. It is one of those historical events about which innumerable different stories could be told, catching more or less of the truth that lies in essence hidden. The smile could betoken insanity, with hallucinations of freedom or food. It could be that Elie's father had received the beatific vision and was now prepared to die in peace. But I offer another reading, not because it must be true, but because it opens doorways in the mind.

My reading is that Elie's father, having determined his exact place in the 'inventory' of the universe, had discovered that that place and that inventory had no meaning… and then smiled, and found content. I am reminded of the enigmatic, far-distant smile of the Buddha. It is as if the death camps bring home the truth that the Buddha realized pre-emptively on his first encounter with suffering: all is vanity; all is meaningless and mad striving. But we can let go of all this, to the unconditional bliss of Nirvana, the blowing out of the light. Not the apprehension of a transcendent reality, but a grasp of the emptiness, the Void (*Sunya*) that embraces all things. Nonetheless I would not say that this is exactly what the smile means; the smile is beyond meaning, as is Nirvana.

In the opening poem of this chapter, the swan presents an image of the tangle of sin we weave in our own deluded minds. This tangle contrasts with the unwoven (uncreated), crescent (growing), moonlike light of Christ, as yet unnoticed, but mirroring the reflection of the swan's own arched neck.

For Buddhism, of course, it is not that evil is a delusion that masks the goodness of reality. Rather the whole idea of a real world 'out there' is a delusion. It is because I want to hold onto things (*tanha*, grasping) that I come to believe there are things out there to hold on to, and a me to hold on to them. But this belief in turn reinforces the grasping in a continuous cycle that has no ultimate basis. The belief generates the chains of bad karma, whereby bad deeds bring their bad results in a cycle that has no beginning. But this deterministic cycle offers a possibility of freedom: if I realize my illusion, and cease to grasp things to reinforce a delusory ego, I can be free. For the word *Sunya* conveys both emptiness and plenitude, like the roundness of the cipher '0.' There is no permanent thing, only a flux like the sea, wholly empty, utterly full. There being no things, no success and no failure, in the words of the Heart Sutra (see Chapter 8): 'What can go wrong?'

In this case release from evil comes simply by my ceasing to believe in it. But in practice that is far from simple. It requires all the disciplines of meditation, mindfulness and single-pointed attention to the here and now. And as Simone Weil pointed out:

> There is something in our soul which has a far more violent repugnance for true attention than the flesh has for bodily fatigue. This is something that is much more closely connected with evil than is the flesh. That is why every time we really concentrate our attention, we destroy the evil in ourselves. (2002, p. 72)

So evil is fundamentally distractedness, inability to attend to what is before us and around us. That may seem a very light way of treating the kind of behavior we find in Kaplan's Nazi. But is it so light a matter? Had the Nazi attended to the rabbi in front of his eyes would he have been able to do what he did? Was it not the fact that he was distracted by his deluded idea of what a Jew was that made him behave as he did? Was he spitting on a real person, or on his idea of evil?

In one variation of the view under discussion, the betrayal of the good takes place in the relationship between beings who are in themselves good. Though different people may have the best intentions, still the relationship between them may go tragically wrong, through misunderstanding or through the conflict of incompatible goods. All people intend the good: as Socrates argued long ago, nobody willingly and knowingly chooses what she knows to be evil or harmful. Even Hitler and Stalin believed their policies were the right ones, and terrorists believe in their causes. But we are all in the grip of different illusions about what constitutes good. These delusions pit us tragically against each other, in conflict over rival versions of the good. In the end, as both Socrates and the Buddha would emphasize in their different ways, harmful acts always harm the doer most of all.

The solution may lie, then, not in having the 'right' understanding of good and evil, because such understanding is beyond us, and the more we think we have it, the more we are likely to do harm in the light of it. Rather, we need to be freed from ideology itself. There are hearteningly many cases where people in the Holocaust did not collude with the Nazi effort, but hid and protected people from their persecutors, at great risk to themselves. But significantly in most cases this was not because of their own ideology, or their abstract disbelief in the Nazi ideology. In the majority of cases it was because they knew the persecuted Jews and others personally, so that it became simply obvious that they must protect their friends, or simply their fellow humans (Koonz, 1987). Human familiarity and fellow-feeling was what undercut the delusions of ideology and propaganda. Perhaps this is what those mysterious words of St. Paul are about: 'rarely will anyone die for a righteous person –

though perhaps for a good person someone might actually dare to die.' (Rom. 5.7) For most of us, it is not 'just causes' and their righteous representatives that make us want to risk our lives, but common or garden goodness. Ordinary goodness subverts the delusions of the 'righteous'.

2. Scientifically Explained

Modern secularism would tend to support the idea that 'evil' is a delusion, but for its own reasons. We noted that one crucial aspect of evil is its resistance to explanation. At the start of Chapter 4 four characteristics of 'evil' were suggested: enormity, intentionality, irrationality and inexplicability. We could summarize by saying 'evil' is the name we give *to extremely harmful deliberate actions whose reasons we do not understand and which we cannot explain*. Once we can explain the action – for example, as the result of such and such a kind of mental illness – though we still see it as harmful and wrong, we cease to see it as evil. Once we see the abuser as acting out the very same kind of abuse he himself received in childhood, we still condemn the act but we see him less as evil, more as a victimizing victim. If we could understand all that caused Kaplan's Nazi to act as he did, we would still feel revolted by his action, and would by no means exonerate it, but we would see him less as evil, more as the victim of the terrible social and political forces that had so misshaped him.

We are still lamentably short of understanding all the wellsprings of human choice and activity, but a secular understanding would assert that we must go on aiming to do so. Such a viewpoint would suggest that we believe in an 'evil of the gaps.' 'Evil' is a superstitious way of filling a gap in our understanding of why people behave as they do, a gap we ought to leave empty until science has filled it. In the benighted past, it is argued, we traced all sorts of suffering to the workings of 'evil' witches, and burned them at the stake. Now scientifically dominated cultures see the witch as a purely social creation, prevalent at certain times in history for sociological reasons. There are no witches now – for such cultures – not because they have all been killed but because good scientific explanation has replaced the notion of the witch. Of course, there are still pre-scientific cultures that abuse children because they are believed to be witches, and there has been a resurgence of *Wicca* in cultures that believe themselves to be post-scientific. But these are matters the secular mind laments. (And thus far, I am with the secularists.)

The hope remains one day science will make the terrorist, the serial killer and the sexual predator disappear too, as scientifically we come to see them as the products of conditions in society, in the family and even in the brain, which can be changed for the better. We noted in Chapter 2 how deeply traumatized people may split off the vulnerable, feeling parts of themselves, leaving a cold and punitive caretaker in charge. Possibly those we call 'evil' because of their incomprehensible psychopathic behavior may become comprehensible, once we see them as people in whom the splitting off is complete, and the feeling part of the self is annihilated. Only the cold caretaker is left, determined to punish in others the disturbing reminder of a vulnerability that has been eradicated from the self. Hence the banal character of men like Eichmann, and the flat two-dimensional lack of human depth which Eagleton (2010, p. 51ff) sees depicted in fictional psychopathic gangsters like Pinkie in Graham Greene's *Brighton Rock*. Psychological accounts (e.g. Theweleit, 1989) of the rise of psychopathic fascism in the SS and similar organizations have sought to show how the trauma and humiliation of Germany in and after the First World War precipitated just such a process.

The secular understanding also dispenses with the idea that natural disasters can be evil, because quite simply if there is no God then there is no agent responsible for them. Horrific things happen in nature: not only earthquakes and hurricanes, but the birth of deformed offspring, and the kind of wasp that Darwin noted, which lays its eggs in caterpillars, to hatch and eat their way out through the bodies of their host. These horrors are profoundly disturbing, but if there is no God there is no intention behind them, so they are not rightly seen as evil. There is 'nothing personal' in the hurts that befall us, except in the case of the ones that conscious agents deliberately cause.

The secular notion is often criticized for removing our responsibility, and making us the deterministic puppets of social forces. And it can be seriously questioned whether a world where our communities, families and brains were scientifically 'engineered' to avoid the emergence of evil would not also inevitably destroy freedom and many other good things. But explanation does not have to be deterministic. To understand someone helps us to forgive them, but it does not absolve them from their responsibility for what they did. There is still a dimension of freedom that science cannot take away from us, and should not try to, because though our freedom often has tragic and evil consequences, it bears also much that gives creativity and meaning to our lives. Chapters 6 will discuss this further.

Often those of a religious frame of mind dismiss too easily the tremendous amount of good the secular approach has done for us. In earlier times events like famine and disease would be ascribed either to the wrath of God or to the machinations of evil spirits and witches. We put on sackcloth and prayed, or we burned witches, but still famine and disease went on happening. Now through science we are able to trace the real causes of such things and begin to eradicate them. If our world is disenchanted, less full of magic, it is also less haunted, less full of supernatural things to fear. That makes us less likely to blame groups like Jews and witches when things go wrong, and less likely to feel shame about aspects of ourselves that are simply natural, part of our evolutionary make-up. The main temptation of the secular is a blithe optimism that leads us to hide or disclaim the ills that science cannot yet solve, and to disown or downplay all that remains mysterious, including the dimension of responsibility.

3. Original Sin

Historically the main battle of this secular viewpoint was against the Western Christian notion of original sin. The idea that we could ultimately explain 'evil' and so cure it and progress beyond it was resisted by those who saw humanity as suffering from a deep and incurable flaw, so that the best we could do was contain the consequences of this ineradicable flaw. In modern times the 'left' wing has tended to represent the secular view that science and education could overcome suffering, and change human nature for the better, the 'right' the more conservative and 'religious' view that we are stuck with both suffering and our corrupt nature. Chapter 3 has already touched on the consequences of these viewpoints, but now we need to look more closely at the idea of original sin as an account of the origin of evil.

The idea is often identified with the story of the taking of the fruit by Adam and Eve in the Garden of Eden. But this story appears in the Hebrew as well as the Christian Bible, yet Judaism has no doctrine of original sin. Nor, for that matter, has Eastern Orthodox Christianity. It was Paul, the early Christian convert (or Jewish apostate, depending on your point of view) who set Adam in opposition to Christ:

> Just as sin came into the world through one man, and death came through sin, and so death spread to all because all have sinned... Death exercised dominion from Adam to Moses, even over those whose sins were not like the transgressions of Adam, who is a type of the one who was to come [Christ].

> (Rom. 5.12, 14)
>
> Since death came through a human being, the resurrection of the dead has also come through a human being; for as all die in Adam, so all will be made alive in Christ. (1 Cor. 15.21–2)

Paul seems to be using the language of typology rather than causality. He is not saying the sin of Adam *caused* all other sin – Romans 5.12 seems to treat sin as something we all do in our own right – or even that all sins are necessarily *like* Adam's. But he suggests a kind of participation or solidarity in human sin and death, which Adam's sin and death prefigure, just as there will be a participation in the risen life, which Jesus' resurrection prefigures. Death is personified as something that 'spreads' and 'has dominion,' seeming to operate by its own causality and reign. We do not die because of Adam, but we die 'in' Adam, in the same way as that in which we are made alive 'in' Christ.

The rich and evocative, but imprecise language here has admitted of many streams of interpretation, but best known to us in the West is Augustine's notion of original sin. Sin is identified with concupiscence, a desperate possessive craving, such as led to the taking of the forbidden fruit. It represents a catastrophic takeover by our desires, and a turning away from God. Augustine placed a special emphasis on the sexual aspect of the catastrophe. Man's (and it does seem to be a special trouble for men) sexual organs cease to obey the will and mind and exhibit a life of their own; and it is through sexual reproduction that the original sin of Adam propagates. This disobedience of our sexuality to our reason is God's fitting punishment for our original disobedience to God. But unleashing desires beyond our control, and destroying our free will, it is a punishment that generates yet further sin and therefore further punishment.

Concupiscence is reminiscent of the Buddhist *tanha,* and the self-perpetuating cycle of sin and suffering not unlike karma. However, Augustine's cycle of evil is driven by God's need to punish our sins, whereas the Buddhist cycle is driven by our own ignorance and delusion. In both Augustinian and Buddhist perspectives, however, evil has no original substance and is merely a lack or privation of good, though producing a real causal chain of effects. When a rose is blighted, or a child corrupted, something really happens; but the evil adds no new reality to the rose or child; it consists only in a diminishment of good. There is less reality there than before. But there really is less reality: the diminishment is real.

In both perspectives, freedom is possible only once we recognize the depth of our diminishment by evil and our loss of freedom, so that we begin to take responsibility for our lives and become free. But in the Buddhist case this happens (in the main) by our own insight, in Augustine's by taking hold of the liberation from original sin won by Christ on the cross. And in the Buddhist case evil exists only in the deluded mind – or we might say, as the deluded ego itself – while in Augustine's it exists in the choices, and hence actions, of the egocentric will as it chooses against God, betrays reality, and resists its own final good.

Augustine's theory has dominated the Christian West, Catholic and Protestant alike. But in modern times it has been much criticized from within Christianity as well as outside it. Matthew Fox (1983), a Dominican priest expelled for his views, has opposed to original sin a concept of 'original blessing.' Meanwhile feminists have suggested that Augustine sees sexuality, and the operation of sin in general, from a narrowly male perspective. The doctrine seems to be fatally flawed by a combination of three factors.

The first is the impetus it gives to a shame about features – including our sexuality – that are natural to our humanity and our animality. The second is the way it sees God as *bound* to punish our disobedience, as if God were limited by some law of retributive justice that circumscribes his power to forgive. Moreover the punishment involved includes punishment of the majority of humankind in hell, where there is no question of future reform or redemption, so the punishment has no possible future good in mind. Retribution becomes the norm, the eternal essence of God, whereas forgiveness becomes that which God contrives (for a few) by the incarnation of the Son and his atonement on the cross. Chapters 7 and 9 will contend, to the contrary, that indiscriminate forgiveness is of the very nature of God, while law and punishment belong to the structure *we* need to contrive to make such forgiveness effective among us.

The third point emerges once we ask the question why God would create a garden with a snake and a fruit, foreknowing that his command would be disobeyed and the bliss for which he created us would be thwarted? Can we really let the buck stop with Adam, or Eve, or the snake, or Satan who the snake was later taken to be, when God is the all-powerful creator of them all. As Sidney Carter put it in his well-known hymn, *Good Friday*:

> It was God that made the Devil
> And the woman and the man
> And there wouldn't be an apple
> If it wasn't in the plan.*
> *© 1968 Stainer & Bell Ltd, 23 Gruneisen Road, London N3 1DZ, England. Reprinted by permission.

If we believe, with dualism, that evil is an independent power not created by God, or if we believe with the Gnostics that God is not the creator at all but a goodness far beyond creation, then indeed the buck can stop at some place other than God. But if we believe with Augustine that God made the world good, and evil is only the privation of good, then why would God allow this privation, which we symbolize by the presence of the snake and the forbidden fruit in the garden of bliss? Augustine and others have been led by such considerations to push the buck further back, to Satan, the angel who chose against God, enviously desiring God's power for himself, and who later appears as the serpent in the garden. But again, why should God create an angel capable of such destructive envy? The question is not answered by Augustine himself; we turn now to Christian views that have taken the bold step of letting the buck stop with God.

4. Lucky Fault

In his theological classic, *Evil and the God of Love* (1968), theologian John Hick contrasts the Augustinian understanding of evil with a different tradition of interpretation deriving from another teacher, Irenaeus of Lyons (c115–c202), and more widely followed in Eastern Orthodoxy, which largely rejects any notion of original sin. Irenaeus' approach was developed in his conflicts with the Gnostics, against whom he wished to affirm creation as the loving act of a good God. But Irenaeus obviously could not deny the presence in creation of much that is painful and evil. How could a partly evil world be reconciled with a wholly good God?

In response to this question, Irenaeus argued that the evil served a good ultimate end. We were created good, but frail and fallible, like children, so that through the experience of suffering, sin and repentance we might come to the fullness of Christ in a manner that would not have been possible if we had been created finished and perfect. That is not to say God caused Adam to sin. Adam, Irenaeus believed, might not have sinned, and might have come to glory sooner and with less pain. But God created Adam fallible enough for sin to be a possibility, and when he did sin, the divine purpose was not thwarted.

In the West, then, we often take for granted the pattern of good creation followed by catastrophic sin followed by the remedy, Christ. But in the East this has at least been balanced by a view that suggests a continuous trajectory of growth, from a creation that is good largely in potential, through the fall into sin, to the coming of Christ who brings creation to fullness. It is easy to develop this kind of understanding of creation and fall in ways that harmonize with an evolutionary perspective, along the lines bravely sketched by Teilhard de Chardin (1975). We can see the world not as having a perfect beginning which got spoiled, but as having primitive beginnings full of potential for good, and developing through the emergence of life and of consciousness – which brings with it the capacity consciously to reject the good, as well as the consequent capacity for guilt and shame – towards the fullness of Christ. Christ is then seen as much more than a mere response to unexpected disaster; he is the destiny of creation from the beginning.

Such a view of Christ as the destiny of the universe irrespective of sin has had its Western protagonists in theologians like John Duns Scotus (c1265–1308). And it is the Western liturgy of Easter Night that *rejoices* in the sin of Adam as 'lucky' or 'happy' (*felix*) because it necessitated the redemption by Christ:

> O happy fault, O necessary sin of Adam
> That brought forth so great a Redeemer.

Yet by and large Irenaeus' account has not prevailed in the West. To rejoice in Adam's sin is not to underestimate the catastrophe; in many ways the darkness of sin is *more* emphasized in the East, where loss of grace, suffering and death itself are not – as for Augustine – an extraneously imposed punishment, but the inevitable consequence of our own catastrophic turning away from God, inward to self-reliance and downward to enslaved attachment to creatures.

> Deprivation of grace is not the cause, but rather the consequence of the decadence of human nature. Man has obstructed the faculty in himself for communion with God,

> has closed up the way by which grace should have poured out through him into the whole creation.
> (Lossky, 1973, p. 133)

Nevertheless in Orthodox theology Christ by his own death and resurrection restores the image of God in us, enabling us again to receive grace and eternal life, bringing us to *theosis*, the participation in God for which we were made. Our turning away is in turn overturned, taking us not back to Eden but forward to the state we were created to grow towards. So for all the gravity of its account of sin, this Irenaean perspective has an overall optimism that contrasts with Augustine. Irenaeus falls short of saying God caused sin as part of his plan for Christ to come, but we could say that *chaos and freedom to turn away are within the providence of God,* not something providence struggles against.

Something of this understanding is expressed in the poem that opens Chapter 4, where sorrow is seen as productive of joy right from the beginning, from creation itself; though there are hints of other understandings in that poem too, perhaps.

Two modern thinkers have boldly restated the Augustinian view in ways which, I believe (though they might disagree) brings them much closer to an Irenaean perspective. One is the Roman Catholic theologian James Alison, discussed in Chapter 2. He has urged us (1998) to reinterpret original sin through Girard's understanding of mimetic rivalry and the need to scapegoat. Instead of an initial disobedience leading to a sexually propagated sin, he suggests an initial fall from natural animal desire into mimetic rivalry. This mimetic desire propagates through society not through reproduction, as for Augustine, but through imitation. But mimetic rivalry leads to violence and death, not as an extrinsic divine punishment (as seems to be the case in the story of Adam and Eve) but as an inevitable consequence (as in the story of Cain and Abel, which is very significant for Alison). Moreover, Alison sees everything from the perspective of the resurrection. We need 'original sin' only as the account of what the resurrection of Christ releases us from, so that Alison speaks, from the Easter perspective, of 'the joy of being wrong.' The notion of death as a consequence of sin rather than punishment for it and the emphasis on the good outcome align Alison with the Irenaean perspective and with the tradition of the 'happy fault'.

5. The Choice of God

The other, contrasting modern thinker is the protestant Karl Barth. Like Alison, and like Irenaeus, he starts from the perspective of Christ; all theology, for him, is done to enable us to enter the redemption Christ brings. But Barth seems to take the bold step which Irenaeus did not quite, of placing the buck with God and the very activity of creating.

> God... and his activity take place in a definite opposition, in a real negation, both defensive and aggressive... God elects, and therefore rejects what he does not elect. God wills, and therefore opposes what he does not will. He says Yes, and therefore says No to that to which he has not said Yes.
> (2004, III/3, section 50, p. 311)
>
> Nothingness is that which God does not will. It lives only by the fact that it is that which God does not will. (p. 352)

In other words, the very act of creating is a choosing of some things to be that means a rejection of others as not to be. Barth speaks of God creating with his right hand, but as having also a left hand containing the evil he rejects in creating. But in this case what God rejects takes on a kind of reality of its own; it is described as '*das Nichtige,*' something that 'lives' as that which God does not create, and therefore (one would have thought) does not exist!

In his excellent little book, *Evil* (2007), Paul Ricoeur clarifies the ambiguity involved in Barth's thought at this point.

> If, in fact, the goodness of God shows itself in his having fought against evil from the beginning of creation... isn't God's power sacrificed to his goodness? Conversely if God is Lord 'also with his left hand,' isn't his goodness limited by his anger, by his rejection? (p. 63)

In the first case – that is, if we take the word 'lives' in the second Barth quotation seriously, and regard 'Nothing' with a capital 'N' as a kind of dark and sinister thing – the result is almost a cosmic good-versus-evil dualism. God by creating plunges into an ongoing struggle with the chaos he does not will. He is then all good but not all powerful.

If on the other hand we take the non-existence implied in 'nothing' seriously, and refuse to make no-thing a kind of thing, the result is an odd inversion of the notion of evil as a privation of good. It is no longer a question – as it is for Augustine – of agents within creation who choose against being and for destruction. Rather, creation itself arises out of a kind of privation of what is not chosen to be, a negation of negation! Barth makes creation sound more like an act of angry rejection than of choosing love. Or at least, anger and love coexist in God as the ultimate source of good and evil. God remains the all-powerful source of everything, good and evil alike; but in that case he causes evil, albeit by his act of rejection.

The confusion here may be thought to be resolved in the light of Barth's understanding of the death of Christ, where God as it were takes 'the nothing' into himself in the destruction of his own son, which as it were frees us from the shadow of nothingness cast by creation. God, having rejected the nothing in creation, takes it into his own story in the act of redemption on the cross.

But the ambiguity in fact persists. Is the 'nothing' which Christ accepts a real evil, a Satan dualistically opposed to God? Or is this 'nothing' non-existence itself? In the death of Christ, does God embrace non-being in the sense of ceasing to exist?

In the former case Barth is operating on the ancient model that sees Christ as winning, on the cross, the ultimate victory over the real evil which God has struggled against since the beginning of creation. But in the latter case we see something more like God accepting the death penalty. The Sidney Carter song quoted above is actually presented as the words of the impenitent thief crucified beside Jesus. The thief's speech goes on:

> It's God they ought to crucify instead of you and me
> I said to the carpenter, a-hanging on the tree.*
>
>

But of course in orthodox Christian theology the carpenter *was* God, the very person of the incarnate divine Son, a-hanging on the tree. So in the person of Christ, God can be viewed as accepting the penalty for the destructiveness inherent in his very creation of the world, taking from us the ultimate blame, and the penalty of death, for the sins we ourselves do as part of that irreducibly ambiguous creation. What follows from that would be the kind of view expounded by Slavoj Žižek (2009, p. 43ff), who follows the 'death of God' theologian Thomas Altizer in seeing the cross as the final self-emptying of God as a separate existence from us. For Žižek, Christianity represents the first and most convincing form of atheism!

Wiesel suggests (2008, p. 77) such an understanding from a Jewish perspective. He relates the slow, painful death of a boy in the concentration camp hanging on the gallows alongside two other suspected saboteurs.

> For more than half an hour he stayed there, struggling

> between life and death, dying in slow agony under our eyes. He was still alive when I passed in front of him. His tongue was still red, his eyes were not yet glazed.
>
> Behind me I heard [a] man asking:
>
> 'Where is God now?'
>
> And I heard a voice within me answer him:
>
> 'Where is God? Here He is — He is hanging here on this gallows...'

We could interpret this in two ways. One is the familiar Christian idea that God suffers and even dies alongside us in Christ. Theologian Marilyn McCord Adams (2006) makes this the basis of her account of how Christ overcomes what she calls 'horrors.' These are terrible events that threaten to shatter the meaning of the lives of those who perpetrate and suffer from them – a category overlapping with but not identical to 'evil' as defined in these chapters. God is ultimately responsible for creating a universe in which horrors can occur. In the torture and death of Christ, she argues, God undergoes horror, making horror part of God's own story, God's own experience. Christ's resurrection and return to the Father ensure that even the worst of horrors need not undermine meaning, but can actually become the means to union with God. Chapter 6 will argue that such a view presents Christ as the tragicomic victim and hero who gives ultimate meaning to the meaningless.

But Wiesel was a Jew, and it is unlikely that this Christian interpretation would be his intent. His own interpretation of the voice within him is probably much less comforting: the sense that in the horror of that boy's death, all hope of God has died forever. Certainly the Holocaust meant the end of the relationship with God for many Jews. For many, God was guilty of failing to fulfill his part of the covenant, and stood condemned. But if this were the whole truth (which of course it is not) it would surely mean a second triumph for those who persecuted the Jews. Not only would the Jewish people and culture perish within Europe, but among the survivors Jewish faith itself would perish.

I am not sure what Barth would have made of Carter's song or Wiesel's gallows scene, and I am fairly sure he would not have liked Žižek at all. But nor would he have liked being thought of as a sophisticated Manichean dualist. Yet it seems to me (and to Ricoeur) that he avoids these alternatives only by remaining obscure. Be that as it may, the notion of evil as a shadow cast by God's choice for good is strangely reminiscent of another thinker Barth would not have liked, Carl Gustav Jung and his notion that all our choices of good create a dark 'shadow' in the psyche. The right and left hands of God – choosing and rejecting – look a little like self and shadow!

However, it occurs to me that the left and right hands might be thought of not as good and evil, or chosen and rejected, but as order and chaos. The world in all its goodness is (in Christian orthodoxy) not created as order out of chaos, but made out of nothing. But it is made, I suggest, with the two hands of order and chaos. God always works, so to speak, with both hands together. When we hold onto one hand and try to push the other away, what occurs is the destruction of good we call evil.

Creating with Both Hands: a Model of Good and Evil

Which of our many models of good and evil are to be preferred? Doubtless there are situations in which different models of evil are more useful or appropriate than others. The problem with the great 'real evil' understandings is that they write our hurts in stone, imposing one grand narrative of what evil is like and who embodies it, when we need to be able to see evil nimbly, and change tactics and strategy carefully, according to what we actually observe. To see Nazism as an 'evil' to be combated by the 'good' Allies may have been less far from the truth than milder accounts; but the saturation bombing of Dresden and other German cities, the brutal rape and pillage by the advancing Soviet armies, and the atomic bombing of Hiroshima and Nagasaki makes it impossible to see the Allies as undiluted angels of light. To see, for example, the Israeli-Palestinian conflict in 'good versus evil' terms (as so many do, one way or another) is naïve and dangerous. And to see our difficulties with the boss in those terms would be frankly paranoid.

So it may seem more profitable, in our search for good ways to respond to hurt and harm, to look at those nimbler understandings which locate evil in the human mind, or in human activity and process. Each of these models seems to have some truth in it. But should we simply be eclectic pragmatists, just taking 'off the shelf' as it were the approach that seems to fit a given situation? As this is a book about practical responses, that might seem the best approach. However, if we were to adopt that approach we would involve a purely subjective choice of model, and leave us, in the end, not far from the subjective view of good and evil that I earlier dismissed as being totally *im*practical as a way of directing our response. Could we not do better, and find a model that somehow draws the best aspects of the models we have considered into a unified and coherent model, which contains the nimble flexibility we are looking for?

I think we can, tentatively, do so. For it seems to me we already have the seeds of such a model in the idea – suggested at the end of Chapter 4 – of order and chaos as the basis of reality. On the one hand there is form, pattern and structure in space, and predictable, law-governed behavior through time: the kind of thing the Chinese call *yin*. On the other hand there is chaos, unpredictability, the sheer welter of matter and energy doing its dance: the Chinese *yang*. Creation – new life and being and goodness – arise when order and chaos come together, the former's structure guiding the latter's energy towards flourishing. In Aristotelian terms, form and matter combine, the former providing an entelechy or 'inward purpose' that guides the latter towards growth. Or as Nietzsche put it, describing works of art and their creation, there is a need to combine the 'Apollonian' sense of order, rationality and restraint, which many of us identify with Ancient Greece and its sun god Apollo, with the Bacchanalian revelry and orgiastic energy of the wild and no less Greek deity, Dionysus.

The Christian God is of course neither Apollo nor Dionysus. But he creates the world, I suggest, with the Apollonian right hand of order and the Dionysian left hand of chaos. In Mahayana Buddhist terms we could say that beings exist through an interdependent co-arising in which elements of chaos come together in ways that supply their own ordered structure. It seems to me that the Buddhist approach prioritizes chaos and sees order as arising out of it, while the theistic approach – in most versions – prioritizes the order in the mind of God as he shapes the chaos to his ends. Our model does not demand that we describe the world in the theistic or the Buddhist way; it is compatible with both, and suggests something in between that is hard to state.

On this model goodness and being always involve both order and chaos. But order and chaos can relate differently. Order can work on chaos from within, in the *entelechy* which Aristotle describes. But equally, it may impose itself on chaos from above or outside, in what we could call a *hypertelechy* (purpose above or in excess). Order is then in tension with chaos, as it were battling to subdue it, while chaos becomes catastrophe, an overturning of order. This is the situation we call 'evil,' and as we have argued, it is the privation of good. Because goodness and meaning can only arise out of order and chaos, this evil possibility has to arise as part of the very process of creating a good world (or in Buddhist terms, the very process whereby a good world arises). If order and chaos can harmonize creatively, resulting in good, meaningful reality, there has to be the possibility that they strive discordantly, in the 'evil' way.

On an inanimate level we can see this destructive dissonance in earthquakes and the like, and in genetic malfunctioning leading to deformity. Here chaos subverts order, or a lower level order proves chaotic and destructive of a higher level order. But we see it conversely when species become tightly ordered so as to fit a very limited niche. When environmental change happens, the fit proves too tight to allow the random newness of adaptation, and the species becomes extinct. So we speak of 'evil' in the natural world, though only in relative terms, as an excess of chaos over order or vice versa that inhibits the flourishing of a species.

On the human level, some ineluctable kind of harmony between order and chaos must be what underlies human freedom. Though our free will is a mystery, it is obvious that to be free we must contain an element of unpredictable chaos, but that this must harmonize with a degree of order whereby we can predict what is likely to emerge from our actions. If we were totally ordered we would be deterministic automata; but if we were wholly chaotic we would be too out of control to make anything happen. In freedom, our order is the entelechy that shapes our spontaneity towards achieving its goals.

But again this very marriage of order and chaos that is freedom is what can turn evil, in a sour dualism where order crushes spontaneity, and spontaneity disrupts order in meaningless ways. Such dualism manifests as what the Buddhists describe as *tanha*, craving, in which our spontaneous energies are circumscribed in closed circuits of greed, rage and delusion. As in the 'Fade,' energy is not ordered toward what is new and open, but channeled in on itself in a closed order that admits of no escape, leading it always back to the same place. And this is what Augustine's 'original sin' consists in: the repetitive 'inclination of what has more being for what has less being,' the desire that turns vulnerably creative beings either into safe, mechanistic automata, or into raging beasts. The first three chapters have shown how a conflicting dualism between order and chaos can manifest itself: in the pushing away of chaos by the forces of order into a place of blame; in an inner dualism for which chaotic parts of oneself become a cause of shame; and in the deep split whereby individuals disclaim any part in chaos and hide away in a frozen, self-contained order of their own.

Table 1: Virtues and Vices according to the Working Model

		GOOD	'EVIL'
		Eutelechy: cool virtue	**Hypertelechy: cold sin**
ORDER	**Energy**	Peace	Repression
	Survival	Courage	Pride
	Appetite	Detachment, Self-control	Obsession, Possessiveness
	Relationship	Faithfulness	Hatred, Blame
	Will	Justice	Domination
	Knowledge	Wisdom	Denial, Disclaimer

		Entelechy: warm virtue	**Dystelechy: lukewarm and hot sin**
CHAOS	**Energy**	Spontaneity, Play	Sloth, Cynicism
	Survival	Hope	Fear
	Appetite	Joy	Greed, Lust
	Relationship	Love	Shame
	Will	Humility, Gentleness	Envy, Rage
	Knowledge	Inspiration	Delusion

Table 1 classifies some virtues and vices according to this model. I have depicted the order or yin as white, and chaos or

yang as black. (This reverses the Chinese shadings, but seems to accord better with Western feelings of order as sunlike, Apollonian, and clear, and chaos as dark, Dionysian and mysterious.) It shows the ways in which, in a person, order and chaos may relate to produce good or ill, in six aspects of life: energy (the basic pattern by which a person structures her life), survival (the person's way of maintaining her identity), appetite (attitude to things than nourish us), relationship with other people, will (what a person tends to choose and desire) and knowledge (how a person experiences and understands the world). Each area has two virtues and two vices: for example energy may manifest as peace (energy well ordered), repression (energy dammed up), sloth (energy lost) and spontaneous play (energy breaking out). You may find it helpful to ponder the other groups of four.

The virtues on the top right represent what I term 'eutelechy,' literally 'well-purposedness.' Typically they are the 'cool,' grown-up virtues that come from the kind of order that contains an element of chaos. The order is aware of the chaos, but encompasses it and it brings into harmony, so that the order steadily grows nourished by spontaneous elements of chaos. Peace is aware of aggression but reconciles it; courage acknowledges what threatens survival but overcomes it; detachment and self-control know the attraction of good things but are not compelled to partake; faithfulness is aware of difficulty but maintains a relationship through thick and thin; justice acknowledges conflicting requirements but can hold them in a fair balance; and wisdom has learned from both good and painful experience.

By contrast 'hypertelechy' (to use the term just defined) involves what could be called the 'cold' sins listed on the top right, where the white 'order' surrounds and strives to contain a growing circle of 'chaos.' It is manifest in the repression of negative-seeming instincts, in pride (demotion of the reality of others), in obsession and compulsion, in blame and hatred (projection of negative elements onto others – see Chapter 1), in domination (will to power and control over others) and in denial and disclaimer (shutting hurt out, as discussed in Chapter 3).

The vices on the bottom right represent what we could call 'dystelechy,' (purpose gone wrong, functioning badly). Here chaos destroys order in some way: as shown by the dark chaos sweeping round the edge of the white order and increasing. The person rejecting order may lose energy and purpose, seeing nothing as worth striving for, as in the 'lukewarm' sins of sloth and cynicism. He may recoil from a chaotic-seeming world to protect his own order, as in fear. His weakening sense of purpose may be replaced by strong instincts like greed and lust; he may internalize disorder, as in the shame described in Chapter 3; or he may seek the destruction of goodness in others, as in rage and envy. Here we are describing the 'hottest' sins, which seem to emanate from the guts rather than the mind. Finally, the person may lose all orientation and pursue imaginary goals of his own, as in delusion.

At the bottom left is entelechy (Aristotle's inward purpose). Here chaos is shaped from within by an emergent order – symbolized by the white blob in the center of the dark chaos – generating the 'warmth' and natural strengths we find in growing and living things. The basic energy involved in entelechy is the kind of innocent playfulness that charms us so much in children. Survival is sustained by the hope that can grasp good possibilities in the midst of chaos and despair. The appetite finds joy in the abundance of life, while the relationship to others is love, both passionate and compassionate, something we cannot produce by order, but can nurture. The will acquires humility, the 'earthiness' that allows the self to belong gently to the world without rivalry. In terms of knowledge, the long experiential haul of wisdom is balanced by the momentary spark of inspiration, including imagination, insight and intuition: all 'in' words like entelechy itself, denoting order emergent from within chaos and wild dreams.

Combining the Models

This is just a crude initial sketch illustrating a little of the potential of this model. The rest of this book does not depend on accepting the model, and it was not written by applying this or any other preconceived model of good and evil. I arrived at this model after writing those chapters, but when I arrived at it, it seemed to make explicit what had been implicitly in my mind as I wrote them. Whether the model is true, you must assess mainly on whether it makes sense to you after you have read them. But something can be said at this point about the way this model draws on the best, as it were, in the other models we have discussed, and supplies a way of thinking of and feeling about evil that is flexible but coherent.

The model shares with the views discussed in Chapter 4 a cosmological dualism. However, the dualism is between order and chaos. Regarding good and evil the model shares the 'asymmetry' of the views discussed in this chapter. Good is aligned with a creative harmony of order and chaos, and evil with destructive dissonance. The issue of good versus evil is not a matter settled in terms of victory versus defeat; rather, both victory and defeat are aspects of an 'evil' warfare, while good lies with reconciliation and harmony. That is absolutely fundamental to Part 2 of this book.

That said, within our model there will be times that look like a struggle of 'flesh-versus-spirit.' In overcoming the dystelechy of a lazy or lust-ridden soul, a person may need to exert a strong effort of will to restore direction and control. But there will also be times when the 'system-versus-nature' model looks more appropriate. When dealing with the hypertelechy of a totalitarian regime, non-violent acts of spontaneous protest and disruption, a sense of humor, and what I call 'wily innocence' are called for. But both responses are predicted from the model, which thus encompasses in itself a nimbleness lacking in the good-versus-evil kinds of dualism.

One root of our model is the yin-yang image, which offers the kind of dualism it most closely approaches. Indeed, one way of pursuing things further would be to read the *I Ching*. Though widely used simply as an oracle, the book combines the wisdom of the Taoist and Confucian traditions into a series of 64 images. Each image represents a different way in which yin and yang – in our terms, order and chaos – may come together and interact with potential for good or ill. Far from merely predicting an inevitable future, the image is an invitation to the person to reflect on her situation and discern the ways in which she, by her own choices, can release the potential for good. The *I Ching* shows us a world not of good and evil forces doing battle, but of working with the continuing interaction of order and chaos. Goodness lies not in 'siding with the good' but in the way the 'superior person' brings the best out of a situation through her flexibility and wisdom.

So the yin-yang does not indicate a good-versus-evil dualism. There is no suggestion that the 'superior person' should not always pursue the morally better option. But discerning the right option is a much more complex and subtle matter than a good-versus-evil dualism would suggest.

At the same time, though order and chaos are presented in this model as interacting in a cycle, this does not predetermine the matter of whether life as a whole, or good and evil, repeat in an eternal cycle, as in Buddhism, or give rise to an ultimate fullness of good, and in Christianity. Just as the cyclical nature of local time – our days and years, determined by the motions of the earth – does not decide the issue of whether time on larger scales is cyclical or linear, so the cyclical interaction of order and chaos does not determine whether out of this interaction good, or evil, will progressively predominate, or alternate in a cycle.

So much for the views discussed in Chapter 4. The question

remains whether my model combines the good features of those discussed in this chapter. I suggest that it does, as can be seen if we focus on the issue on how we see the evil in the action of Kaplan's Nazi.

1. 'Evil' consists in a privation of good. It happens when order and chaos conflict and prevent the arising of good or effect its restriction or destruction. The Nazi's act was 'evil' because it was a deliberate attempt to undo the good, to destroy the rabbi as the human being he is, to make him go against the meanings that give him life, or in Jewish and Christian terms to deface the image of God in which he is made.
2. 'Evil' is manifest as ignorance and deluded craving. This is obvious in cases of dystelechy, where our true goals are lost sight of, but is also an aspect of hypertelechy, where ideologies poison our natural humanity. The Nazi was so blinded by ideology that he could no longer see who and what the rabbi really was. He spat, not on the image of God, but on his own corrupt idea of the Jew.
3. 'Evil works through a human psychology in ways that can be scientifically traced. Though cosmological in scope, our model of virtues and vices is psychological and sociological. It could be enhanced by observing and tracing the ways in which the aspects of virtue and vice lead to one another. The Nazi did not simply choose 'out of nothing' to make the rabbi spit; his action could be better understood if we knew his own psychology and biography, and how and why he had become a Nazi. This analysis would not enable a complete understanding; there would remain something terrible and incomprehensible in his act, which has to do with free will and responsibility. Science could not absolve him, but it could make him recognizable as a human being disturbingly like ourselves.

4. 'Evil' involves 'original sin' in that it is something we choose to do, yet our choices are not free but constrained by the chains of cause and effect that largely write our history for us. In terms of our model, we have a bias towards letting order and chaos come together badly, preventing our own and others' full flourishing. There is a historical causality that led to the kind of ideological blinding, the collective delusion that enabled the Nazi (though it did not force him) to make this individual choice. Though it is particularly horrible, there is continuity between such acts and all sorts of 'ordinary' everyday bullying.
5. At the same time 'evil' is 'lucky' not in itself, but because it springs from what can be turned to good. It results from a bad marriage between order and chaos, forces which can be married well so as to give birth to new being and goodness. Of course there was nothing at all happy or lucky in the Nazi's act. All the same, confronted with it we need to fasten on an all important dimension of hope: to refuse to allow the holocausts and other atrocities to triumph by taking away our joy and celebration in the deep goodness of all that is real. That is the basic message of the psychologist Viktor Frankl, who advocates, in the face of all he suffered in the Holocaust, a 'tragic optimism' (2004, see next chapter).
6. 'Evil' is a possibility inherent in the arising of being and goodness, or to put it in the theistic way, not God's direct choice but an inevitable consequence of God's choice to make the good that can only be made out of order and chaos. These accounts encourage us to enter a redemptive process in which the evils of the world are truly felt for what they are, but also turned to whatever good may come from them. Even the rabbi, devastated as he must have been, can be cared for and restored; even the Nazi may come to true remorse in which he begins to make good the

evil he has done. This may seem unlikely, but we should never lose hope.

So much for my model. It may or may not convince you at this stage; I hope it will by the end of the book, though as I say, the rest of the book could contain truth even if the model is wrong. But we do not live our lives by models; it is narratives, our ways of telling our human story, that really speak. The 'good versus evil' model is convincing partly because of the exciting stories of slaying the monster that express it for us time and again. Are there stories that express our model in this way? In Chapter 6 I shall argue that there are: the narratives of tragedy and comedy. If we lived by these stories, I shall suggest, we would respond better to hurt and harm.

But after all this talk about evil, maybe we need some relief! Maybe we need to focus a little on the good, and on the non-violent innocence I believe to be the polar opposite of 'evil'.

Summary

1. In contrast to the vision of the world as a dualistic mixture of good or evil, or even mainly bad, mainstream Christianity affirms the goodness of creation. Nothing that exists is evil in itself; evil consists in the destruction of good, the prevention of flourishing, or the inclination toward lesser being. But how does this destruction, prevention or inclination arise?
2. In Buddhist traditions evil is at root delusion or ignorance. Plato and others agree – nobody wants to do evil as evil; evil arises through false ideologies of where good lies.
3. For modern scientific and secular understandings, the term 'evil' merely wraps in myth our incomprehension of why people do certain kinds of harm. Once we understand the causes of such harms, we can cure them.
4. Augustine held a darker view – we all inherit 'original sin' –

an original wrong choice for which God's punishment is a predisposition to desire with results that he must, again, punish. This view has been much criticized.

5. But an alternative Irenaean understanding sees sin as arising from our immaturity and opening up a way to grow deeper into God. Alison interprets 'original sin' in terms of mimetic desire and its consequences, which are joyfully overcome in Jesus' resurrection.
6. But this may mean the 'buck' stops further back, with God's original act of creation. Karl Barth's obscure sayings can be interpreted in this way, suggesting either a cosmic dualism that Christ overcomes when he takes evil into himself on the cross, or the idea of a 'nothingness' that is the shadow side of God's choice in creation.
7. The accounts of evil offered so far are not incompatible, but can be brought together into a 'yin-yang' model of good and evil as differently emergent out of order and chaos. This offers a way of mapping out the virtues and vices.
8. This model draws positive features of the different understandings into a coherent and flexible manner of understanding even the most radical evil. This model is implicit in the discussions of Part 2, though the validity of Part 2 does not depend on accepting the model.

Part 2

How Can We Respond Well? Towards a Wily Innocence

As summer clouds before the rain halo
the sun that hangs in truth far beyond in
infinite azure, so you, Lady
are corona enthroning Light
in light.

But he plays at Eden's gate, too near
the sword: the cherub fire plays on your mind,
yet you cannot draw him back
(who drew you like the sun
draws cloud from water, up), you must offer
him; and he, Days Ancient, wend
his child-way to that altar
where the sword goes in his side – your heart –
and Bethlehem caves
paradise in. This new thing I
the old must sing, before I go.

Presentation (Luke 2.21–40)

In Matthew's Gospel, when Jesus sends his newly commissioned disciples out to heal people and declare the nearness of God's kingdom, he lets them take even less than the average wandering ascetic: no money or pack for sustenance, no staff for protection, no sandals. They are to be absolutely vulnerable and dependent on whatever charity they may receive. And he declares, 'I am sending you out like sheep into the midst of wolves; so be wise as serpents and innocent as doves,' (Matt.

10.16).

We might ask why they had to be so defenseless, like sheep sent to preach the gospel to wolves who would inevitably tear them apart! Even mentally it seems they were to be *akeraios*, meaning 'without harm' – which could mean harmless but also unharmed, uncorrupted, unblemished. Both meanings reside in the term usually used to translate the word: 'innocent'.

But having wondered that, we might additionally wonder why or how this innocence could combine with *phronimos* – wise, discreet, prudent, or circumspect – looking around warily for danger, and slipping away like a snake if any is spotted. How can good disciples be doves and snakes at once? It helps a little to know that the ancient serpent was itself an ambiguous symbol, representing on the one hand temptation – as in Eden – but on the other hand, wisdom and healing, and even Christ himself. In John's Gospel (3.14) Jesus compares himself uplifted on the cross with the healing serpent uplifted in the wilderness. The natural symbolism of the serpent – as something that glides stealthily and leglessly low on the ground, with venom that can kill but also provide the basis of healing medicine – itself suggests both evasive cunning and wise discretion. But these connotations still seem remote from dovelike innocence.

It was not the only occasion when Jesus is recorded as commending what may have been innocence. Perhaps this is what he meant when he touched children and blessed them, and in Mark's version embraced them – actions probably as alien to the patriarchal correctness of his culture as it is to the political correctness of our own, for certainly the disciples did not approve – and went to declare, 'Whoever does not receive the kingdom of God like a child shall not enter it.' This is narrated, with variations, in all three synoptic Gospels (Mark 10.13–16; Matt. 19.13–15; Luke 18.15–17). This affirmation of children is more or less unique to Jesus; we find nothing like it in the teaching of the time, though in the quotation at the beginning of this book the prophet Isaiah (11.6–9) sees the coming kingdom of non-violence as being led by a child. But why do we need to become children, and it what respect? Does 'innocence' name it?

There is certainly an innocence, an aspect of the non-violent sheep among wolves, in the way Jesus goes to Jerusalem, the place of his death. I have tried to capture in the opening poem something of the way of the Christ-child that is too close to the original innocence of the Garden of Eden, and hence liable to be killed by the cherubic swords that prevented human beings from re-entering it (Gen. 3.24). Yet Jesus himself was agile and wily in the way he won most of the arguments with the religious authorities. Do we see in him something of the wily innocence he commended to his disciples? How else might he and they survive the spiritual and physical vulnerability they had chosen? Does this suggest a way that we too might be vulnerable to hurt, and yet not come to harm or do harm in turn?

I shall explore this possibility a little as a way to introduce Part 2 and its unfolding of ways of responding well to evil, hurt and harm. I shall first say something about the ambiguity of the child in modern culture, then explore what might be valuable in innocence, and finally say something about the 'wiles' we need to learn if we are to retain – or perhaps rather attain – innocence.

Angels, Animals – or Wily Innocent Heroes?

There are three main ways in which we can think of children: as little adults-to-be, as half-tamed animals, and as innocent angels. Probably through most of history the first option predominated. Children wore little versions of adults' clothes, and they often worked in factories and fields alongside adults. If grown-ups had to take special care of them, it was in the same way that one might take care of a small plant that needed protection till it grew big and strong. But with the Romantic movement and the idea of original innocence, children became a bit magic: enchanted messengers of a purer world, terribly vulnerable to the corruptions of adult society. They started to wear special clothes to enhance this aura of innocence. But from time to time cases like the Bulger killers and the Yorkshire boys, mentioned above, have revealed an aspect of children quite incompatible with this. The press has been remarkably quick, as noted, to pick up on the idea that since they can't be good angels, such children must be the opposite: wild animals if not demons. The idea of the demon or witch child is of course not new; sadly it is currently propagated in some African churches, leading to the horrific abuse and isolation of children believed to be evil. In a milder form it informs the notion – thankfully preached more than practiced by my parents and grandparents – of 'spare the rod and spoil the child': the idea that a child is a wild animal that needs to be broken in, tamed and civilized.

What is interesting, however, is that just recently several films have picked up on stories of young people in a way that seems to fuse all three of these ideas, presenting children or early adolescents as heroes who in their battle against darkness are at once sophisticated little adults, innocent angels, and rather wild and dangerous. I think of Lyra Belacqua, in Philip Pullman's *The Golden Compass,* and the hugely popular Harry Potter from the works of J.K. Rowling. Both Lyra and Harry are 11 years old when they start their adventures, and in the corresponding films played by 12 year old actors. Then there are older stories also recently translated into film: the child heroes and heroines of *The Lion, the Witch and the Wardrobe,* the first of a series of film adaptations of C.S. Lewis's *Chronicles of Narnia;* and Frodo – in Tolkien's *Lord of the Rings.* He is a 33 year old hobbit whose name means 'wise,' but in the film composed half a century later, this character is played by an innocent, teenage-looking actor, Elijah Wood.

All these young heroes and heroines share many features in common. They are profoundly innocent, in the sense that they are forever being amazed or even terrified by the world they explore; their eyes are forever opening in wonder. They have, not a courage hardened through experience, but a tough determination and a sense of justice that has yet to be contaminated by cynicism and defeatism. But they are also wily, with an instinctive, almost animal sense of where danger lies and who is to be trusted, and a readiness to think up on the hoof strategies for outwitting and confusing their enemies, even if this involves lies and deception. And in some contexts they behave like young adults, though imbued with this innocent yet dangerous aura.

There are many reasons, doubtless, why books like these have become bestsellers and been made into blockbusting films eagerly devoured by many who are not children – myself included. But one reason may be that the wily innocence of their lead characters represents a quality we in contemporary society feel we want and need. While 'virtuous' is hardly the word that springs to mind with Lyra and the other heroines and heroes, we would hesitate to dub their wily innocence as just 'sinful' or 'wicked.' For we recognize that, if they are to overcome 'evil' that seems infinitely more powerful than they are, they will need to be wily as well as innocent. And we, as we face the White Witches, the dark Lords and the bureaucratic 'magisteria' of our time, need to develop their kind of wily innocence.

After a crisis in my life I wrote about the beginnings of recovery:

> A crude cheeky little girl rampages within me now, making rude signs at all caretaker-demons. In her glorious provocative pure and innocent nudity, she is the heart of me that has never grown up, and never learned to be truly responsible. Now, given an altogether different sort of discipline, she will... God is not only the ordering Father *and* nurturing Mother *but also* the wild chaotic Child: the God of maverick dreamers and tricksters like Jacob and Joseph. God is the one who sails close to the wind, and rides upon its

wings (Psalm 104.3), who forms light and darkness, good and ill (Isaiah 45.7), who is Yin and Yang in their wonderful interaction.

Now looking back I can see the discovery of the wily warrior child within me was only a *stage* to recovery. The 'altogether different kind of discipline' we discover when we reconnect with our inner child needs huge time to grow up and become responsible, just as any actual child does. The process of remorse as described in Chapter 7 – developing a true sense of the reality of others and the harm we have truly done them – cannot be circumvented. The child needs to learn wily wisdom and subtlety, not only in order not to be harmed, but in order not to be harmful in her wild rampages. That said, the image of the child – not only innocent, or wild, or a little adult, but all three at once as we see in these screen images – may represent something in ourselves we need to recover if we are to be healed of harms.

The Trickster is an ancient image that combines divine innocence and diabolical cunning in the same way. One example was Hermes who was a messenger between the human and divine, and held a staff with two serpents coiled around it, one poisonous and the other containing the antidote. Another is the youthful Ariel in Shakespeare's *The Tempest*, creating magic illusions and fooling people on behalf of his master Prospero. Yet another may be the Satan of the Old Testament, before Christians identified him with the wholly evil Devil: Lucifer the light-bearer, a dark angel who does Yahweh's dirty errands for him like afflicting Job. Such figures combine wily cunning with something childlike and innocent, and Jung has noted their strange role in reconciling people with their 'shadow,' opening doors in the closed places of the mind, or as we might put it, loosening the interlocked battle of internal order and chaos and marrying them in new and healing ways. (See Kalsched, 1996, p. 38–40.)

Aspects of Innocence

I have spoken of innocence as if we all agreed on what it is, but any glance at a dictionary that records usage will reveal that the word carries many meanings, some positive, others negative. Some have more to do with ethics and the way we behave, others more to do with our state of knowledge or our way of seeing the world. I will just summarize some of these meanings, so that we can then see what in them might be important in a response to hurt, and what might or might not be compatible with wily innocence.

The ethical meanings listed in *The Shorter Oxford English Dictionary* include

- The legal state of **not being guilty** of an offense. Not in itself relevant to our discussion.
- As described above, **harmlessness and non-violence**. Obviously this is of the essence of what this book is seeking.
- **Moral purity**. The state of not having been harmed, blemished or corrupted. This could be relevant, but Chapter 3 noted how the search for moral purity can be dangerous in the way described by Rose and West.
- **Sexual inexperience**. Not obviously relevant, though both Buddhist and Christian monasticism have treasured it. Perhaps this is because of associations with innocence generally; but I am not sure that celibate people are necessarily always innocent in other ways!
- **Non-responsibility** – a state like that of Adam and Eve before their 'fall' of not knowing the difference between right or wrong. Not the same as 'Irresponsibility' which means knowing the difference but not caring about it. This would seem to be something inimical to a responsible approach to hurt and harm.
- **Unselfconsciousness**, including lack of shame, like Adam

and Eve naked in the garden. Once again this is not 'shamelessness,' which is actually being aware of one's shameful state but not caring. Unashamed nakedness of character does seem to be one aspect of the innocence Jesus requires of his disciples as they embark on their mission, and may provide us with an important clue.

The last two meanings contain an element of lack of knowledge or awareness, and lead us to the 'epistemological' aspects of innocence:

- **Ignorance**, just not being aware. To deal with hurt one must be aware of it as hurt, so ignorance as such is not to be desired.
- More positively, a **fresh perception**, uncluttered by too many concepts and preconceptions, ability to see through the emperor's new clothes, or to paint with an 'innocent eye.' This suggests Buddhist mindfulness, and will prove important in Chapter 8.
- **Uncalculating naivety.** This makes children charming, but also terribly vulnerable. It is not a quality we see in Jesus. His parables show a familiarity with 'the ways of the world,' and it was not failure to see the dangers that led him to the cross. I suggest it is one area where we need to be wily and prudent of we are not to be overwhelmed by harm, but respond well.
- **Spontaneous trust.** Children tend in the main to trust people, though sometimes they can show an instinctive and valid mistrust. Some argue that Jesus uses children as an example of trust in God, but this seems to me over pious. Trust is a charming quality, but needs a strong dose of savvy discernment if it is not to make people vulnerable to harm.
- **Wonder, imagination and playfulness.** These are the

> qualities that often came to mind when I asked people what they associated with innocence. We treasure them in children, but often we lose them as we become adult. Then cynicism destroys a sense of wonder, or routine destroys imagination, or a sense of duty and the need to work leaves little time for play. But Plato saw leisure and play as the places where we go on learning, and Jesus certainly showed a taste for enjoyment and playfulness. If we are to make something good out of the hurts we receive we will need all the wonder and imagination we can lay hands on. Chapter 6 will explore the playfulness of the tragicomic clown.

Innocence emerges, I suggest, as something with many aspects we ought to value, but some we need to be wary of. On the ethical side we ought to treasure non-violence, purity and lack of self-consciousness and shame; on the cognitive, an open, spontaneous, uncontaminated grasp of reality, enriched by imagination and playfulness. All these features, especially the wonder, seem to me to be summed up in the picture I took of family member Beth Stoddart (now Wright) (**Figure 1**). On the other hand innocence can be gullible, vulnerable and irresponsible, involving a kind of ignorance we need to grow out of. Moreover if we pursue innocence in the sense of purity too much, we may actually lose our non-violence, and become discriminatory and condemning.

Figure 1

Wiles That Make Us Innocent

A Sufi wish (of which I cannot trace the source) urges us to 'become that which you were before you were, but with the memory and understanding of what you have become.' The art we need, if we are to respond well to our hurts, is one that somehow keeps hold of the innocence we partly see, and partly imagine in children, but combines this with the prudent wisdom we can only learn through long experience of life.

But 'keeps hold of' may not be the right words. People who cannot let go of their childhood, and are forever trying to look and be young when they are old, are generally rather sad, and laden with nostalgia for something that probably was never as good as their projections make it seem. Jesus did not urge us to *revert* to being like children, but to *become* like children. He was not commending regression, but growth into a state that is in some way like that of children, or like our image of our childhood.

In practice this will mean acquiring 'wiles' that are quite different from what children normally possess. One of these wiles is a general circumspection, the serpentine prudence Jesus commends. There may be times when being a non-violent martyr is necessary – as it was for Jesus – but it is not appropriate to precipitate ourselves into martyrdom just because of stupidity or lack of proper care for ourselves as the vessels of divine love. Jesus did not simply send his disciples like sheep among wolves; he *told them* that was what he was doing, and gave them detailed instructions on how to cope with this situation without getting 'eaten'! He concluded with the significant instruction on dealing with humiliation and hurtful rejection as one deals with the dust on one's feet: shake it off (Matt. 10.14...) In the gospel this instruction is explained in terms of a vindictive motive, quite contrary to the teaching of Jesus elsewhere, that rather destroys the point about letting go of harms.

In terms of the model suggested in **Table 1** (Chapter 5) you will notice that the virtues of innocence are all on the bottom left: they are the warm virtues of entelechy. If they are to grow well and not degenerate into dystelechy, I suggest, they need partnering with the cooler 'grown-up' virtues of eutelechy, which conversely need to retain the virtues of innocence if they are not to harden into hypertelechy.

The remaining chapters will focus on four grown-up 'wiles' or virtues that are not the kind of quality we normally find in children, but which serve to preserve or awaken a childlikeness nonetheless. In the process the negative reactions discussed in the first three chapters are overcome.

- Chapter 6 will explore a notion of responsibility that is much more adult than the 'blame' that is often so habitual among children. But it will develop this as part of a tragi-comic approach that bounces back from suffering with the wily innocence of the fool, free from recrimination and blame
- Chapter 7 will look at actions most children and many adults find painfully difficult: remorse and forgiveness. Through these processes innocence can be restored, as we learn what children often do know: how to make pearls out of the grit around us and within us, and be free from shame.
- Chapter 8 will explore how traditions of meditation and prayer – things children rarely do when forced, though their spontaneous wonder often has the quality of both – can enable us to dissolve the hold of the past and dwell in the perceptual innocence of the present. It will also explore how such detachment reverses our tendency to disclaim hurt.
- Chapter 9 will explore the healing of memory through time and especially traditions of healing justice, in which

truthful memory leads finally to a restoration of innocence and a forgetfulness of wrong which is (eventually) a childlike blessing.

- Chapter 10 will draw the threads together under headings suggested by the Beatitudes of Jesus, the Eightfold way of the Buddha and the Fruits of the Spirit in St. Paul, resulting in a ninefold pathway for finding innocence in experience, and responding well to life's hurts.

Chapter 6

Responsibility without Blame: Tragedy and Comedy

To get to the center of life,
go to the edge: out in the deep ocean
find the Skellig Rocks of the heart.

To quench your thirst,
go to the desert, where sunstroke chills, light
blinds, and wind sweeps
the dunes of the soul.

To find true morality,
ask the prostitute, the drug abuser
or the corrupt and bankrupt
businessman: what sustains life
without hope or pride?

What is real
has no power
over the imagination. No resonance
in daily chatter confirms it. The confident
do not notice it. The darkness comprehends it
not.

To get to the great
look at the small: the brazen markings
on the orchid petal, the green sheen
of the dung beetle, the little shoot
growing through the masonry

of the tower block.

To learn about grace,
ask the disgraced
vicar who has taken to the bottle,
why he still prays; why
God still exists.

To get to the center of life,
go to the edge.

Tao of the Edge

The following chapters will look mainly to the Buddhist and Christian traditions for the resources to respond well to evil and hurt. But in a book of this kind it would be foolish to ignore the great resources that derive from another source, one that has mingled with the Christian tradition to nourish the typically Western responses to harm: the traditions of tragic and comic drama that derive from ancient Greece. Though all cultures know both the depth of suffering and despair, and that strange eruption of mirth that we associate with humor, only in Western culture do these elemental feelings take the cultural shape we call tragedy and comedy.

On the face of it, the apparent superficiality of comedy and the hopelessness of tragedy are deeply opposed to the serious hopes that religions like Buddhism and Christianity seek to engender. But this chapter will argue that Buddhism and Christianity are truest to themselves, and closest to each other, and (most relevant to this book) best able to inspire a positive response to evil and hurt, when they espouse a kind of tragicomic perspective. The Jesus of the oldest Gospel is best seen as a tragicomic figure. The teachings of both Jesus and the Buddha have been overlain by their traditions with a varnish of solemnity and devotion which is anything but tragic or comic.

But in Buddhist traditions like Zen and in the lives of clownish Christian saints like Francis we see the original laughter and tears breaking through.

'Tragic' and 'comic' originally denote forms of drama, but have come to mean, more widely, views of life, and thirdly and more loosely, particular kinds of event. Newspapers readily describe traumatic events as 'tragedies' without any apparent thought of dramatic form. This book as a whole is concerned with the tragic and comic in the third sense: with how particular pains and hurts can be approached creatively as comic or tragic, or both. But to learn what might be wise and creative in our response we need to learn from the traditions of drama and the views of the world they conjure up – the tragic and comic in the first and second senses.

This is what the first four sections will explore, looking first at the structure of tragedy, and at the fear and pity it inspires, then at comedy as a dramatic form, and finally at the nature of comic humor. The middle three sections look at the relation between tragedy and comedy and the two faiths which this book draws on. For it is important that the resources we draw on in this book are not an incompatible 'pick and mix,' but blend in a coherent vision. So I look at Christ as a figure that combines the tragic and comic (though in a different way from modern tragicomedy); and I ask whether Christianity and Buddhism are best understood as tragicomic in outlook. The final three sections explore the potential of the Buddhist Christian tragicomic vision so far developed. I argue that such a vision offers a way of holding people accountable without loading them with blame; that it enables us to contemplate the truth of our condition with a healing realism; and that it opens up positive responses to hurt and harm.

The Tragic Journey

Say what you will, the greatest boon is not to be;
But, life begun, soonest to end is best,

And to that bourne from which our way began
Swiftly return.
The simple playtime of our youth behind,
What woe is absent, what fierce agony?
Strife, and the bloody test
Of battle, envy and hatred – and at length
Unloved, unkind,
Unfriended age, worst of all, and last,
Consumes our strength.

So stand, not I alone,
But all, and he,
Our much-tried friend,
A rock in a wild, north sea
At winter's height,
Fronting the rude assault
Of all the billows of adversity
That break upon his head from every side
Unceasing – from the setting sun,
From dayspring, from the blaze at noon,
And from the pole of night.
(Sophocles, *Oedipus at Colonus*, 1.1227–48: in 1947, p. 109)

In these lines from the chorus in Sophocles' last play, lamenting the sufferings of Oedipus, we find two core features of tragedy: an unrelentingly pessimistic view of the world as full of pain and hurt of every kind; and the noble image of the tragic hero, pitted against those sufferings like a rock in a wild sea. All is negative, it seems, except the soul of the hero, who confronts world pain without hope of overcoming it, but with a glory in his own being. In Oedipus' case this glory is about to lead to the apotheosis in which he will be taken up as a god, in a divinization that makes explicit what is perhaps implicit in many tragedies. There is nothing at all divine in the extreme

Figure 2: The Tragic Journey

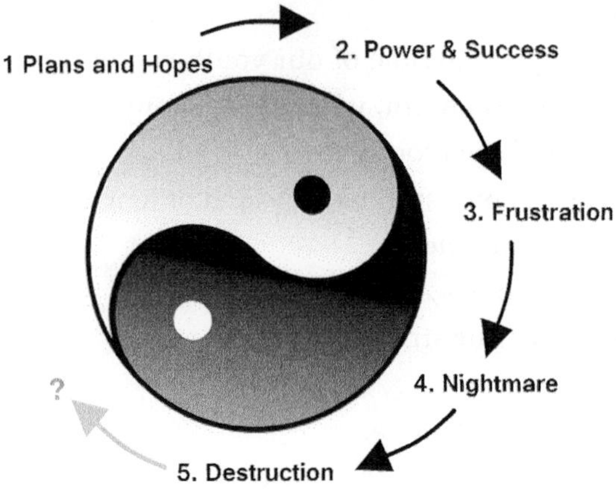

sufferings which tragic characters like Oedipus, Antigone, Lear and Gloucester (blinded in *King Lear*) undergo, but there is something godlike in them as they suffer.

There is certainly a broadly common pattern that gives shape and direction to the suffering. According to Christopher Booker (2004, p. 156) – generalizing a little, as he tends to – there are five stages in the unfolding of a tragedy. I have found it instructive to map these stages onto our yin-yang symbol in **Figure 2**. In the first stage, the 'hero' with at least the reputation for virtue climbs toward power and achieves dreamlike success (Oedipus defeats the sphinx and becomes king; Macbeth takes the throne; Lear partitions his kingdom). By the second stage, however, we sense there is something rotten about this power, as it relies on repression and disclaimer (Macbeth starts having to murder more people; Lear, rejected by his daughters, begins to rage; the truth about Oedipus' murder and incest gets out). At the third stage, cracks have opened letting in a chaos that will not go away, whose ultimate cause is the hero himself (Duncan appears, seeking vengeance; Goneril and Regan commit their atrocities). By the fourth stage this has turned to nightmare. Chaos, rage and dread engulf the tragic hero (Oedipus is blinded and banished; Lear wanders in the storm). The fifth stage sees the hero wiped out, often in an orgy of destruction (Oedipus dies at Colonus; Macbeth is killed; Lear dies with Cordelia dead in his arms). But I wonder if there is not often at the end of tragedy the beginnings of a sixth stage. Very often the characters that remain at the end of a tragedy voice suggestions of a world cleansed by the downfall and ready for a new beginning; and as noted, there can be a sense of the deification of the tragic hero.

Whether the process follows these stages exactly, in tragedy it always seems to be the case that something arises to turn the central figure's dreams and hopes into nightmare and destruction. In some cases that element is an alien 'fate,' in others it is a 'fatal' seed implicit in the hero's own bad choice. But in most if not all cases there is the kind of pattern that our figure makes clear: an evolving dynamic of order and chaos that works through the main protagonists. In Buddhist terms this process whereby flawed actions feed back into the suffering of the agent would be called karma. There is something here that leads us to see the hero as acting out a destiny that is greater than himself, even if it is of his own making; and that something tends to make the hero noble or even godlike, even if like Macbeth and Othello he is a sinner.

Goat-Songs and Scapegoats

How do we explain the way, despite his moral flaws, both the hero and his downfall strike us with awe? In a pithy phrase which has formed the basis of a huge amount of literary theory (see *Aristotle and Catharsis*, in Michel and Sewall, p. 252–75), Aristotle described tragedy as

> through pity and fear completing the purification (*katharsis*) of such kinds of suffering (*pathemata*). (*Poetics* 49b 28)

The balance of pity and fear is reminiscent of the numinous

balance of fascination and terror which the Lutheran theologian Rudolf Otto identified with religious awe and the idea of the holy (2004). The contrary feelings keep our minds in a kind of orbit around the tragic hero as around an awesome holy object. We pity his sufferings, but pity alone would pull us down – as gravity pulls a planet – into compassionate identification with the hero, whose sufferings would be full of pathos but without dignity. Pity in this sense can dehumanize and degrade a person into the mere object of our need to help. But we also fear the features that led to the pain: the violence, the ambition, the pride, or perhaps simply the brooding sense of fate and doom that hangs over him. This fear on its own would act as a centrifugal force, like that which pulls a planet away from its sun. But the balance of forces keeps us in orbit, as it were, unable to approach too close because of our dread, unable to flee because of our compassion. The result is a characteristic tension between identification and shunning, in which we are able to see the hero as alien yet like ourselves.

But how does this tension lead to the catharsis Aristotle described? This is more controversial. To some it suggests something sacrificial about the hero's suffering and death. The word 'tragedy' derives from the Greek for 'goat song,' and some have conjectured that tragedy may have grown out of a sacrificial ritual involving goats (though others have speculated that at the early festivals goats may have been given as prizes for the songs that were the antecedents of tragedy). Whatever sacrificial origins there may have been, they were certainly lost by the time Aristotle wrote, and he does not himself connect catharsis with sacrifice. But he does connect it with the numinous mixture of fear and pity, otherness and likeness, which we have identified.

René Girard comments:

> The qualities that make a 'good' tragic hero are precisely those required of the sacrificial victim. If the latter is to polar-

> ize and purge the emotions of the community, he must at once resemble the members of the community and differ from them; he must be at once insider and outsider, both 'double' and incarnation of the 'sacred difference.' He must be neither wholly good nor wholly bad. A certain degree of goodness is required in the tragic hero in order to establish sympathy between him and the audience; yet a certain degree of weakness, a 'tragic flaw,' is needed to neutralize the goodness and permit the audience to tolerate the hero's downfall and death... Having accompanied the hero part of the way, the audience suddenly perceives him as wholly 'other' and abandons him to his fate, his superhuman ignominy and glory. (2005, p. 307)

So perhaps the balance of awe and dread in the hero of the goat-song purifies us in the way the scapegoat does. The fearful sufferings of the hero are his but ours also; they are the consequence of his own fault but also deep and fatal fault lines in the world that pre-exist him, causing a dread that balances our mercy. The tragic hero is unique, but Chapter 1 suggested that every criminal who is punished suffers both for deeds for which he was responsible, and for the deep social flaws that made him the kind of person he was. In the tragic hero we contemplate our own evils, framed in a way that enables us to hold them in the silent tension between dread and compassion, in something like the meditative and therapeutic stillness discussed in Chapter 8.

Revel-Songs, Confusion and Resolution

In Greek drama, counterpoised to the 'goat song' is the 'revel song' or comedy. 'Comedy' for most of us these days means the kind of thing comedians do – telling jokes, performing funny stunts, and making us laugh. This whole process is a lot more mysterious than we usually realize, and it is highly relevant as a (generally) good, creative way of coping with the pathos and bathos of life, as we shall see in the next section.

But though these elements were always there in classic comedy, its essence was the telling of a different kind of story from that of tragedy. Comedy moves characteristically in a three part movement from happiness to confusion, alienation and hostility – sometimes dreamlike, sometimes even nightmarish – to the dispelling of delusion, realization of identity, resolution, reconciliation and the restoration of friendship, and nearly always marriage (c.f. Booker, p. 150). **Figure 3** relates this to our yin-yang model. The point to note is that the movement around the circle is shallower than the tragic trajectory, but gets further. The confusion and delusion involved in comedy are nothing like the devastation and death in tragedy; but whereas tragedy ends with the merest hint of regeneration, the climax of comedy is the denouement in the last act, where recognition breaks forth like a new order from the midst of chaos and confusion.

Figure 3: The Comic Journey

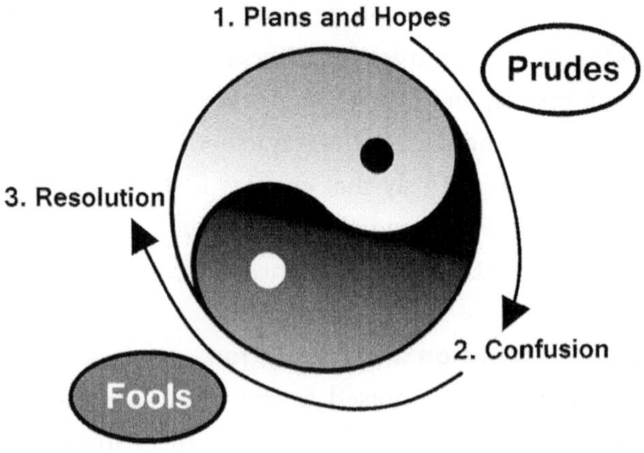

The diagram also shows the role of what I call the 'prudes' – the tightly controlled puritans, full of 'hypertelechy,' who often cause the move of the heroes and heroines into suffering and confusion – and their opposites, the fairies and fools who often outwit the heroes and heroines in the confusion stage, but also often aid them on their way to realization. More of them in the next section. If you know a few comedies, whether a Shakespearean play like *Love's Labours Lost, Much Ado about Nothing* or *A Midsummer Night's Dream,* or one of the many romantic novels and films that take up the same pattern, it should not be hard to identify these stages and character types.

Comedy then is a different kind of plot in a different kind of world from tragedy. In terms of evil, tragedy suggests the Gnostic vision of the whole world as flawed and full of evil, which runs through the main character and finally causes his downfall. The only suggestions of good are the (generally excessive, and always ruthless) justice of this process, and the way the hero for all her faults seems to contain the awesome spark of the divine. Comedy suggests the very different view, discussed in Chapter 5, that all hurt comes from confusion and delusion in a world that is primally and ultimately good, but light and dreamlike.

> Our revels now are ended. These our actors,
> As I foretold you, were all spirits, and
> Are melted into air, into thin air:
> And like the baseless fabric of this vision,
> The cloud-capp'd tow'rs, the gorgeous palaces,
> The solemn temples, the great globe itself,
> Yea, all which it inherit, shall dissolve,
> And, like this insubstantial pageant faded,
> Leave not a rack behind. We are such stuff
> As dreams are made on; and our little life
> Is rounded with a sleep.
> (Shakespeare, *The Tempest* Act 4, scene 1, l. 148–158)

Many of the grand narratives by which we tell our history are 'comedies' in terms of their pattern, albeit comedies that demand to be taken very seriously. Christianity speaks of a primal fall followed by the dark and nightmarish confusion of a world full of sin, resolved by the coming of Christ, the unraveling of the mysteries, and the new love and clarity of the Kingdom of heaven, sealed by the marriage of the Lamb to his Church. Marxism speaks with (qualified) sympathy of the Middle Ages when craftsmen and women had ownership over the work of their hands, followed by the dark confusion, injustice and alienation wrought by capitalism, to be overcome in the coming socialist utopia when people will once again live in solidarity and with ownership of their work. Feminism, again, conjectures about an initial golden age when women had equal or superior rights and the Mother Goddess was worshipped, through the dark ages of patriarchy and 'phallocracy,' to the coming age of liberation and the end of the oppression of women, and with that, the end of all oppressions. Angela West would be quick to point out that such 'comedies' are only telling half the story, omitting the tragic aspect of our human condition; and that 'comic' ideals have a way of generating their tragic 'flipside' in practical consequences.

Humor, Fools and Clowns

But as well as having happy endings, comedies provoke mirth. They create that complex set of physiological reactions – universal to human beings and unique to them and perhaps the higher primates – which we call laughter.

What makes us laugh is usually someone's humiliation. A proud and dignified bishop slips on a banana skin and falls on his bottom – we relish the way the man with lofty and spiritual pretensions is revealed as very material and bodily! Titania falls in love with Bottom, disguised an Ass – again, her romantic tones are brought low by being directed, unwittingly, at an animal. In the *double entendre* of a joke a crude, physical meaning emerges alongside the lofty, intellectual or spiritual one. Such laughter is crucial to the kind of comedy we call satire, which typically targets those I have called 'prudes' – people full of the cold vices of hypertelechy, pride, domination, repression and blame, desperate to keep the chaos in and around them in check – in which case the laughter enables the chaos to emerge and come out on top, bringing the prude down to the entelechy of the fool.

Both the comic and the tragic hero suffer. But in tragedy the response of pity is held in tension with our fear at his dark or even evil side; while in comedy and satire, pity is juxtaposed with something like relish or triumph at the other's expense. This results in a much more restless, eccentric orbit. Where the tension of tragedy leads to stability, that of comedy leads to the shifting, unstable sense we associate with laughter, as we leap from the one, dignified perspective to the other, base one, and back, without being able to hold these perspectives serenely together. Sometimes, as in satire, the relish ousts the pity, and the laughter is merciless and cruel. Paradoxically, in other cases, the laughter intensifies warmth and empathy – and this is typically when the hero is a 'fool'.

Many cultures have developed figures who have made a profession of being laughed at, but as Enid Welsford has pointed out (1968), it is in Christian culture that the figure of the court fool is particularly to be found. The origins of this development are obscure, but Welsford traces it back to the New Testament and its tendency to 'turn the world upside down' with the notion of a foolishness that is wiser than that of the wise (1 Cor. 1.26–8, 3.18–20) and a Kingdom of Heaven breaking out among the most down to earth of people.

Welsford also notes that whereas the tragic heroes and heroines belong entirely to the dramas that are so often named after them, the fool – who transgresses the boundary between the holy and the profane – often stands not at the center of the drama but at the boundary where the drama meets the 'real world' of the audience, inviting them to pull fun at the figures prancing on the stage. There is no drama named after Falstaff, but in several history plays he is the real focus of our affection. We can imagine this huge and earthy figure winking knowingly at the audience, just as in pantomimes it is the comic figures who draw the audience into participation.

This brings to mind another element of laughter, which is a kind of transcendence. When we laugh there is a sense in which we step outside of serious engagement in the drama of life, and see what is going on from another angle, which we significantly call the 'funny side.' I remember a teacher describing how one of her duties was to supervise the children in their obligatory worship at a particular church. The service was benediction with the Blessed Sacrament which is supposed to inspire great awe and devotion to the consecrated bread of the Eucharist. But she found it hard to stop the children's giggling. What to the pious was awesome was to the children, unfamiliar with the symbolism, a weird clowning about in odd brightly colored clothes, with strange smells and gestures. Unable to enter the drama, they saw everything from another side, the funny side.

To laugh is to oscillate thrillingly between what sociologists call 'emic' and 'etic' perspectives, that is, between what things mean to participants and what they might look like to a stranger. The fool and his modern successor – Charlie Chaplin and Mr. Bean, as noted in Chapter 4 – are kinds of perpetual strangers on the earth, outsiders unable to handle things in the proper 'insider' way, putting their own idiosyncratic 'spin' on things. Like children, they unmask pretensions, and blur the boundary between cunning and innocence, and order and chaos. The witty and playful-seeming remarks of the fool in King Lear are full of scathing perception. If the tragic hero shows us the dignity of humanity surrounded by sorrow, the fool presents human indignity, even our own, as something that does not destroy, but discloses, true human dignity.

Jesus and Tragicomedy

As views of the world and of human dignity, therefore, tragedy and comedy are very different. As story structures, tragedies end unhappily in death while comedies end happily in marriage. Tragic heroes are central to their tragedies, while comic fools stand at the edge. The tragic tension creates stillness, while that of comedy is shifting and unstable. Comedy and tragedy seem opposed.

They are, it is true, united in the kind of 'tragicomedy' that seems to have come to replace tragedy in modern times. However the modern tragicomedies of Samuel Becket, Harold Pinter, Bertolt Brecht, Jean Anouilh and the like are really neither comic nor tragic in the traditional sense. They neither trace the darkness within a hero to its fatal consequences, nor pass through dark confusion to joy and light. On the whole they are simply plays about ordinary people leading sad but amusing lives. Such tragic and comic elements as there are in them cancel out. When, in Samuel Becket's *Waiting for Godot,* Gogo prepares to hang himself using the rope that holds his trousers, and they fall down, the slapstick humor undercuts any tragic awe, while the attempted suicide makes us guilty about our laughter. So we are imprisoned in a suffering quite without redeeming features.

As a result, 'the mixture of grief and embarrassment and pity and derision, if spicy and rarely dull, is in the end melancholy and dispiriting. It demonstrates disillusion; it rarely incites to action. It can therefore fairly easily become comfortable, self-pitying and morbid,' (Styan, 1968, p. 295). So, confronted with modern tragicomedy, 'one takes care not to go to heaven, nor to descend to hell. One believes neither in purgatory nor purification. One can *neither face nor forget reality, neither weep nor laugh*. One squints, grins, and gradually the heart freezes,'

(Kaufmann, 1969, p. xix, my italics).

So modern tragicomedy tends to represent a kind of 'lowest common denominator' in which tragedy and comedy subvert each other, and make a tragic or comic story or world view problematic. But could comedy and tragedy combine in a different way, melding as stories to pool their complementary truths? I shall argue that this does happen in the precedents of tragicomedy to be found in the earlier Gospels.

As he goes to his crucifixion, Jesus is not in any way presented as a tragic hero. He does not declaim against his enemies or argue his case, like Oedipus or Antigone, or rage in the storm like Lear, or deliver soliloquies like Hamlet, but is mainly silent. The physical and mental suffering is minimized and largely implicit, and in some ways the depiction is closer to the Monty Python film, *The Life of Brian,* than it is to Scorsese's *Passion*. (Though not *very* close to either!) In the scourging and the mocking by the soldiers, it is not the physical pain that is stressed but the humiliation in which Jesus becomes a clown, a figure of cruel fun:

> They clothed him in a purple cloak, and plaiting a crown of thorns they put it on him. And they began to salute him, 'Hail, King of the Jews!' And they struck his head with a reed, and spat upon him, and they knelt down in homage to him. (Mark 15.17–19)

This passage is omitted from Luke's Gospel, which makes more of the human dignity of Jesus and his serenely heroic words of forgiveness from the cross; and it is attenuated in John's, which emphasizes his divine dignity. Likewise only Mark (15.29–30), and Matthew following him, describe the bystanders mocking Jesus for not being able to use his divine powers to come down from the cross. In Mark and Matthew it is as if an element of comedy is brought in to emphasize the pitiable degradation of Jesus.

Even at the crucifixion, elements like the soldiers casting lots for Jesus' robe strike an oddly comic note. This is well developed in the Medieval mystery plays, which even find a funny element in the crucifixion:

1st Knight:	Why crack ye so? Fast on a cord And tug him to, by top and tail.
3rd Knight:	Yea, thou command us, lightly as a lord; come help to haul him, with ill hail.
1st Knight:	Now certes that I shall do, Full snelly, like as a snail. (Harrison, 1985, p. 140)

The comedy here, however, enshrouds a bitter tragedy, which according to Biblical scholar Louis Ruprecht is the dominant note of the earlier Gospels.

> The synoptic gospels were indeed Christian tragedies... Jesus' collisions with the religious and political authorities of his day are exacerbated by the collision between his will and God the Father's. That collision detonates Mark's whole Gospel, and the heart of that collision is the Gethsemane prayer.
> (2008, p. 85–6)

Ruprecht shows how in the tragedy that is Mark's Gospel the hero falls into a fatal conflict with the religious and secular authorities, is deserted by his followers, and in Gethsemane (14.32–42) is presented as being in deep tension even with God and his own tragic destiny. On the cross he cries out, 'My God, why have you forsaken me!' (15.34). And though the tomb is found empty, in the original form of this Gospel there is no encounter with the risen Christ. The final, grammatically brutal sentence conveys dread rather than hope: *ephobounto gar*, 'For they were afraid' (16.8).

Ruprecht argues that the Gospels of Matthew and Luke are basically elaborations on the tragic gospel of Mark, but that of John represents a totally new departure. Here, tragedy is replaced by a 'good versus evil' narrative in which God incarnate and the children of light do battle with the children of darkness. Mark's tragic sense, which summons us to compassion and awe, is replaced by the familiar dualism that categorizes people as good or evil, and summons us to the kind of imperialistic conquest in the name of Christ and light and truth, which is all too familiar from the Church's history.

It seems to me that Ruprecht captures some truth here, but oversimplifies. It is true that Mark's Jesus inspires a typically tragic mixture of compassion and amazement bordering on dread. There is a sense of tragic catharsis, which Paul and later the writer of the letter to the Hebrews captured in the idea that Christ was a kind of ultimate sacrificial scapegoat for the sins of all the world. We might add to this the way Jesus, like the Greek tragic heroes, engages in tense and hostile debate with his enemies: though distinctively and significantly not in Mark's Gospel after his arrest. (It is in John that Jesus continues to debate right to the end.) And there is in Mark, as in tragic heroes, a deep sense that it is *necessary* to suffer and die – that these things are foreordained and cannot be avoided – though in a strange way this enhances rather than limits our sense of the hero's freedom. But in the case of Christ this necessity seems to spring from the way the world is rather than from tragic defects in his own character: Christ seems to bear the sins of the world, carrying the weight of a global *karma*.

It is even possible to discern something of the fivefold structure of tragedy in Mark's Gospel and even more in that of Matthew, which is believed to be based on the five books of the Pentateuch. To begin with there is great hopefulness of the infancy narratives, the baptism of Jesus, the Sermon on the Mount and many healing miracles. This leads into a time of dreamlike success with a triumphant ministry in Galilee. Then begins the frustration stage, with hostility among the religious authorities, misunderstanding by the disciples, and the prophecies of the coming passion. Christ begins to undergo the 'alienation or ostracism from the safeguard of licensed being' which George Steiner ascribes to the tragic hero (cited in Felski p. 15–16). This leads into what with some exaggeration could be called a nightmare stage, with dark prophecies of the catastrophic coming of God's kingdom and stark, challenging parables about the dangers of rejecting the Christ. Finally we have the stage of despair on the cross and ensuing death. But then – to say the least – there is far more than the usual hint of regeneration!

In all these ways, Jesus does what Marylyn McCord Adams (2006) sees as necessary if the divine is genuinely to enter the domain of human horror. If we accept the bare bones of the traditional understanding of Christ as the Word of God in real human flesh, one might be tempted to say he thereby converts human horror to divine tragedy, turning what would otherwise be the meaningless suffering of all those millions who have met with horrible deaths under a pretence of state justice into something that God undergoes as the tragic unraveling of his own creation.

But of course to put it this way is to ignore balancing elements that develop within the same structure. Matthew's infancy narrative includes not only hope but the massacre of the innocents, a kind of foretaste of what is to come on the cross. Contrariwise the 'frustration' elements at the third stage are seen by Christ as opportunities, and at the heart of this stage is the transfiguration (17.1–13), where the discourse with Moses and Elijah concerning his coming passion is accompanied by his glowing with the divine glory. And the despair and death open the way to the resurrection of many saints (27.51–3) and 'on the third day' to that of Christ himself.

Even Mark includes such hopeful elements. Neither his Gospel nor any of the others can be described simply as tragedies in the Greek sense. If it is retorted that not all Greek tragedies were without hope of regeneration either, it remains clear that the Gospels also contain much that pertains to comedy. It is not just that they have a happy ending (if only a hint of such in Mark) but also that this happiness brings the disciples out of their misunderstanding and confusion in the comic way. The element of misrecognition and then recognition of Christ is characteristic of comedy, and is particularly notable in the Emmaus story (Luke 24.13–35) where the disciples travel several miles with Christ, and even talk sadly about his death and the rumors of his resurrection, before they recognize him in the breaking of bread.

The 'clownish' elements in the depiction of Jesus have already been noted. Like the fool, Jesus possesses innocence, humor and naivety, and he acts outsides the then current constraints of decency and order. His 'alienation... from the safeguard of licensed being' can be seen as comic as well as tragic. Like the fool he carries a self-made kind of authority that enables him to see through the 'emperor's new clothes' and unmask hypocrisy. In several ways he is like the children he commends as entering the kingdom. All the same, it would be a mistake to see Jesus *only* as a clown or child, any more than we can follow Ruprecht and see him just as a tragic hero.

He is both. He is, I think, the kind of figure that the French painter George Rouault (1871–1958) glimpses with many icon-like depictions of Christ as a naive kind of holy clown (**Figure 4**). Seeing Christ in this way – combining tragedy and comedy in a face that is at once cartoon-like and sober, innocent and wise – seems to make artistic sense. And more than that. My first encounter with these pictures, as a Buddhist agnostic in my late teens, was one of the factors that made me feel Jesus Christ might be worth following. In these pictures – and perhaps in Jesus – the tragic and comic do not seem to undermine each other in the way they do in modern tragicomedy. But is there a way of working out and testing this glimpse beyond the world of art, in a way that is compatible with the Buddhist and Christian traditions?

Photograph by Ben Sutherland, 2009. Reproduced under Creative Commons Attribution Share-Alike License: http://creativecommons.org/licenses/by-sa/3.0/

Christianity, Buddhism and Tragedy

Some, like literary critic Lawrence Michel, argue strongly that Christianity is not compatible with tragedy.

> Profound ambiguity in the presence of evil; human life as a predicament; standing under judgment; assurances called into question—these things generate the tragic frame of mind, the tragic sense of life... But Christians believe in the efficacy of the Incarnation and the Resurrection and the

> Redemption... The Gordian tragic knot has been cut... At the root of the question of living in a vale of tears, then, there is a basic incompatibility between the tragic and the Christian view. And nothing has yet come forward which can be called, without cavil, both Christian and Tragedy at the same time. (in Michel and Sewall, 1963, p. 232–3)

In similar vein, George Steiner has argued that tragedy requires a total pessimism and an aristocratic culture, which are undermined by the optimism and egalitarianism which modernity and its many therapies inherit from Christianity. As he scathingly puts it, 'social psychiatry is no answer to Oedipus,' (cited Felski p. 4). On such a view, the tragedies of Shakespeare and Racine, though produced in a Christian culture, are either too devoid of hope to be 'Christian,' or else too Christian to be true tragedies.

However, if tragedy is defined as Steiner would like, in terms of the sheer absence of hope, there are not even many Greek tragedies that fit the bill. Though in tragedy the suffering is depicted in a remorseless, heart-rending way, we have noted that in most tragedies there is, at the end, a hint of restoration; though not in a way that lessens our regret or sense of the brute reality of harm. It need not be seen as impossible to continue the tragic trajectory upward until it ends in a real hope (though again, a hope that does not cancel out or justify the harm). Conversely, though we have seen that the trajectory of comedy typically moves through illusion and confusion rather than deep pain, death and loss, it would not be impossible to imagine a narrative that moved in the comic way from initial hopes to final recognition and reconciliation but through a much darker middle stage.

Such a narrative would not be tragedy as we know it or comedy as we know it, but a kind of tragicomedy quite different from the modern version. It would be comedy added to tragedy, not comedy and tragedy cancelling out. It would be the

Christian narrative, at least in the form as shown forth in the early Gospels.

But if the storylines could be extended in this way, what of the characterization. Would tragedy and comedy so combined produce coherent characters? Well, both tragedy and comedy show us a figure who is both familiar and alien, who falls victim to bewildering forces which he or she may have unleashed but is not entirely responsible for, and who represents a version of the scapegoat: either the tragic scapegoat who purifies us through pity and dread or the comic scapegoat who becomes the butt of our jokes. The central characters of tragedy and comedy come together in a quite coherent and recognizable figure: someone not unlike the tragicomic Jesus as depicted in Rouault's 'icons'.

But what of the other faith we are tapping as a resource? Arguably no religion takes the tragedy of the world more seriously than Buddhism. Its starting point – that which drove the Buddha onward in his search for enlightenment – was the inescapable reality of birth, suffering, old age and death, and the impermanence of everything, which means that even joys and the things and people we love are momentary, and suffused with the tragic fear and knowledge of their passing. Buddhism could be regarded as the most tragic of all religions, since it offers absolutely no consolation in terms of gods or features of the world that might bring happiness. Happiness has to be found only in oneself, through the renunciation of striving and attachment.

Accordingly there is much in the poetry of Buddhist-influenced countries, notably China and Japan, that expresses intense sadness and longing (the Japanese call it *yügen*) in the face of the transience and emptiness of all things. And there is humor in Buddhism too, especially in Zen with its *koans,* which are rather like jokes that, when the punch-line is grasped, may send the seeker into enlightenment with peals of laughter.

However, Buddhism has produced no drama that can be called tragic or comic. Why not?

Perhaps the answer is that tragedy requires not just suffering, but a sufferer, a hero who tragically endures the suffering, with whom we can both identify in pity and recoil from in awe. Buddhism invites us to take a quite different path, namely to abandon the self and its suffering and achieve insight into a reality that transcends personality. The Zen influenced *no* drama of Japan, for example, emphasizes transience, but in order to move towards insight and release from suffering.

Moreover Buddhism does not, like the tragic and comic narratives, begin with a pristine state of hope from which there is a fall. Suffering and bad karma have existed from beginningless time. The fall-and-return scenario so prevalent in many major religions is absent from Buddhism. There is no good beginning and – in Mahayana Buddhism at least – no good ending, only a world of time and suffering (samsara) in parallel with a timeless unconditioned bliss (Nirvana). So whereas the Christian tragicomedy focuses on the figure of Christ, who is both human and divine, and both tragic and comic, the Buddhist approach takes away from such central heroes, away from drama which is inevitably personal, and away from narrative approaches as such, towards a cosmic emptiness that is full, a world of suffering that is also at the same time the world of bliss.

If Christianity offers a tragicomic narrative that takes us fully round the 'wheel' of order and chaos, combining the extent of the comic journey with the depth of the tragic, Buddhism invites us to take our stand outside the wheel altogether – or perhaps at its still center. Rather than travel with Christ through suffering to joy, we are invited to contemplate the coming and going of good and evil, order and chaos, as an ebb and flow we are part of yet not part of, because 'we' ourselves are just ebb and flow also.

So despite its unblinkered, tragic sense of suffering and its element of mirth and bliss, Buddhism cannot be called 'tragicomic' in the same way as Christianity. But that is not to say the Buddhist vision is incompatible with Christian tragicomedy; it may be that if one wants to express the Buddhist insights as a story, the story would have to be rather like the Christian one.

Tragicomedy and Truth

But now we must turn to the crucial questions. Is tragicomedy as so far explored true to how things are? And does it help us deal with hurt and harm? This section will argue that the Christian tragicomic story contains important truth; the next will argue that one of the most important truths it contains lies in the way it enables a separation of the kind of responsibility we need to hold on to from the kind of blame that causes such harm; and the final section will argue that this and other important truths in the tragicomic perspective enable us to deal better with harm.

Many argue that a tragic view of life (rather than say a comic or an optimistic one) is the least disillusioned and most truthful and honest view. In this spirit the philosopher George Harris argues (2006) that reason has much to grieve about. The past contains immeasurably more suffering than happiness; it evidences a huge human capacity to inflict suffering; and our future prospect is of an inexorable deterioration of the conditions that make civilization, and in the long-term life itself, possible.

However, in this bleak context of large scale cosmic history, Harris argues that a limited degree of progress is possible.

> The issue for us should be about how to construct a life that is on balance good, a life that, however far from utopian, contains more good than bad. Moreover, we should see our point in history as one in which that is still possible… We are

> living in a marvelous biological and cultural window of opportunity for the possibility of good human lives, lives that can be on balance good, though riddled with much pain and sorrow. That itself is a remarkable, highly improbable fact... It should be celebrated. (p. 287)

What Harris suggests here is not far from psychologist Viktor Frankl's 'tragic optimism.' For Frankl, the tragedy is that the world is full of suffering, guilt and death. The optimism means that there is always the possibility of '(1) turning suffering into a human achievement and accomplishment; (2) deriving from guilt the possibility of changing oneself for the better; and (3) deriving from life's transitoriness the incentive to take responsible action,' (2004, p. 140). Frankl's is by no means a blithe optimism derived from a denial of pain; he lost his wife and parents in the Nazi concentration camps, and suffered terribly there himself. He exemplifies in his person as well as his teaching an unflinching grasp of the depth of life's tragedy. But where some other writers on the death camps have seen any kind of affirmation as an evasion, Frankl immerses the tragedy in a 'comic' sense of the human power to make meaning out of life.

But in view of all this, is tragedy the whole truth? Does comedy celebrate something tragedy misses? We tend to feel that tragedy is more 'profound' than comedy, so that it must be 'truer.' Comedy can be seen as a trivial escape. But is this partly because we feel tragedy in 'deep' parts of our being, in our guts, in the 'bowels' of compassion and in stomach-churning fear; whereas we laugh by means of a quivering higher up in our lungs and throats. Are there ways in which comedy represents the truth, and ways in which tragedy may represent an escape from the delightful superficiality of things into a false profundity? Is the 'superficiality' of the fool in King Lear, for example, not closer to deep truth than the vengeful manic raging of the dispossessed Lear? Does Lear himself not learn from his fool to be more magnanimous, more 'great in soul,' more embracing of all the dispossessed?

How does one answer such a question? It surely cannot be quite right to do what Harris does (though not Frankl), and make this a question of the 'balance' of good and evil in the universe. The world cannot really be a contest which tragedy wins if there is more evil than good in it, and comedy if there is more good than evil. For how can we compare different kinds of good and evil? To use the philosophers' term, goods seem to be 'incommensurable' with evils, and even with other kinds of good.

How do we say which is 'best,' a glorious sunset, a wonderful meal with friends, a passionate embrace or a Mozart symphony? And how can we determine whether the goodness of such things 'outweighs' a car accident, a murder, or (to use Dostoyevsky's example) the tears of an innocent child? As I look out on my garden, with its many kinds of leaf and flower, each flowering in its own right time, and consider the many kinds of birds and insects, the frogs, dragonflies and sticklebacks to which it is a home, I encounter an almost heart-wrenching beauty. When, as I do so, I hear the news on my radio of floods and atrocities and terrorist attacks, my heart is wrenched in a different way. It would be absurd to say the beauty of garden 'outweighed' the bad of the news. Or that it did not. Good and evil are not on a continuum but, as noted, asymmetrical. That is why it is perfectly reasonable to see history as broadly a story of progress, and equally reasonable to see it as a story of continual decline, or to see it as a flux in which different kinds of evil and good come and go.

There is a subtle point at stake here. Order and chaos are (in terms of physics) on a continuum. Crudely, it is obvious that the chaos involved in blowing up a family cancels out exactly the order involved in their existence. The end result of creating then destroying the family is zero: no family. But it is far from clear that the goodness manifest in the family – the whole range of virtues and kinds of happiness and the long, loving work involved in the life of the family – is negated by the evil involved in the brutally quick act of destroying it. There is a sense in which no amount of evil can destroy the goodness that was manifest in something, even if it can destroy the bearers of that goodness. The evil and the goodness are not comparable; they are not, like order and chaos, on the same scale. That makes it a nonsense *both* to try to justify harms in terms of future goods, *and* to try to show that in such and such a case the harms cannot be justified. We just cannot do the equations.

That is why comedy and tragedy are not competing visions, one of which is 'false' if the other is 'true.' Both involve responses we need to learn if we are to respond well to the world in its mix of suffering and goodness. Without comedy, tragedy can make us too overwhelmed by the sorrows of the world to act to end them, while comedy without tragedy can entrance us with the idea that 'all's well that ends well,' and lull us into inaction just the same. Comedy alone might make us think of evil as just a passing state of confusion soon to be dispelled, while tragedy forces us to acknowledge the really devastating effects of our confusion. But tragedy, by divinizing the hero pitted against the ills of the world (even if some of them are of his own making) can engender a rather grandiose conception of the individual ego. Comedy deflates this ego and puts us back where we belong – in the thick of humanity and down-to-earth materiality.

Christianity, I have argued, offers us a kind of tragicomedy in which suffering is fully faced and acknowledged yet taken up into what Christians might call the divine comedy, in which suffering is seen as the suffering of the Source of all being, who will transform it into the raw material of our ultimate joy. That transformation does not 'cancel out' the sufferings, which remain (as we shall see in the next chapter) a cause of tragic remorse; but it does mean that conversely the tragic suffering does not cancel out hope. Mahayana Buddhism states this mystery less dramatically and more impersonally, by affirming that the world of suffering is not 'cancelled out by,' but *is* the world of Nirvana. We could say, in the same way, the world of suffering is not cancelled out by, but is the world of bliss; the tragic world is the comic world.

Fated Freedom and Innocent Sin

But what a tragicomic perspective offers is not only a narrative that is true to a world that contains both good and evil. It has something remarkable to say about our part in doing good and harm; our status as agents. Philosophy has long struggled to answer the question of whether our actions spring from our own free will or from some kind of necessity (whether predestination by God, the gods or fate, or deterministic causes acting in nature or society). We have seen how modern debates often focus on whether harmers are responsible agents or conditioned victims. Tragedy seems to say both.

> As many critics have noted, what distinguishes tragedy is an uncanny unraveling of the distinction between agency and fate, internal volition and the pressure of external circumstance. According to Jean-Pierre Vernant and Pierre Vidal-Naquet, 'the same character appears now as an agent, the cause and source of his actions, and now as acted upon, engulfed in a force that is beyond him and sweeps him away.' Northrop Frye observes that 'tragedy seems to elude the antithesis of moral responsibility and arbitrary fate.' And Schelling writes in an earlier moment of 'an actual and objective conflict between freedom in the subject on the one hand, and necessity on the other, a conflict that does not end such that one or the other succumbs, but rather that both

> are manifested in perfect indifference as simultaneously victorious and vanquished.'
> (Felski, 2008, p. 11)

So, for example, Oedipus' sufferings are actually *both* the consequence of his own actions, *and* the acting out of the fate decreed by the oracle. It was his action that killed the man on the road, but the fact that this man was his father was not known to him, but the manifestation of his fate. Likewise his marrying of the Queen Jocasta, who unbeknown to him was his mother. In the same way Antigone chooses to bury her brother, in obedience to the moral law but in defiance of the human law decreed by the state, so bringing about her execution. But neither her brother's death nor the law of the state were her choosing; though she acts freely, she certainly feels she has no choice. Conversely with Macbeth, Othello and Lear, their sufferings certainly result from their defects – ambition, jealousy and pride respectively – but there are also elements of fate involved. In Macbeth this is clear from the witches' oracles; in Lear, it is chance that brings about the death of Cordelia, so creating an intensity of suffering that is disproportionate, one feels, to the original crime, and in which she herself suffers innocently.

Tragic heroes, then, do make choices to do what they do. But as they do so, a fate or destiny larger than they are is working its inexorable way out. Characteristic of tragedy according to Paul Hammond (2009) is an uncertainty about the protagonists' autonomy; about whether it is they who act, or the gods who act through them; and about where to draw the boundaries of the self and the human. Philosophy has never given a satisfactory answer reconciling freewill and determinism. Nor has tragedy given an answer in terms of rational explanation, but it has presented us in drama with the impenetrable truth that we are both determined and freely choosing. In a sense every punished criminal, and each person who reaps the consequence of her bad decisions, is tragic, incurring suffering for wrongs she has done but which have also 'done' her, causing her to act in the way she did.

This perspective on responsibility, crime and punishment is one of the ways in which tragedy presents us with the truth, and so enables a response to suffering that is positive yet realistic. It makes nonsense of the blithe modern optimism which assumes all evils can be solved, but equally disables a fatalistic resignation that gives us no choice. In contrast with the dogmatic optimism and simplistic conspiracy theory of some political activism it offers 'a more self-reflexive politics, attuned to the ambiguous and complex relations between time and action, intentions and contingencies, determination and chance,' (Felski, p. 19, commenting on David Scott). Against those feminists who argue that tragedy encourages fatalism, Kathleen Sands argues that the abyss of meaningless pain with which tragedy confronts us 'does not generate beauty or meaning; instead, with incomparable intensity, it generates the desire for them,' (in Felski p. 86–7). So it strongly motivates action, but not by means of encouraging optimistic delusions.

Chapter 5 looked at the idea of original sin, and the Introduction to Part 2 explored notions of innocence. But tragedy often presents us with people in a state of *innocent sin*, causing harm that cannot be avoided even with the best of intentions. It shows us 'the catastrophe, not just of innocent suffering, but of innocent fault,' (Kathleen Sands in Felski p. 84). To be sure, tragedy also presents us with people like Macbeth who make sinister choices and face their just consequences. But Oedipus has to face up to the harmful consequences of choices that had no harmful intent. Hamlet is torn between his sense of duty to avenge his father, and his own natural gentleness and restraint, which resists the shedding of blood. Even Macbeth does not desire harm as such; but he cannot resist a naïve craving for the fame and glory that he childishly sees as his good, only to find to his horror that following this craving precipitates him into a spiral of increasing evil. In their different ways their tragedies present us with people being led into conflict and negativity though their desire is good – or at least, not harmful. They sin – in that they incur harm for themselves and others through their choices – but they are innocent in that they desire no harm.

I would argue that we read the gospels best when we do not demonize Pilate and the High Priests, so turning the Passion into a brutal contest between the bad Jews and Romans and the good Jesus. Rather we need to grasp the good that the priests were seeking: the survival of a very beleaguered and fragile Jewish identity and faith, menaced by a huge and callous empire and now shaken to its foundations by Jesus' casual treatment of Judaic law and tradition. And we need to see also the good Pilate was seeking: the maintenance of an empire that he may have seen in the same way as we British once saw ours, as the main source of rationality, legality, justice and goodness in a world darkened by superstition. The good of Jesus is sacrificed to the things other authorities saw as more important. Therein lies the tragedy.

Martha Nussbaum argues that here, too, tragedy presents us with a difficult truth that we can recognize from everyday experience.

> That much that I did not make goes towards making me whatever I shall be praised or blamed for being; that I must constantly choose among competing and apparently incommensurable goods and that circumstances may force me to a position in which I cannot help being false to something or doing some wrong; that an event that simply happens to me may, without my consent, alter my life; that is equally problematic to entrust one's good to friends, lovers, or country and to try to have a good life without them—all these I take

> to be not just the material of tragedy, but everyday facts of lived practical reason. (1981, p. 5)

Better than any naive duality between the good and the bad, tragedy shows us how the world is. It enables us to unite our zeal for our own goods with humane understanding of the rival goods of others, and a chaste wisdom about how even our zeal for the good can cause harm.

A Tragicomic Response to Hurt?

The Marxist literary critic, Terry Eagleton (in Felski, p. 346) tells a parable, based on the request of old Oedipus, blinded as a punishment for his unwitting sin, to be allowed to enter the city of Athens.

> Oedipus, broken and blinded, stands before Colonus... His presence now poses a question to the nearby city of Athens. Is it to gather this unclean thing to its heart, or cast it out as so much garbage? Is it to dismiss this beggarly king as a monster, or find in his disfigured visage an image of the monstrosity of the human, which is to say of itself? Can it bring itself to pity what it fears? Will it discern in the death-in-life condition of the dispossessed the shadowy outline of a new way of living, one which preserves a pact with failure and mortality? Then Theseus, ruler of Athens, deciphers the riddle. He knows that by making this obscene thing into the cornerstone of the polis, a great power for good will inevitably follow.

So Oedipus becomes an unusual kind of scapegoat, one that was not driven out but welcomed in. In the ministry of Jesus we find the same kind of thing happening. Society's scapegoats were welcomed to the table fellowship of the King. And in his own resurrection, the disciples who had turned away from him in horror welcome him back into their midst. It is this welcoming of the marginalized – not just out of charity, nor out of the false idealization previously discussed, but as those who hold a part of the meaning of life which we have denied or lost – that is celebrated in the poem that opens this chapter. Comedy and tragedy represent ways of welcoming and celebrating the scapegoat, in the one case with our mirth, in the other with our tears and dread.

Eagleton goes on to relate this to Western alarm at the terrorist and other violence that often seems directed at it by the non-Western world.

> The West has yet to learn this tragic lesson. It cannot recognize in the fury at its gates its own monstrous violence come home to roost. It is unable to decipher the symptoms of weakness and despair in that annihilating rage, and is therefore capable only of terror rather than pity.

In other words, the West has lost both the tragic and comic perspectives, and with it the Christian way of making the stone the builders rejected into the cornerstone of the building. We have reverted to starker and simpler dualistic perspectives in which our good stands challenged by the forces of alien evil. Terror – and anger and blame – dominate our response to the fury of those who demand an equal share with us of what the world has to offer.

A tragicomic perspective is one that welcomes Oedipus and other similar scapegoats back: the criminal scapegoat into the community he has harmed, the psychological scapegoat into the community of the soul, and the global scapegoat into the community of the Earth. I suggested in Chapter 1 that Buddhism with its beginningless karma and Christianity with its original sin see the one who does harm as being immersed in harm and passing it on. The buck does not stop with the harmer or criminal or anyone else, and we should not heap blame and shame upon him. Yet the harmer is responsible for his harm; for we are all to be held to account for what we do. Philosophy may not be able to unravel this paradox, but tragedy and comedy present us with it and enable us to see that it must somehow be true. Chapter 7 will explore how the tragicomic sense of solidarity in sin – the sense that people are responsible, but none is ultimately to blame – may enable us to feel remorse and offer forgiveness. And Chapter 9 will explore what follows from this tragicomic perspective for the way we treat criminals and others who do great harm.

Sands suggests (in Felski p. 83–4) that 'tragedies are to history what trauma is to time,' and that 'tragedy, as an aesthetic form, consigns trauma to a ritual space where, rather than being silently re-enacted, it is solemnly voiced and lamented.' In other words tragic drama may do for the wounds of the community what listening with positive regard, and – in a different way – meditation may do for personal wounds. Chapter 8 will explore further how practices of mindfulness may create a space where people experience harms done and suffered without false consolation, so setting them free from the compulsion to repeat harm in endless cycles.

Tragic heroes like Oedipus and Lear, and in a different way Job, come to innocence through 'staying astride their humanity' (Jung's phrase, quoted below in Chapter 8) in their sufferings. In tragic drama they – and we in empathy with them – find a place where there is no longer a compulsion to fight or flee the pain. They – and we – are able to suffer innocently, without consolations, justifications, or impetus to revenge.

But the tragedy is that the innocence tragic heroes eventually discover through their pains does not survive the brutality of the world. Though they have come to seem divine, they perish with their wounds. That aspect of tragedy does not hold out hope for us in our wounded state. Here we need to learn from the anti-hero of comedy, the clown or fool, who suffers misfortune time and again, yet retains a paradoxical mixture of pathetic vulnerability and indomitable ability to 'bounce back,' making us weep and laugh at the same time.

To sustain the innocence in suffering found in some tragedy, we need this comic resilience. So innocence in the face of suffering may be best found in a tragicomic narration of life, which, without in any way glorifying or justifying evil, suggests ways of creating, not a total Utopian good, but nevertheless some good out of it. Christianity has at its heart the tragicomic narrative of Jesus. And Buddhism holds the tragic and comic together in its different story-transcending way.

Summary

1. Buddhism and Christianity contain features that are clearest in the forms of drama that originate in pagan Greece: tragedy and comedy.
2. Tragedy is not just pessimism: in tragedy we see evil forms of order undermined in successive stages by the chaos that is inherent in them.
3. Tragedy invites us both to identify with its heroes and heroines in compassion for their sufferings, and to shun them in fear as we would a scapegoat. We contemplate their suffering as their fault but also belonging to something larger, which includes us.
4. 'Comedy' refers originally to drama in which characters move through conflict and illusion to happy resolution. Christianity and many modern narratives of liberation are in a sense comedies.
5. But 'comic' also refers to humor and laughter and to the clown or fool – another kind of scapegoat who juxtaposes fine order and embarrassing chaos together in an unstable union that is different from tragedy's movement from order to chaos.

6. In modern tragicomedy the tragic and the comic often cancel each other out to produce nihilistic degradation. But the early Gospels present Christ as a tragicomic figure in a more positive way.
7. For some, Christianity and comedy are inconsistent with the pessimism of tragedy. But tragedy often contains seeds of hope. Horrors can be enfolded in an ultimately 'comic' perspective. Christianity at its best is tragicomic. Buddhism also holds tragedy and comedy together, but not in the form of a tragicomic story.
8. Tragedy presents us with the truth of our condition, but only when complemented by comedy.
9. Tragedy shows how the sins that cause the downfall of the hero and others with him may not be his fault, inviting us to see people as responsible but not 'to blame'.
10. A tragicomic perspective can enable us to welcome the scapegoat back into our midst, treat criminals with respect, and preserve an innocent response to harm.

Chapter 7

Solidarity beyond Shame: Remorse and Forgiveness

Dark bread of daybreak, my dark love will break you,
my love will betray you, will love you
to death.

Because I love in you more
than the joy of human desiring, I hand
the man over to the men who stand
so ready to mock. I must set your cup
to my lips and must drink you
into mine and the others' life
so brutal, to save us.

Because I love your spirit that moves
without thought of me or the morrow, free
through Passover moonlight, I whisper
your name, and watch the inhuman forgiveness
drop from your eyes, to betray me
as friend.
(*Judas hands Jesus over to the authorities*)

In the final scene of most comedies, and some tragedies, there is forgiveness and reconciliation. In comedy this is part of the return from confusion to reality that is the concluding movement: the misconceptions that have led to harm are resolved and the protagonists see each other in a new and truer light. In tragedy the process is often different, part of the regeneration wrought by the tragic hero's death. Seeing the carnage created by bitterness and feud, the protagonists turn from blame of the enemy to remorse at their own part in violence, and resolve to heal their differences. A classic example is the reconciliation of the Montague and Capulet families at the end of *Romeo and Juliet*.

Without remorse, those who harm go on harming. Without forgiveness, those who are harmed go on hurting. Any account of how to deal well with hurt and harm will need to look closely at the processes of forgiveness and remorse.

This chapter will look first at forgiveness, exploring *when* it is appropriate (for example, before or after remorse and restitution?), *what* it is (what happens when we forgive), and *who* it is that can or should forgive. Then it will turn to the question of remorse. First it will ask about the object of remorse: *what* remorse is aware of. Then it will ask about the *who* of remorse – the subject who experiences it. Finally it will ask a question about remorse and forgiveness together: *how* through them innocence can be restored to a relationship, and how this process can be enabled by a tragicomic perspective.

When Should We Forgive?

The Jewish writer Solomon Schimmel describes (2002, p. 8) a significant happening that took place during a session of the South African Truth and Reconciliation Commission. This commission offered an amnesty to all on either side who had committed crimes and atrocities in the course of the struggles that led to the end of apartheid, provided they made a full and truthful confession of those crimes. A white police officer tearfully confessed to having ordered two houses to be set on fire with seven black adults and five children inside. All were killed. His confession was greeted with tears and eventually a standing ovation. A Jewish rabbi then interrupted, saying that it was ridiculous to commit such a sadistic crime and then simply say sorry and expect forgiveness. Christians responded angrily, one saying that Jews do not know how to forgive.

According to Schimmel, this event highlights significant differences between the Jewish and Christian approaches to repentance and forgiveness. For both faiths forgiveness is very important. But in the Jewish and Islamic traditions forgiveness follows repentance, which includes restitution to those one has offended and satisfaction of the demands of justice. And one cannot forgive sins people have committed against others. Forgiveness is a right reserved to the victim, and to God since all sins are sins against God. Because human beings are made in the image of God they have free will and are therefore to blame and accountable to God for the sins they commit. It is a sacred duty to call people to account for their sins, and to punish them according to the law. Though penitence and forgiveness are desirable outcomes, they do not circumvent the demands of the law.

I am not familiar enough with Judaism and Islam to know whether Schimmel is right. And there are those who would put Christianity in the same tradition. But James Alison contends that 'in the most traditional framework of theology, forgiveness precedes confession,' (2003, p. 36). Christ came in God's name and announced the good news that sins are forgiven. He gathered to himself a community that contained many who had sinned, and it is far from clear whether they had all repented. There are many examples of this, especially in Luke. On one occasion, Jesus said to the tax collector Zaccheas – whose trade would have led him into collusion with the Romans, collection of more tax than was due in order to line his own pocket, and probably brutal intimidation of his own people – that he would eat at his house. In this culture, table fellowship implied reconciliation. It was in response to this prior forgiveness that Zaccheas repented and promised generous restitution of all he had dishonestly appropriated (Luke 19.1–10).

Christians also believe Jesus gave his disciples authority to announce forgiveness in God's name, and the Church in its Catholic, Orthodox and many Protestant forms offers absolution of sins in the sacrament of reconciliation – though it has to be said, only, *after* these sins have been confessed. Meanwhile classic atonement theory declares that Christ on the cross has borne the punishment due for all human sin. Chapter 9 will discuss this further, but for now the vital point is that the forgiveness won on the cross obviously precedes the repentance through which this forgiveness is claimed for sins committed in the present day.

Modern secular approaches to sin, repentance and forgiveness vary. For some (like the philosopher Immanuel Kant) the demands of individual accountability and retributive justice are so strong as to rule out all possibility of forgiveness. For others, more liberal minded, people are simply the products of their society, and it is society, not the individual, that is called to repent and change when crimes are committed as a result of poverty or bad upbringing. In both cases – but for opposite reasons – the perpetrator's remorse and repentance slip away from their centrality in the Christian, Jewish and Islamic traditions.

Where does Buddhism stand on this issue? Buddhism would agree with Judaism that we are free and therefore accountable for the way we live. In Mahayana terms we all have 'Buddha nature' and are capable of achieving enlightenment by our own reason and effort. However, Buddhism has no equivalent of the Jewish *Torah,* a legal system whereby those who choose and do wrong are punished. In this context justice is essentially something we are called upon to create on behalf of God. Buddhism has a different kind of law, the *dharma,* which is not divinely ordained but part of the way the world is. Good and bad deeds will reap their reward according to the law of karma, a cause-and-effect process in which we do not intervene and should not try to. Inevitably, it is believed, we will come to experience in ourselves every suffering and unhappiness we have caused in others. Sometimes this is described in terms of the way evil acts will cause evil to befall the perpetrator – the mean-minded man who is lonely in old age because he has alienated all his former friends; Hitler perishing at the heart of the storm of war he had unleashed. But it is also described more subtly. I have heard it said by Tibetans that the Chinese interrogators who torture and kill their people must be crippling their own minds and spirits in a devastating way, or must actually be acting out of a spirit already devastated by bad karma. (This chapter will later on consider the harm sin does to the sinner.)

In such a context, justice is best left to work itself out. Explorer Peter Matthiessen comments on the Buddhist Sherpas who acted as guides on his expedition in Nepal:

> because of their belief in karma... they are tolerant and unjudgmental, knowing that bad acts will receive their due without the intervention of the victim. The generous and open outlook of the Sherpas, a kind of merry defenselessness, is by no means common, even among unsophisticated peoples. (1978, p. 40)

For such a 'merry defenselessness' the focus is not on vengeance, but on building up good karma for ourselves, which in Mahayana tradition can be transferred to others. This requires that we develop a total love for all beings, good and bad alike, including enemies and all who have done us harm, equally and impartially. Only this can release us from the suffering induced by the enemy. Revenge is a sword that wounds the one who holds it all over again, even (especially?) when it does not touch the enemy. And ultimately what is sought here is release from the ego that is so easily harmed by the world's inevitable hurts.

This is why, though there is careful examination of conscience in Buddhism, and confession of sins – often to a fellow monk or retreatant – there is no equivalent of absolution. For Theravada Buddhists there is no way of avoiding the karmic consequences of sin; the sinner has to work through them himself without another's intervention. For many strands of the Mahayana, on the other hand, forgiveness is already there: in the unconditional vow of Amida Buddha for the Shin Buddhists; or in the possibility of achieving Enlightenment and realizing the Buddha nature that was always free from sin (see Thompson, 2010, p. 179–81).

The Jewish and Islamic perspectives stress our accountability to one another as free egos; it is as a harmed ego that I seek just retribution and restitution from the ego that deliberately harmed me. But the Buddhist perspective would urge us not to see what is going on as a matter of egos at all, but as a karmic process in which we are all imprisoned, but from which we can freely choose and endeavor to be released. Once we find release, we will still feel hurt but not harm. Hurt, as defined in the Introduction, is the experience of physical or mental pain, which may leave a wound. Harm is the damage done to us, as persons, by this hurt or wound. If there is no ego to be harmed, there is no harm, only the hurt.

This may not be an easy possibility for us ego-bound persons to imagine. But Anthony de Mello tells a parable (1982, p. 116–7) of a Zen master who was accused by a village girl of being the father of her child. Angrily the villagers took the child to the monk and harangued him. All he said in response to their accusations was, 'Very well, very well!' They left the child with him, and he ensured she was well looked after. But his reputation was in ruins and nobody came to him for instruction any longer. Long afterwards the girl admitted that the real father was the lad next door. The villagers returned to the hermit begging forgiveness, and offering to recompense him and take the child to her true parents. But all he said as he gave the child back was, 'Very well, very well!'

Some may find such loss of any ego that could be harmed (or benefited) appalling, while others may see in it the essence of liberation. We might want to speculate on whether the villagers and the girl went away feeling forgiven, or whether the Zen master's detachment would mean that their guilt would remain unresolved. But any reader of the gospels, with Jesus' commands to love enemies (Matt. 5.44) and to be perfect like the father whose sun shines and whose rain rains on good and evil people alike (Matt. 5.45) will recognize the same kind of appalling or liberating challenge. Buddhists see the world as inherently just, while Christians like Jews see justice as something to do with a transcendent God who commands us to make justice in the world. Buddhists see their goal as release from the ego that can be harmed, while Christians like Jews see the goal as loving relation between a person and a personal God. Nevertheless, despite all this divergence, the Christian ideal regarding unconditional forgiveness and impartial love of all seems to me closer to the Buddhist ideal than the Jewish. (That is not to say that Buddhists and Christians have always and everywhere lived up to those ideals!)

What Happens When We Forgive?

But whether we see forgiveness as unconditional, or conditional upon remorse and recompense, will depend on our answer to a prior question: what *is* forgiveness. In particular, what difference does forgiveness make? What does it change? What ends, and what begins, when forgiveness is offered? What comes to an end when forgiveness happens? Is it remembrance, anger, desire for punishment, mistrust, impenitence, or something deeper?

Firstly, is forgiving a case of forgetting? Consider a case where a man gets a woman drunk, takes her to her home and rapes her in her own bed. Next morning she wakes up with a terrible hangover, but no memory of the last night. Has she forgiven the man? Of course not. We can only forgive something we are aware of, something that hurts. The struggle to forgive for Miroslav Volf (whose experience was described early in Chapter 1) was not a struggle to forget the officer, but to *remember rightly*. For him as a Christian commanded by Christ to love his enemy, this meant being able to 'remember abuse as a person committed to loving the wrongdoer and overcoming evil with good,' (2008, p. 11).

So when people say, as they often do, 'I can forgive, but I cannot forget,' they are not contradicting themselves. Of course, they are actually usually saying something more subtle and complex than, 'I can remember that you did x to me, but I forgive you.'

If it is not forgetting, is forgiveness a kind of overlooking, a turning away and not noticing, or ceasing to regard an action as unjust or a crime? When people apologize the response often comes back, 'There is nothing to forgive.' But that is not a case of forgiveness. The one who forgives must remember the harm done to them as a harm; forgiveness is not lenience or failing to take harm seriously. When the father forgave the terrorists for the Omagh bombing in which his daughter had just died, he was certainly not saying such things do not matter or that his daughter's life was not important to him and it was a light matter to take it away. A declaration of forgiveness is always an imputation of guilt. That is why to those who (correctly or incorrectly) do not think they have done any wrong, the offer of forgiveness can be perceived as an insult.

For as James Alison points out (2003), there is a false, aggressive kind of forgiveness that avoids the need for repentance altogether. It arises when victims – be they Palestinians or Jews, or gay people addressing the Church, or whoever – simply declare forgiveness (as it were!) on their oppressors. This is really a way of saying, 'I am better than you. Not only am I your victim – and therefore innocent where you are guilty – but I am doubly innocent because I forgive you and do not wish you any harm, even though you have harmed me terribly and refuse to repent!' Such forgiveness is false because it is a way of claiming exalted victim status (as described in Chapter 3) without actually making oneself vulnerable in the way true seekers of reconciliation have to do. True forgiveness must establish equality, righting the injustice of the crime, creating a state where the two can look each other face to face without humiliating the offender to inferior status. Often it is expressed by shaking hands, or embracing, as equals.

Is forgiveness, indeed, something we can achieve or do at all? Does it happen by a deliberate choice or act of will? I think not. There appears to me to be no distinction between wanting to forgive, and forgiving. As soon as we want to forgive, we have done so. Something has happened in our 'heart' or emotional life from which the desire to forgive springs. Of course there may be some things this desire makes us want to do, like seek the person out, shake hands, and achieve reconciliation. But the forgiveness must already be there to motivate this activity.

This is not to say that forgiveness may not require effort. The act of saying 'sorry' or 'I forgive you' can change a whole relationship in a moment, and open up possibilities of life that just were not there before. But to come to that moment, in a way that makes sense and carries this potential for change, normally involves huge moral effort both before and after that instant, to make it real. But this is mainly an effort to change one's own heart: to see anew and more widely and deeply, and to live anew in the light of what one newly sees. Not always – the Omagh father seems to have managed to forgive instantaneously. Perhaps for a saint like the Buddhist hermit, the effort of changing the heart is all behind him, so that harmful actions are now seen immediately in a forgiving light. But for most of us it takes much longer to effect the emotional change that forgiveness involves.

What change in our emotional life might this be? Does forgiveness mean ceasing to be angry, grieved or offended by a hurt done to one? It often does involve that, but not necessarily. The father just mentioned would be abnormal if he did not continue to feel grief and probably anger about the loss of his daughter. We can forgive an unfaithful partner, for example, yet not cease to feel rage or grief or both. On the other hand forgiveness does seem to imply an ending of hatred. You cannot meaningfully say, 'I hate you for doing this to me, but I forgive you.' This is presumably because anger is just a natural response to hurt, whereas hatred is an attitude to the one who caused the hurt that is quite incompatible with forgiving that person. If we hate someone we often want to do them harm, or find ourselves pleased to hear of some harm that has befallen them. When we forgive, our anger or grievance relinquishes the desire to retaliate. We hurt because of the sin, but we no longer hate the sinner. That of course involves placing a distance between the sinner and the sin, such that while perhaps still being angered or hurt by the sin we can still love the sinner or at least wish her well.

This brings us an important step closer to understanding forgiveness. Forgiveness involves seeing the sin in a context wider than our hurt, and the sinner as a wider and deeper reality than just the hurt they have caused us. And in this context, we find ourselves able to relinquish any desire to avenge the hurt we have received, to repay hurt by hurt.

Does that mean that we cease to desire the offender's punishment? Not necessarily. I might relinquish a desire to see the offender hurt, but still wish him to be punished according to the law. This could be because of a desire to maintain the law. I might feel that making an exception would undermine the deterrent effect of the law. Or I might reflect that it would introduce an element of unfairness, if those who were forgiven by their victims were spared punishment while those who had committed less serious crimes were punished because their victims would not forgive them. Or more profoundly, I might feel that it is for the offender's own good to serve his sentence – that to waive the sentence might actually be to harm him. This might be especially true in cases where the offender shows no remorse. If allowed to go free he may simply laugh at his victims and commit similar crimes in the future; however, by being given 'time for amendment of life' he may come to repentance and a new and better kind of life.

For all these reasons an ethic of forgiveness does not necessarily imply an ethic of amnesty, of 'letting people off the hook.' This seems to me to be a point that every good parent and schoolteacher knows: that it is of the utmost importance to children to administer justly and fairly the rules that have been agreed, and this may include punishment, but that does not mean there is any desire to hurt or harm a child who does wrong. Indeed such a desire would undermine any sense of fairness.

Another try. Does forgiveness mean a restoration of trust? Again, not necessarily. It is true that without forgiveness, trust cannot be restored, but not vice versa. Suppose a friend of mine, as a favor, drove my son home from school, crashed and caused my son's death. Suppose that it later emerged that the accident was his fault. I might one day come to forgive his negligent driving, or I might even forgive him immediately despite my anger and grief, because I saw that the death was not intentional but resulted from the kind of negligence I know I too can sometimes be guilty of. But I would probably never let him give my other children a lift. The forgiveness involves my seeing the person in a wider light in which his actions are seen as non-malicious, but that wider light may still include elements I cannot trust, like my friend's poor driving skills. The forgiveness might enable my friendship to continue, but the friendship will have to negotiate around the elements I cannot trust.

These reflections have, I hope, brought us to the heart of what forgiveness is. Paradoxically it involves a kind of rebirth in the victim's 'heart' or emotional life that allows the perpetrator to exist in a wider perspective than that contained by the hurt he has done. We might even call it a 'repentance' in the victim, in the sense of a change of attitude (*metanoia*), a turning away from the perspective of the hurt. This may be facilitated by the repentance of the perpetrator, or it may facilitate it. The perpetrator may reframe his own story, such that he no longer says, 'I did this and there was nothing wrong in it,' or, 'It was wrong but I did not do it,' but, 'I did that and it was harmful, and though I am the one who did it I now wish I was not, and wish never again to be the doer of that kind of thing.'

And that may be what enables the victim to see him as having another possible or actual story other than the story of the crime. But it may be that the victim's ability to tell the wider story about the perpetrator is what enables the latter to tell it too, and so grow bigger than he was. This is rarely possible for humans, but as we shall see, it is what Christians believe God does in relation to us through Jesus Christ. Miraculously, we can sometimes do it too.

> When we forgive those who have wronged us, we make our own God's miracle of forgiveness. Echoing God's unfathomable graciousness, we decouple the deed from the doer. (Volf, p. 208)

But who are this victim and forgiver? So far we have been speaking mostly in terms of a person who does harm and needs to repent, and a victim who may forgive. In many but not all situations this is a simplification, since people have harmed and need to forgive each other, though not always to the same degree. That of course is something hard for those involved to evaluate, and this is often what makes forgiveness difficult.

People often say something like 'I apologize for what I did, but you must admit you were partly to blame...' And that kind of apology can be difficult to respond to. The other person does not know what to consider: the issue of whether she should forgive, or the issue of whether she should be penitent herself.

So the questions of when people should forgive, and what forgiveness is, cannot be resolved without asking...

Who Should Forgive?

Chapter 2 introduced the story of Carla and her abuse by her father, but did not relate how that story ended. As the father who abused her neared the end of his life, reconciliation became very important for Carla. She longed to hear her father give voice to the matter on which he had throughout his life remained so silent: to say a simple sorry and to receive her forgiveness. But this was tragically short-circuited. All she heard from her father was that he had gone to the priest and made his confession, so everything was now all right. Her father, having been told officially by the Church that God forgave him, could avoid the difficult and painful path of seeking the forgiveness of his daughter.

> The great secret... had been for the priest's ears only and would not be discussed with the people he had hurt. It was too much to expect him to break his heart right open; even the knowledge of his impending death wasn't going to breach his reticence. I cried inside, for both of us. What does it take, if leaving the body, the planet and your family for ever doesn't break down resistance? But in those last remaining days, he was loving and tender to all of us, giving us embraces which touched our hearts very deeply. He was showing love, and we could feel the realness of it. And yet he wouldn't die a totally happy man, choosing instead to cling to his faith, which promised total forgiveness through confession to a priest. (2004, p. 383)

Carla's situation is not unlike that of the victims of the many priests who have effectively been absolved of their abuses against children and placed 'safe from harm' in a parish far removed, with their victims sworn to silence. Most victims do not love their abusers in the way Carla continued to love her father. For many, retribution continues to be an aim, though for others the aim may simply be to receive acknowledgment of the trauma they have undergone and assurance that the priests will not go on to traumatize others in the same way. But the basic pattern is the same in the way it removes the need, and therefore the motivation, for abusers to experience remorse and a reconciliation – if at all possible – with their victims. And that in turn precludes a total happiness that only reconciliation can bring: which is why Carla 'cried... for both of us.'

The Church believes in a God who loves us unconditionally, whose Son Jesus announced to all and sundry the forgiveness of sins, and who commands his Church to continue forgiving people in his name. That sounds a wonderful and comforting vision. But in the case of Carla's father, the pronouncing of forgiveness seems to have short-circuited a process that might have brought about greater change. A truly remorseful father might have found a deeper forgiveness, that of the one he had harmed, and love might have triumphed more truly over hurt, bringing healing balm to the wounds his daughter bore and, doubtless, those he himself bore in his soul.

So is it the case that forgiveness can only come from those who have been hurt? If so, whither the all embracing and unconditional love of God, and whither the Gospel of Christ? But if not, must our redemption await the forgiveness of all those we have harmed? And could one hard-hearted person halt our progress for all eternity over one relatively trivial offense he cannot find it in him to forgive?

Intuitively there is a good case for saying that forgiveness has to come from those we have hurt. That is why the only sins for which we can really 'forgive ourselves' – in that odd but often used phrase – are those that have only hurt ourselves. I am not sure that such sins exist, since actions always take place in a social context. Even the self-harmer and the suicide bring harm to others beside themselves. 'If I were able to absolve myself, I should be claiming that my acts and their meanings could be – as it were – reclaimed, drawn back out of their life in the lives of others' and that would be to wield 'power over those others in whom my past is still alive,' (Williams, 2000, p. 104).

Even God's forgiveness, then, if it is not to be a sheer exercise of divine power in the face of our victims' memories, must somehow be mediated through those through whom we have in some sense wounded God. But our victim may be unable to forgive, for psychological reasons of his own that do not truly reflect the seriousness of our sin, or simply because he is no longer alive. Or he may too ready to forgive for the wrong reasons, unable to appreciate the harm that has been done to him, like the child who blames himself. In that case, perhaps the forgiver needs to be one who knows and loves the victim deeply enough to speak on their behalf out of the valuing discussed above, and who also knows the perpetrator and their whole story.

That sounds like what the Christians believe to be God, the One who loves the victim and identifies with him totally, but loves also the offender and knows his whole story. Ideally God alone is in a position to forgive, and his atonement declares his willingness to do so at huge cost to himself, meaning his own death and rebirth. If God did not (in some deep sense) exist, perhaps we might need to invent her to make up for the deficiencies in our ability to forgive...

At the climax of St. Matthew's Gospel, where Jesus' teaching ministry ends and the passion begins, we read the famous story of the Last Judgment (Matt. 25.31–46). Here Christ judges or forgives not on the basis of divine laws but on the basis of very concrete acts of caring for the sick and imprisoned. He declares, 'inasmuch as you have done it to the least of these, you have done it to me.' It seems to me that only a God who is wholly identified with the victims has the authority to forgive sins committed against them (rather than against divine law in the abstract). And we might add, only a God who equally identifies with the sinners, and knows their whole story as part of his own, can truly judge them. In the Passion narrative that follows this awesome parable, we see exactly what it means for God to enter fully into the story of human sin, to the point of experiencing in Godself the pain of condemnation and God-forsakenness.

If this is so, the Church cannot be wrong to declare what it believes to be divine forgiveness. Where it seems to me to err is when it seeks to administer that forgiveness as an alternative to the human processes of justice, healing and forgiveness. The Catholic Church has been right to proclaim to its abusing priests, in the face of a condemning world, that God still loves them, but altogether wrong to draw the conclusion from this that it must protect them (and thereby itself) from the secular processes of investigation, judgment and penalty. It was right to declare that God loved and forgave Carla's father, but wrong to let him get away with avoiding seeking Carla's forgiveness. Its announcement of forgiveness (God's unconditional reaching out in yearning to set the sinner free) was valid, but its declaration of absolution (actual liberation from the consequences of sin) was premature. That declaration devalued Carla, letting God's love for Carla's father obscure God's love for Carla herself. The Church cannot absolve us from our sins and their consequences. It can only declare God's unconditional love, and show a way whereby – conditionally upon our seriously undertaking the painful processes of seeking forgiveness from and offering it to one another – that love may become effective as absolution from our sins.

One analogy for this is that we are to God as planets are to the sun. God's love shines on us whether we are good or whether we are bad. From God's point of view there is no dark side to us: 'with you the light and dark are both alike,' (Psalm 139). But to us dark and light are not alike. From a human point of view there is a dark side that is turned away from God toward destruction and nothingness. That does not stop the love and forgiveness of God bathing us in its everlasting light, but it does make absolution – our turning toward that light with the whole of our being, which Christ called *metanoia,* change of heart, repentance – a painful and difficult process for us. When the priest declares God's forgiveness, he is sure and certain. What he cannot be sure of, however, is the sinner's repentance. Even the sinner, on his own, cannot be sure of this. For too long we have pietistically assumed that inner feelings of contrition and a token penance are enough. But the old Jewish idea of repentance included restitution and reconciliation. It had a social dimension which neither the priest nor the penitent could be sure of, because it depended on how others responded. In Christian terms it is a mistake to make forgiveness dependent on repentance and restitution, but right to insist that absolution and liberation from the consequences of sin are so dependent.

'To err is human, to forgive divine,' as Alexander Pope's familiar saying goes. Human forgiveness involves something divine: seeing someone as God has always seen them. God cannot forgive us, because he never condemns us – the people we are – but always sees our hurting of others as hurts against our own true selves, and hence against God. In this sense forgiveness is always 'eschatological,' that is, always to do with the ultimate reality of who we are, beyond the changes and chances of this world – changes and chances that often make true forgiveness impossible in this life. Forgiveness and reconciliation always, even when they do happen in this life, involve a death, a letting go and leaving behind of the abusive relationship that bound us in the past – a letting go, often, of a lot of what has defined our sense of who we are.

So the priest was right to assure Carla's father of forgiveness, but he should have required him to do so much more than say a few 'hail Marys.' The father should have emerged fired with the vision of God's forgiveness, which is eternal and unshakable as sunrise, an ultimate reality written in the heavens, but also something that can take root in the here and now of his life only if he seeks forgiveness from his daughter. He would have known, of course, that she might not give it; it is not possible, or desired by God, to force reconciliation. But if she had given it there would have been weeping and lamenting and remorse over the destruction he had long wrought in her life, and a lament for the childhood he destroyed in her, but also the joy of something new, of seeing as God sees.

Carla's father clearly felt ashamed and guilty. This is something the priest was able and right to relieve him of by telling him God loved him despite his sins. But Carla's father should have been released from depressing self-concern not to self-satisfaction or a false 'inner peace,' but to concern for the harm he had done to Carla and the need to make amends and restore, as best he could, what he had long ago broken. To become real, he needed to be freed from guilt into remorse, and from remorse through reconciliation, hopefully, into relationship restored.

So now our considerations turn from forgiveness to consider...

What Remorse Reveals

Guilt and remorse are not popular today. People often speak of guilt as pathological, or self-absorbed. It seems obvious, however, that when a great crime has in fact been committed, a lack of remorse is what is pathological. One wishes Hitler had felt more remorse for the Holocaust, and Shipman more for the series of murders he so cold-heartedly committed. Their lack of remorse is what suggests a pathological self-absorption in their own project, and indifference to the terrible reality of the suffering and destruction they were wreaking.

So for the philosopher Raimond Gaita, remorse stems from that sense of the reality of others as human beings like oneself, on which he believes all morality depends. It can be compared to grief over the loss of a loved one.

> Remorse is a recognition of the reality of another through the shock of wronging her; just as grief is the recognition of the reality of another through the shock of losing her. (2004, p. 52)

As Chapter 2 suggested, remorse is therefore quite different from the fundamentally egocentric responses of shame and guilt, in the same way that grief or mourning is different from depression and melancholy. Sigmund Freud argued that 'mourning recognizes that what is lost is different from the self, while melancholy treats all loss as the loss of something in or about me,' (Williams, 2000, p. 129). In the same way, remorse is a sense of another as being hurt by me, whereas shame and guilt as described in Chapter 3 involve a consciousness of myself as being deficient or harmful. Shame and guilt can accompany remorse, but need not, for the awareness of the other hurting can shut out all sense of self.

Remorse is more than the 'regret' that we so often hear from politicians these days. Regret is a concern for hurt and harm that befalls another, whether or not I have caused it. I can regret the loss of life in an earthquake, without remorse. A politician can regret the suffering his policies seem to have caused without admitting the causal connection and culpability – as when, at the time of writing, President Barak Obama expressed regret over the death and suffering caused by the atomic bombing of

Hiroshima and Nagasaki. He was clearly saying this was a terrible thing to have happened, without wanting to say that the country he represented had done wrong in causing it. Presumably he thought the act was justified in some way.

Likewise I might regret that I did a crime, but if this is were only because I got caught and sentenced to prison, it would involve no remorse. In regret I set a distance of some kind between the regretted action and myself. I suggest that the events should be lamented but that I should not be regarded as lamentable. It is a bit like asking people to hate the sin but love (or at least respect) me the sinner – except that I do so by protesting that it is not really sin that is involved. This is why when leaders like Obama express their 'regret' at the loss of civilian life caused by bombs dropped on their cities, the civilians themselves are often outraged rather than appeased. (Perhaps terrorists are more honest in not even – usually – expressing regret at the death and suffering they cause; when they do, it sounds hollow.)

Like Gaita, Rowan Williams links remorse to awareness of injury.

> To say that one of our major cultural bereavements is *remorse* is to raise the question of whether we are still capable of seeing failure and betrayal as inner and personal wounds, injuries to a person's substance. (2000, p. 97)

It is not clear whether the injury in question is to the 'substance' of the one harmed or the harmer; the context suggests the latter. But remorse surely involves both. It is feeling the harm we do to another as evidence of harmfulness in ourselves, 'such that another's loss becomes – not the same as mine, but the cause of loss to me,' (p. 129). For remorse, unlike regret, implicates the agent personally in the suffering of the other. As Gaita puts it, it involves people suffering 'in guilty recognition of what they have become.' The remorseful person does not separate herself as sinner from the sin; she regards herself as being the kind of person that has done that despicable thing – that is, a despicable person. After a wrongdoing, remorse asks not only 'What have I done?' but, 'What has become of me?'

So remorse involves several aspects of a sense of reality. It involves a sense of the *reality of the other* and of the harm we have done them. It involves a sense of *what we have come to be* through the act. And behind that lies a sense of what we once were and might still have been but for the act.

But remorse also involves something Gaita does not actually mention: a desire for something that cannot be. Remorse, like regret, and like grief over loss, wishes the past to be different. In all these emotions we want something that has happened – my destructive action, or the loss of the one I love – not to have happened. This counterfactual desire can be extremely painful because we know at the outset that there is no way in which what we want can be achieved. But with remorse there is something worse. Because what I did in the past has made me what I am now, remorse implies a desire that I be other than the person who did it. Remorse involves a kind of grief for the loss of myself, for the loss of innocence, the loss of the me I once knew and respected.

But there a hope lies buried. I cannot change what I did, but I can, perhaps, change the person I have become. That is why remorse enables forgiveness: because it enables the other to believe I can become other than the person who hurt them.

Corruption, Hope and the Who of Remorse

Remorse suggests something we do not like to hear: that we cannot so easily separate the sinner from the sin, and as the conventional wisdom goes, hate the sin but love the sinner. The remorseful person does not make that separation. He recognizes what is surely the case: that we are not some kind of spiritual essence that sails on untouched by the deeds we do. We are made by what we do.

> A man who lies to himself, and believes his own lies, becomes unable to recognize truth, either in himself or in anyone else, and he ends up losing respect for himself and for others. When he has no respect for anyone, he can no longer love, and in him, he yields to his impulses, indulges in the lowest form of pleasure, and behaves in the end like an animal in satisfying his vices. And it all comes from lying – to others and to yourself.
> (Dostoyevsky, *The Brothers Karamazov*, Book 2, Ch. 2)

So Dostoyevsky's character Fr. Zosima describes how apparently trivial dishonesty can corrupt a person's whole character. In a more extreme way, the person who kills another, perhaps in a 'permissible' setting like warfare, has to become the kind of person that does not find it impossible to aim a gun to wound or kill. And tragically that person may then find maiming and killing easier in other settings. To change from being the kind of person who hates to cause suffering, pain and death in another to being the kind of person who enjoys doing so is not as difficult as we would like to think. For many, it only requires training by repeated doing. The doing changes our being. This is what we call 'corruption' – another moral concept we do not hear so much of these days, which perhaps we ought to add to Rowan Williams' list of our culture's 'lost icons.' It is why we should not trust politicians who tell little 'terminological inexactitudes' (to use Winston Churchill's delicate phrase) or are unfaithful to their partners, even if these matters seem far removed from the demands of office.

Buddhism has long been aware of the possibility of corruption, which it describes in terms of the *sankharas*, our mental formations and habits.

> These are very important for Buddhism because they are not tendencies we have but tendencies we are. Instead of being 'my' habits, their interaction is what constructs my sense of 'me.' Then we are punished not for our sins but by them. People suffer or benefit not for what they have done but for what they have become. (Loy, 2001)

So the sense of being punished *by* our sins for what we have become through doing them – rather than *for* specific sins we have done by an external God or Principle of Justice – is central to Buddhism. It is also what we see at work in the downfall of tragic heroes, and it is what remorse acknowledges.

In view of the possibility of corruption, we need to qualify Butler's criticism of the way in anger we tend to see people only in terms of the harm they did us. It is true that we should see people in terms of the balance of good and bad in their characters. We should not see someone as 'a liar' or 'a murderer,' but as someone who has lied or murdered, but who also perhaps did many good things. But we also need to recognize that some sins do actually change the kind of person we are. And it is not just terrible atrocities that do this, but sins like lying and deception. Catholic theology distinguishes 'mortal' from 'venial' sins; venial sins are sins that come and go, while mortal sins are those that strike at the heart of what we are.

Just as it is easier to let iron rust than to make it pure again, it is easier to become corrupt than to change back to what we were: to become once again the kind of person who would not lie, or kill, or torture. It is possible, but it involves more than practice; it involves the pain of remorse. There is an asymmetry here which has to do with the asymmetry explored in Chapter 5 between good and evil. Because evil is an undoing of being, it is relatively easy to learn to do. The material for evil to work on – our own goodness – is already there for the evil act to undermine by force of habit. But because evil is destruction and deprivation of being, to restore what we were involves a new creation of something out of the nothing we have created in ourselves. That is one reason why Christians ascribe repentance and restoration to the grace of God, not human effort alone.

A simple analogy is a bridge across a wild torrent made of rope and rafters. We only need to cut a few ropes or girders and the whole bridge will unravel and cease to be usable as a bridge. But to put it together will be less easy. Things will no longer be in place to knot and weave the bridge together again. A whole new scaffolding may be needed to reach from one shore to the other and temporarily hold things together. And we will need people with the skills of making bridges to do their work – much harder to come by than people able to cut rope! In the same way our degeneration into bad ways may be relatively quick and easy, but our restoration to the good people we once were requires the pain of remorse, and perhaps the superhuman 'scaffold' of grace, able to span the abyss.

So is it more realistic to despair of the restoration of hardened evildoers? Gaita urges to the contrary (p. 7–8) that we should not treat anyone as despicable 'filth' even if they have done truly despicable deeds. But he contends that this is not because we believe in some part of them that has not become contaminated. We should not refrain from treating the concentration camp commandant as filth because, though he tortured people and supervised their systematic killing, he was a good father and husband, said his prayers, was kind to animals and loved good music. We know this was true of some of the commandants; but did that make them a bit better than those who were bad fathers and had poor taste in music? Jews and Christians speak of people being sacred, however wicked they are, because they are made in the image of God. Others speak simply of our duty to treat all people with respect, whatever they have done. But this is not because of some good part of the person that persists whatever evil they do. In the same way, when we say that a bridge is reparable it is probably not because part of it is still working as a bridge; even the part that is still working may need to be destroyed to restore the bridge.

Gaita argues that the reason we should accord respect to all is because no one is beyond the reach of 'a sober remorse' (2004, p. 8). By this he means a remorse, that is not self-dramatizing or self-absorbed, but clearly focused on the realities just described: the other person, the harm they have suffered because of what you have done, and what you have become through doing it. Gaita is saying it is not so much that people, however wicked, retain something valuable in their character, but that they are to be valued absolutely and unconditionally, despite their own 'valuelessness' in legal, moral and social terms. This relates, perhaps, to the point made in Chapter 3: how Jesus associated with the outcast not because they were actually nice innocent people underneath, but because even the wicked are to be loved and valued and hoped for. To declare all human beings sacred and worthy of respect is to say that we should never give up on anyone.

Statements about unconditional human worth, and being made in God's image or having Buddha nature, are therefore statements about our end and the possibility of attaining it despite all the bad in what we do and become: in short, our redeemability. The strength of Christianity and the Shin version of Buddhism is that for them the source of our confidence in people's redeemability is not people's own qualities (which may seem beyond repair, as in the likes of Kaplan's Nazi) but God's (or Amida Buddha's) love and power to save, which are unshakable and beyond doubt (unless qualified by the belief that some will be lost or punished everlastingly in hell). On the other hand, even God cannot transform us without something happening in us: namely, our *own* remorse. Another's remorse and repentance cannot lead to our transformation. And trust in the other's power to transform us does not let us off the hook of working out what it must mean in our own case.

Secular perspectives like Gaita's own – without God, grace or the power of the Other — are of course capable of asserting unconditional worth. But what about Hitler in his bunker, committing suicide before the Russian forces arrive, or Stalin lying on the floor after his final heart attack, while nobody dares enter the room without his answer? So far as we know there was not, in these final moments of their lives, time for the remorse required for the millions of deaths they had caused, let alone for the amendment of life that would restore in them what Christians call the image of God. Is a secularist who believes in no life beyond the grave not bound to say they died as the filth they had become through what they did? Christians – at least those who believe in purgatory – leave open a metaphysical way whereby they might come to and express a sober remorse, and so recover the innocence they had destroyed by their lives on earth.

And Buddhists would be able to affirm that they, like all sentient beings, were destined for Nirvana, and had countless future lives to work away the bad karma their terrible lives had accrued. When Buddhists speak of the Buddha nature this is surely what they mean. They cannot mean some everlasting essence of the soul that remains intact through change – how could a Buddhist believe that without believing in a self at all? For Buddhists there is no eternal 'heaven' or 'hell' but in a sense our many reincarnations in this world constitute purgatory, the place of suffering and remorse and the hope of new life.

How to Become a 'New We'

Though like grief in terms of its sense of the reality of another, Gaita argues that remorse is quintessentially solitary. With other griefs we can find solace in the fact that others have suffered this way too. But

> remorse... sticks with us, although corrupt versions of it merge readily enough into a sense of common guilt, where all are guilty and so none is... Someone who is true to her remorse will always reject, as inappropriate, consolation that is based on her recognition of the guilt of others... It should be no consolation if what we did was also done by the best of people. (p. 47, p. 50)

With remorse, it is false comfort for me to say 'well there are plenty of others who have been unfaithful... murderers... or whatever.' The guilty should not find relief through sharing their experience of guilt with that of others. In that sense remorse involves a deep loneliness, even a 'dying to the world' (p. 48).

Now I can see the point being made here, but I wonder if bereavement does not include the same kind of loneliness and dying to the world. It is true that others have lost loved ones, just as others have committed wrongs, but this one unique irreplaceable relationship has been shattered or betrayed – by death, or by my wrongdoing. Though there are comforts in solidarity they cannot undo this painful uniqueness, as every bereaved and remorseful person knows.

And ultimately the loneliness of remorse – like that of bereavement – is common. It is what all humans are liable to experience because they are mortal yet loving, and sinful yet caring. If we move too fast along these lines we arrive at self-deception. Saying that there are lots of other sinners like me can be a way of avoiding remorse altogether, since it can be a way of saying I'm not really that bad after all. But in the desolation of a real grief over what is my responsibility and mine alone, there is solidarity, because in the words of St. Paul, 'all have sinned,' (Rom. 3.23). All sensitive and aware human beings therefore know this sorrow I am feeling. And we can add to that what we noted, that (original) sin is bigger than me, something in which I participate or collude. So if it is to be truly realistic and not egocentric, remorse must involve not only a sense of the reality of the one I hurt, and the reality of what I have become through my act of hurting; but also a sense of my sin as part of a whole history of sin, in which it is effect as well as cause.

A tragicomic sense might help in this. Tragedy, as described in Chapter 6, focuses on the individual's sin and fate. It traces how the latter emerges from the former, how evil deeds trap the hero and transform what he is for the worse. We contemplate in fear and pity 'what has become of' Oedipus, Macbeth, Othello, Lear, and see how even the most terrible fall does not efface his human worth. In comedy on the other hand we contemplate the frail humanity the hero shares with us. That is why the hero (or anti-hero) seems to stand on the edge where the stage meets the audience. In the fool we realize our common loneliness as sinners all. In remorse we confront the tragedy of our own self-undoing, but if we leave it there we may retain an overblown sense of our isolated grandeur as 'the chief of sinners.' Comedy deflates us, telling us we are nothing so special as that!

So I ought to be able to grasp in myself through my remorse what I may also grasp in my forgiving of others: a sense of the normality of abnormality. The most moving thing about Walt Whitman, it has been suggested, 'is that he teaches, instead of an absolution of sins, a sort of *patience with deformities* from which human charity might begin,' (Bromwich, 1989, p. 168); an attitude which 'judges not as the judge judges but as the sun falling round a helpless thing,' (Whitman, 2004, p. 37–41).

The Bible frequently describes God as 'long-suffering' towards sin and full of loving-kindness. The Medieval mystic, Mother Julian of Norwich, elaborates:

> Though we sin continually he loves us endlessly, and so gently does he show us our sin that we repent of it quietly, turning our mind to the contemplation of his mercy, clinging to his love and goodness, knowing that he is our cure, under-

> standing that we do nothing but sin... If there be anywhere on earth a lover of God who is always kept safe from falling, I know nothing of it—for it was not shown me. But this was shown: that in falling and rising again we are always held close in one love.
> (1980, p. 55 – Longer Text 82)

Shin Buddhists speak with similar tenderness of our foolish 'bombu nature,' which cannot achieve its own liberation but needs the grace of Amida Buddha. All Buddhists, of course, accept the noble truth of *dukkha* – best understood as the painful 'unsatisfactoriness' of existence. And the Protestant Christian tradition is founded on Martin Luther's insight that to be human is to be unjust – incapable of leading a life that does not do someone an injustice, and so transgress God's law of love – so that we cannot perfect ourselves but need God's undeserved grace. These varied traditions are unanimous in their opposition to the widely held modern assumption that it is possible to lead a perfectly wise and fulfilled life.

So when penitence is humiliating, and forgiveness proceeds on the basis of a fundamental moral inequality between the entirely 'innocent' victim and the entirely 'guilty' penitent, it generally proceeds on the basis of falsehood. Not always – child abuse is a clear case where we should not try to ascribe any guilt to victims who are either too weak to resist physically, or too innocent to resist morally one vested with superior authority in their eyes. There are other similar cases, and we should certainly not assume that in every crime it is really a case of 'six of one and half a dozen of the other.' But even where one person is entirely innocent of the crime in question, that person is unlikely never to have committed harm themselves. Therefore true forgiveness proceeds on the basis of ultimate solidarity. Forgiver and forgiven are both sinners engaged in freeing each other from the deadly hold of their past and building a new relationship beyond recrimination.

> Forgiveness... is... not a hermetic self-sealing off from the other whom I declare myself to be nothing at all like. On the contrary, forgiveness turns out to be a creative moving toward someone *whom I am like* in such a way that they will be free from death *with me* so that together we will be a new we. (Alison, 2003, p. 42)

It is this 'new we' that Jesus – as interpreted in my poem at the head of the chapter – is calling Judas along with the other disciples. But the Judas of my poem resists. His love for Jesus has become a desire to possess him for himself alone. He can only experience Jesus' forgiveness as 'inhuman' and 'brutal.' Preferring Jesus to be dead rather than shared, he betrays him to death, and chooses death for himself too rather than the new we that is beyond death. (But I speculate – beyond the poem – that in the resurrection Jesus' forgiveness broke through the gates of death and hell to reach Judas there.)

Fundamentally it is as one called to joyful innocence, but sharing in common human sin – and moreover sharing in it in a way for which I alone am to blame – that I most keenly and authentically feel remorse. And it is as a sinner myself that I am able most wisely and authentically to forgive. In shame, the wrong I have done overwhelms me, and I encounter the other only as the one who sees into me. Self-consciousness fills my horizon even when I am aware of others. But in remorse it is the other I am aware of in terms of the harm I have done her, and I see myself only in the light of that harm to the other and what it implies about the person I am. In forgiveness, however, the other frees me from this story of myself by allowing herself to tell a wider story of me. In repentance, forgiven, I enter that wider story with the forgiver. A 'new we' is created, and an innocence is restored which neither of us could invent for ourselves.

Summary

1. Forgiveness and remorse are fundamental aspects of a positive response to harm. In some traditions, forgiveness must follow on true repentance including restitution. But in Buddhism and Christianity forgiveness can come first. For Buddhism, when there is no self there is no harm to forgive; for Christianity, God forgives us unconditionally and invites us to do likewise.
2. Forgiveness is not a matter of forgetting, or overlooking a sin. It is not an act of choice or effort, but a state of our emotions. It does not necessarily mean a cessation of hurt or anger or of desire to see punishment done, or a restoration of trust. It is a change of heart in which we see the harmer in a wider perspective than the harm.
3. Forgiveness cannot be offered on another's behalf, unless perhaps on behalf of one we know and love dearly who cannot speak for himself. The Church expresses the unconditional love and acceptance of God, which free us from guilt and shame. But only those we have hurt can overcome the remorse we feel about having hurt them; only through them can a new relationship come, and the Church should not attempt to short-circuit this.
4. Remorse involves a recognition of the reality of another and the harm we have done to them, and a grief concerning the kind of person we have become to do such harm.
5. We cannot completely separate the sin from the sinner, because sins corrupt the sinner. Corruption is easy, restoration is hard. But concepts like 'Buddha nature' and 'the image of God' mean that we should never despair of the possibility of remorse and restoration in ourselves and others.
6. Remorse, like bereavement, is a solitary process, yet it is as universal as sin, and best enabled by a tragicomic sense of our solidarity in foolishness. When we truly forgive we see

the other as like ourselves. So the process of remorse and forgiveness can restore an original innocence and create a 'new we' which we could not create on our own.

Chapter 8

Reclaiming the Real: Mindfulness and Prayer

She is there again, the asylum seeker
chatting in the smoky corner. The other day
we'd flirted. I loved the bright sky
flashing in her Moldavian eyes, and the lazy tones
of her broad and sleepy motherland.
She was selling herself, she said
it was the only way. I was not interested
I said, but lied.

Today I hope she will not notice and disrupt
my respectable English evening with a friend.
But as soon as he goes to buy the round
she is bearing down on me. She is not pretty now
but her ravaged body shines in a strange light,
metallic and transfigured. The sun
has set on her eyes, opening black rimmed
luminous oceans of night. Electric hair
spirals out, charged with danger, like Medusa
turning me to stone.

Breaking the bread
of silence, she offers me like wine
the gash in her wrist, swollen and weeping.
I hate blood, but brace myself to kiss her there.
Erotic, it feels; red, gaping lips.

I am looking for hope, she says. I blush

for her shamelessness, my sudden lust.
A wound in me has opened, but I hate
blood, at all costs I must keep my life
inside. Faces are turned to the priest
with the whore. I have none to offer
I say, honestly enough, but knowing my hunger
could have fed her well. I make excuses
and go to help my colleague with the drinks.
Wounds

Chapter 6 explored the question of how to respond well to hurt and harm in general terms of the world view within which we experience them. Chapter 7 looked at the issue in terms of the interpersonal dynamics of remorse and forgiveness. Two questions remain: what kind of individual practice might express such a world view and make remorse and forgiveness easier; and what kind of society might do so. The latter will be partly explored for Chapter 9. In this chapter I wish to approach the question of how we become people capable of remorse and forgiveness. How do we become the kind of people that will not be hurt by harm, or at least not be psychically disabled by it, and not immediately respond to hurt with either blame or shame? What might ensure that the hurts we receive do not make us bitter, passing on harm to ourselves and those around us, and making us prisoners of our past?

How Not to be Half Psychopathic

We suggested that the psychopath who does 'evil' crimes is one in whom the vulnerable, empathic self has been tormented out of existence. In Kalsched's terms, the inner child has died and only the 'caretaker' remains, desperate to crush any sign of weakness in himself or others. The psychopath relates to nobody else as a reality outside him; he relates only to the stories he tells about others, as possible sources of power, pleasure or danger to him. But he himself becomes less than richly real, likewise confined to the story he tells about himself.

One critic said of Al Pacino's depiction of the gangster who is the 'hero' of *Scarface* that 'the attempts to flesh out a character cut from inch-thick cardboard are hopeless.' But I suggest that Pacino's brilliance was precisely the terrifyingly convincing way in which he portrayed the 'inch-thick cardboard cutout' character of the psychopathic gang-leader Montana. In Chapter 5 we noted Hannah Arendt's description of Eichmann as superficial and banal. Nobody to my knowledge has won an Oscar for their portrayal of Hitler or Stalin (though in 1996 Forest Whitaker did win one for his Idi Amin in *The Last King of Scotland*). It is very hard to portray such characters in a deep or profound way. To be deep they would need to be characters fleshed out with human concern, moral dilemma, awareness of conflicting need, and a sense of their own ambiguities and temptations. (Actually this does happen at certain moments in *Scarface;* it is Montana's refusal to kill children that finally precipitates his ruin.) There is no evidence that these tyrants were humanly fleshed out in any of those ways, so the actor has either to portray them superficially, or falsely.

However, a telepathic visitor from another planet, who had access to our thoughts and feelings, might well see us all on more of a continuum than we would like. At one extreme would be the saint who really does engage with others without mediating myths. At the other extreme would be what we call the psychopath who has no possibility of remorse, because all sense of others' vulnerability is obscured by his own need to cover up his own. As a result he is all the time reacting to the desire, fear or rage others evoke in him. But most of us would be in between. We do experience others, but only through the distorting mists of our own reactions and our own need to protect our story of ourselves. Sometimes these mists part and there are moments of genuine empathy and relationship. But often even in what is often regarded as our noblest moments – like 'falling in love' – we are seeing each other through the lens of our need, and projecting onto others either what we want to be there or what we fear might lurk there.

My relationship with a man who is a bishop, for example, will be mediated through several layers of misty narratives. There will be the narratives various elements of society used to describe bishops. One – probably the most respectful – will be the Church's narrative that says the bishop is a revered successor of the apostles, whose flame-shaped miter proclaims that the Holy Spirit rests upon him as it did on them. Another will be a narrative that regards bishops as tyrants who are mainly to blame for the purveying of unscientific superstition. Then there will be the narratives the man tells himself and others about his relation to these narratives. Some of these narratives will be told in body language. Maybe the bishop sails along, paunch foremost, head tilted slightly back, as if he were wearing robes even when he is not. Or maybe he goes about with a jaded, sheepish, hangdog look as if he wished he weren't wearing vestments even when he is. Or maybe he wears jeans and a T-shirt, exudes bonhomie and invites people to call him Dave, when his real name is Bartholomew. Whichever it is he will be speaking a narrative about how he the man relates to the narratives about bishops. What he cannot do is just be the man and pretend the bishop narratives do not exist.

Finally there are the narratives I am consciously and unconsciously telling as I relate to this man. Maybe my story is that of an ecclesiastical climber; I think of the bishop as a source of preferment and, whether consciously or unconsciously, edit what I say according to what I think will impress him. Or maybe I am a rebel inheriting from my past bitter experiences of fathers and authority figures. The bishop immediately reawakens these narratives and I find myself vacillating between provocation and cringing, as if anticipating some remark that will put me down. Or I may be a successful academic who despises this representative of superstition, and find myself mentally pouncing on his remarks in order coldly and sarcastically to tear them apart for their lack of logic. Then in a quite inappropriate context where the narratives of bishop-reverence prevail, I find to my alarm that one of these vitriolic pounces is being acted out in real conversation by me!

What I am contending is that our responses to one another have a 'psychopathic' element, whereby we relate as cardboard figures in a story with our humanity edited out. Moreover the narratives are fraught with unstated violence: the competitive aggression of the climber, that forces him to disclaim aspects of his humanity that might not please; the shame and rage of the rebel; the icy vitriol of the academic. How can we disentangle ourselves from this miasma of interpenetrating narratives? How might we flesh ourselves out again into our full, complex humanity, free from these imprisoning narratives?

One way might come through the kind of calamity from which comedy and tragedy are spun. If the bishop and I encountered each other in the same massage parlor, or drunk at a gay party, or hijacked in a terrorist cell, narratives contrary to our normal public narratives would have to emerge! We would, perhaps, begin to meet as real people. But these are not the kind of happenings either of us would be likely to aim for...

Mindlessly Spinning Yarns

A factor that makes it harder to meet as human beings is the modern sovereignty of the individual ego. Modernity involves a battle between two narratives already noted in Chapter 4. For the traditionalist 'right,' the ego is locked in a perpetual battle to master its animal nature and become autonomous and responsible. For the 'left,' the battle is between the originally innocent self and the oppressive structures and ideologies the 'system' imposes on it. The left tries to understand the harms people do by reference to their conditioning by the system; the right sees such 'soft' attempts as undermining personal responsibility. What both left and right have in common is a typically modern kind of dualism, in which the center stage is held by a self who has to be 'against' something.

What both fail to see is that the self is its own worst enemy. Anyone who has explored the self through therapy or meditation will know how the self is forever telling stories about itself, and following through programmatic scripts without any of the freedom it likes to ascribe to itself. In Paul Scott's novel, *The Birds of Paradise* (1979, p. 235), the hero concludes by reflecting that he has learned

> how vulnerable is the illusion that a man has of his own importance, not of his importance to others, but of his importance to himself, and how to speak of what drives him to sustain the illusion, of the means he finds to drive himself, of the dark that falls on him when the illusion is gone, is virtually impossible.

What can stop us mindlessly spinning yarns about the world to sustain our own importance to ourselves, and begin mindfully to engage with the world as it is beyond our scripts?

I suggest that the answer lies in a kind of detachment that is the very opposite of disclaimer. The poem – based on a vivid dream – illustrates this as a kind of parable. The prostitute literally wears her wounds on her sleeve, offering her hurt to the priest. A parallel is suggested with Christ offering his wounded body and blood. Some may find the parallel blasphemous, and the priest certainly recoils. He sees the woman as more like Medusa, the goddess who turned those who looked at her to stone. Her wound has opened a wound in him, but he has to disclaim it. 'I hate blood, at all costs I must keep my life inside.' His wounds must not show; as a priest his desire must not be seen. So he denies both wound and longing and turns away. But what makes him need to reject her is his inability to separate her wounds and need from his own. Because he cannot disentangle them in his heart he has to disentangle her from him physically. Had he been more detached, he would have less need to deny her – or himself.

The secret of the healing of wounds lies in a detachment from our and others' self-sustaining narratives that enables us to engage with the reality of both. In Buddhist terms of course the self is only story; the reality there is a karmic wave on the surface of Emptiness, or what Thich Nhat Hanh calls 'interbeing.' The relation between us is more real than any self existing on its own; the charged energy between the priest and the prostitute uncovers the ocean they share, undercutting the priest's story of his own identity.

Detachment may sound like disclaimer, but it is our recoil from pain that drives us to disown and repress it. To be detached is not to adopt some mystical indifference beyond pleasure and pain, but to still our automatic reactions to pleasure and pain and the tales we spin around them. To be able simply to hurt, without recoil or repression, is the very opposite of disclaimer.

Therapy and the Puppet-Self

The role of the therapist and counselor is surely to offer a safe space free from the narratives of judgment, condemnation and shame that have afflicted the client; a space where the client can bring ancient and recent wounds from the darkness of repression to the light of day and the fresh air where they can heal. According to the founder of 'client-centered therapy' Carl Rogers (1951), the 'unconditional positive regard' of the therapist gives the client the psychic space in which shame or guilt or rage can uncoil out of the cramped spaces in which they are accustomed to live, and unfurl their originating hurts. The therapist does not 'heal' the client; the client's wounds heal themselves when given this kind of time and space, just as physical wounds heal themselves when at the right time we take the tight bandages off and expose them to the air.

The process of therapy generally is one of 'remembering in order to forget.' The client is helped to remember rightly the original situation in which harm was done, together with all the feelings of pain, in order that the latter, long repressed, may discharge itself in a safe place that will not impact back on the client in further hurt or shame. The therapist's role is not to intervene or diagnose or comfort – all of which would be to impose power over the client or in some way to take his world and her pain from him – but simply to be there with the client and protect his own space, so that this can happen in his own time.

There is no doubt that therapy and counseling have made a tremendous impact. For many in the secular West they have replaced religion as the place people now turn to for healing of the suffering or disoriented mind. Whereas religion is often perceived – and often rightly – as imposing its own narratives on people's biographies, and so exercising a covert power, therapy and counseling, in their different ways, are seen as empowering the client and putting him in charge of his own life. The 'client-centered' therapist simply helps the client find his own narratives to interpret his experience, and his own values to live by. The 'psychodynamic' therapist will have her own framework – Freudian, Jungian or other – to interpret the client's experience, but even so she will not offer this interpretation to him on a conscious level; the Freudian or Jungian narratives will rather condition the space within which the client is slowly enabled to take mastery of his life. The process is normally one of strengthening the ego (Freud) or the self (Jung) in the face of the often implacable demands of social narratives (Freudian 'superego') and the hidden, unchosen narratives of the unconscious or Freudian 'id.' From being a puppet whose strings are operated by those hidden narratives, the client learns to pull his own strings and live his own life. Some therapies work differently. That pioneered by Jacques Lacan saw the ego as more of a problem to be overcome than part of the solution. But Lacanian therapy is obscure, remote from the mainstream and generally regarded as heterodox.

However, precisely insofar as the client's self or ego is encouraged to be 'in charge,' therapy and counseling are unable to tackle the narratives the ego spins for itself. If what I suggested is true – that the self is its own worst enemy – that is bad news. If Buddhism is right – that the self's need to sustain itself is the heart of the problem, rather than the solution – or if Christianity is right in its more modest claim that the self is conditioned from its birth by original sin and disordered desire, then therapy can only go so far. The ego will take charge of the client's life, constructing its own stories about what has happened in the past to make it what it is, and its own values concerning what to do to make itself what it wants to be. But there is no way within therapy itself of knowing which narratives are true, which values valid.

At the heart of modern therapy is the modern ideal – promoted by Kant and more radically by Nietzsche – of autonomy. Polonius' motto from *Hamlet* (1.3, l.78–82) reigns supreme: 'To thine own self be true; And it must follow, as the night the day, Thou canst not then be false to any man.' But does it follow? Were Hitler and Stalin not true to themselves and their own Fascist and Communist narratives? Would a good counselor have saved millions of lives by helping them resolve their 'issues'? Did their evils arise from a failure in self-understanding and self-regard, or rather from a psychopathic failure to understand and regard the different stories of others, like the *kulaks* and the Jews?

Rowan Williams argues that, contrary to the premises of therapy, our life stories are not something to which we have exclusive ownership rights.

> In a society frequently dominated by the rhetoric of therapeutic self-discovery... it is possible for therapy to become a tool for denial, a way of neutralizing the perspectives of others or retreating into an enclosed frame of reference in which the story of victimization acts as a total explanation and justification for all the contours of a biography.
> (2000, p. 104)

In this way our own deficiencies can be ascribed to evils in our upbringing: so we are not to blame. Or remorse, which might make me aware of the hurt we have done to others, becomes just a suffering *we* have to bear, until through counseling we overcome our 'neurotic' sense of guilt. For Williams, on the contrary, 'the story that can be told of me does not *belong* exclusively to me,' but to the others with whom my life is entwined. For this same reason Angela West (1996) argues that we are born already entwined in society's story of hurt and harm; so 'in what sense are we born 'innocent' of all that happened before we were born?'

After several years of therapy I personally found myself with many possible narratives about the experiences that made me me, and many possible ways of evaluating what to do now, but no way of evaluating which was true and right. All that happened was that more and more interesting narratives of self-understanding were being spun, taking me further and further from real contact with the narratives of others. Though I pulled my own strings, I was still a puppet – getting more and more entangled with myself! That was what made necessary my journey back to Buddhism and its practices of mindfulness, and eventually to insight meditation.

Insight Meditation: Healing in the Now

Familiar to many in the West is *samatha* or tranquility meditation, in which through regular breathing and single-pointed concentration on an object one reaches a state beyond thought. *Vipassanā* or insight meditation is less well known, but has been pioneered in the West by teachers like the Burmese master Sayadaw U Pandita (2002). It has been adapted for Christian use by the American Episcopalian priest John Cowan (2004) and by the Carmelites Mary Jo Meadow, Kevin Culligan and Daniel Chowning (2007).

Vipassanā begins with the same kind of concentrated attention as *samatha*, but when sensations, feelings and thoughts occur they are 'noted' with non-discriminating attention, before returning gently but firmly to the focal object, which is normally the breath. The aim here is to note the thoughts and feelings but not to spin any narrative around them. The experience itself is carefully distinguished from the feeling tone of attraction, repulsion or indifference associated with it, and care is taken not to feed the latter with further thought. For example one notes hunger pains as 'sensation in the belly,' and distinguishes that sensation from the feeling of aversion one has to such pains; and having noted that, one does not get caught up in thoughts like 'I must be hungry,' 'It's a long time till lunch,' and 'It's stupid they don't allow one to have elevenses on this retreat!'

In time, more persistent bodily feelings or mental states begin to clamor for attention. Then the attention is moved for a while to those sensations and feelings, and the practitioner attends to them again with non-judgmental awareness, experiencing them not as something interesting or distressing 'out there' but from the inside, so to speak, entering into their own reality without spinning narratives about them. In a sense the practitioner is his own therapist, offering his own experiences the same non-discriminating yet empathic space that the therapist strives to offer the client.

Sometimes a bodily sensation brings out a feeling: shoulder tension for example may be experienced as carrying a great burden, or as coiling up in shame. Memories – sometimes traumatic ones – may surface in this process. However, it is important not to speculate about what is going on, and not to build up a biographical history around the memories, but to deal with the present manifestation in mind and body here and now. This makes for a big difference between this approach and therapy with its emphasis on remembering past events rightly. The wound generated in the past is dealt with not by delving into the past, but by bringing out the present feeling, the present manifestation in the body, where through a total non-judgmental attention whenever it presents itself, it can gradually – or sometimes quickly and dramatically – be healed.

In this process we learn to deal with the imprisoning wounds of the past as they exist in the body and the mind now, so as to be liberated into life in the present, living in the now with complete mindfulness. John Cowan, who has introduced *vipassanā* to Christians, describes someone who found his meditation practice faltering. His teacher gave no technical advice, but simply told him, 'You are ignoring something.' This man had had an alcoholic father who had shouted at his mother, or been too drunk to take his son to games at school. He remembered all this, but one day the simple thing he had ignored came to him. 'It hurt… No way should that happen to a child,' (2004, p. 76). Suddenly he was in tears, and he wept for days in quiet corners of the retreat center. At last he was able to meditate again.

The most essential factor in our ability to deal well with the harms we have undergone is surely the courage to say honestly and with feeling, 'I hurt' – rather than buying into a narrative like 'you hurt me' or 'I hurt myself' or 'whatever you do you can't hurt me.' That ability is so simple to state and so hard to learn! When we describe a hurtful experience, what men (especially, I think) most often miss out is the fact that it hurt. That is something meditation can help us attend to, as good therapy (so long as it does not get too carried away by the client's narratives) also can.

I have heard sitting meditation described as 'taking our seat in the universe.' It is as if having been here, there and everywhere in our thoughts and feelings – caught in the chain of cause and effect and imprisoned by the narratives we have constructed about who we are and where we are going – we actually find ourselves living in the only moment that exists, now. As the Vietnamese monk and peace activist, Thich Nhat Hanh (2002) says in relation to walking meditation:

> Everyone walks on the earth, but there are those who walk like slaves, with no freedom at all. They are sucked in by the future or by the past, and they are not capable of dwelling in the here and now, where life is available.

In walking meditation one focuses on the detailed movements of the feet and legs in the same way that in sitting meditation one focuses on the inflow and outflow of the breath. After a while in such meditation, I often have the sensation that I am not moving myself along, but my legs and body are the still point of the world, and that with my legs I am moving the earth underneath me. Of course in relativity theory these descriptions are equally valid: I move relative to the earth; the earth moves relative to me. The Polynesians, apparently, when they paddle a boat from one island to another, see themselves as bringing the far-off islands near, and pushing their home islands far away, by their rowing action. In mindfulness, it could be said, we see the here and now as the real point, where the action is. Of course I have intentions, but they are acting in me here and now to bring imagined possibilities into this here and now. And I have memories, but they are traces left in the here and now of my mind of what has already moved away into non-existence. Intentions and memories exist only as what is coming toward or receding from this 'boat' of consciousness paddling in the here and now.

Anyone who has played a sport – tennis for example – will be aware of how important it is to let your play with the racket here and now be for you as the paddle is for the Polynesian rower. That does not mean you forget the state of the game so far, or your intention to win. But you need to release yourself from conditioning by the feelings those factors evoke. If you are feeling, 'Help, I'm not doing well,' or 'I've just got to win this shot or I'm sunk,' or 'He's playing poorly – I can relax,' then the whole tone of your game will deteriorate. You need to be playing not with your stories and feelings, but with your racket.

The Blessing of Unfulfilled Desire

So living in the now does not mean living like goldfish, which are reputed to forget everything that happened more than five seconds ago, so that each time they swim around their bowls they have forgotten they have been at the same place before! We do not abandon all memory and attention, but experience the present as the only moment at which these touch reality. We are able to catch the moment when feelings feed themselves with narratives and so give rise to desires. That subtle process is brought to the light of consciousness, where I can assess it and maybe frame better alternative intentions.

For example, in a seminar someone may haughtily defeat my argument. Without mindfulness I will experience unacknowledged feelings of humiliation and aversion toward that person. Then I will feed that feeling with conscious thoughts of how arrogant that person is, and before I know it – without catching my intention – I will find myself saying something designed to 'put that person in their place.' But if I have a mind trained by meditation I will be able to note the emotions arising in myself, and see the narrative about them constructing itself in my mind, and the intention forming. That offers me several points at which I can intervene. I can attend dispassionately to the feelings of humiliation, but refuse to feed them with the narrative about the person. I can note that narrative forming, but refuse to let it trigger automatically an intention to retaliate. Or I can catch the intention to retaliate before it has actually formed the words designed to humiliate the person.

This makes me free. I can choose to take no action. I can choose a more constructive action – like acknowledging the truth in the person's criticism, but putting my point in a better way that answers it. Or if after consideration I really do think the person needs to be countered in some way, I can pursue my original course, but perhaps modifying it in a way that is more compassionate, and more likely to be received than a cutting riposte.

It is difficult, perhaps, for those of us reared in an ego-centered society – and often burdened with a distorted understanding of Freud – to acknowledge that there can be blessing in deciding not to fulfill our desires. We have come to see freedom as a matter of getting what we want rather than deciding what to want. Deciding not to go after what we desire sounds like repression. But repression is a matter of disowning desires and driving them into the unconscious. *Vipassanā,* by contrast, makes us fully attentive to our desire in a totally non-judgmental way, recognizing that sin lies not in the contents of our minds but in our intentions and actions in the world. But from the standpoint of non-judgmental attentiveness we can make a free decision about whether acting on those desires would benefit us and others or not. And if not, we can bless the desire and let it go. If it comes back, we can say hello again and repeat the process.

If I act out of this freer perspective, I cease to be chained by instinctive animal reactions of fight or flight, and automatic human scripts that describe life as a competitive battle in which I am always having to fight my own corner. I am 'standing astride my humanity,' neither asserting it in pride nor hiding it in shame. Or (unashamedly mixing metaphors) I am taking my own unique seat in the universe, which is neither above nor below all the other seats, but alongside the myriad of other sacred beings in the universe.

Ultimately the goal of insight meditation is to gain deep practical insight– as opposed to merely intellectual assent – into the three characteristics of existence: suffering, impermanence and no-self. As Cowan puts it, meditation leads us to grasp in practice that happiness does not come from the fulfilling of desires. It enables us to say, 'I hurt,' without being seduced by the narratives whereby society tells us pain can be marginalized. It enables us to acknowledge need without believing all our desires can and should be met – that belief that incessantly nags at us and can make our whole life unsatisfactory. It shows us how all things and all desires arise from nothing and lapse into nothing; nothing remains forever. And it fails to show us any permanent center we could call a self; instead, there are just narratives that tell me, 'This is what I want,' and 'That is what they did to me,' and incessantly buoys up a sense of self that has no ultimate basis.

When we first experience these insights it may feel like 'the dark that falls… when the illusion is gone.' But the dark feeling of vertigo gives way to something else. We are like people who think we have to paddle and paddle (and probably push other people underneath us) in order to keep afloat. It seems a terrible thing to realize there is no 'I' that can keep itself separated from the waves – until we realize that without any 'I' there is, here and now, floating, flow, and freedom.

Global Mind

The particular kind of meditation just described is specific to the Theravada tradition of Buddhism. But it is the Mahayana tradition that has unraveled the implications of the insight gained into suffering, impermanence and no-self. It sees reality as empty and without foundation, just there in its delightful 'suchness.' At the common core of the Mahayana traditions is the ancient Heart Sutra, which is recited daily in Zen and many other monasteries. It teaches that 'all dharmas [things] are marked with emptiness; they are not produced or stopped, not defiled or immaculate, not deficient or complete... There is no suffering, nor origination, nor stopping, nor path... there is no attainment and no non-attainment.' In meditation there is no striving to attain a special state, or to promote or suppress experiences. All things are just as they are. They and we are neither perfect nor imperfect, for no ideal of perfection and no self is there to compare. Hurts are a source of neither shame nor pride; they just are, along with pleasures, experienced as such, and not covered with thought. So the Bodhisattva or Buddhist saint, 'dwells without thought-coverings. In the absence of thought-coverings he has not been made to tremble.' He experiences the bottomless emptiness and impermanence of all things without flinching. And indeed, if there is no idea of a thing to cling to, 'what can go wrong?' (Throughout I have used the old translation by Edward Conze, cited in Humphreys, 1960, p. 114–15).

One criticism often made of Buddhist meditation is that it is self-centered. One can be mindful only of the contents of one's own mind. Mindfulness does not open one to the reality of the other and their experience in the way that might lead to the pathways of remorse and forgiveness, and a life beyond the doing of harm. So though it teaches compassion and egolessness, paradoxically Buddhist techniques make one more self-absorbed and less compassionate.

Part of the answer to this is provided by the Mahayana understanding that the mind that experiences is not the ego's mind but Mind. The Yogacara school teaches that all that exists is Mind, which is conceived of as the totality of experience. While I cling to the ego, of course, I see a limited range of experience as 'my experience' happening in 'my mind.' But there is no ego, only patterns of experience traveling across the sea that is infinite Mind.

The rival Madhyamaka school asked, reasonably, why this should be called 'Mind' when it is not some person's mind; is the 'sea' in which everything is going on not a sheer bottomless emptiness? But the idea of universal Mind persists in this Zen koan of Mumon:

> Two monks were arguing about a flag. One said: 'The flag is moving.'
>
> The other said: 'The wind is moving.'
>
> The sixth patriarch happened to be passing by. He told them: 'Not the wind, not the flag; Mind is moving.'
>
> (Mumon, cited in Reps, 1971, p. 117)

In the same way, when mindful insight is achieved we will not experience a hurt in terms of 'you have hurt me' or even 'I have been hurt,' but 'Mind is hurting' – or even just 'hurt is happening.' That may sound incredibly detached and disengaged – can we imagine a victim of the death camps feeling his sufferings in this way? But the converse is that there is now no felt difference between hurt to another and hurt to myself: whether it is someone far away being tortured, or me wounded here and now, the same experience applies: that which we label 'hurt is happening.' That is how a total detachment leads to a total compassion. My sufferings are Mind's sufferings; someone else's sufferings are equally Mind's sufferings, which are as much 'mine' as anything is.

Abraham's God or Philosophers' God?

The ideas of Mind that experiences all experience, and an Emptiness that is the source of compassion, are the closest the

Buddhist traditions get to an idea of God. The theistic faiths agree that there is one Mind that is conscious of all things, but go further, in two ways.

One is that the divine mind actually creates the things it is conscious of, out of nothing, and creates them as material beings following natural laws that the divine mind has also created out of nothing. This makes God more transcendent in terms of being than the Buddhists' Mind. As the creator of space and time and natural law, God is beyond space and time and nature, whereas Mind is more like the immanent vessel of all that is.

The other is that the analogy with the human mind is pressed further than Buddhist Mind. God can love the beings God creates, provide for them, enter into relationship with them, and even (in the Christian tradition) take on the form and nature of one of his creatures, humankind. This contrast cuts the other way, making God more knowable and lovable than Mind, less transcendent and more immanent in terms of knowing than Mind, let alone Emptiness.

Christianity has always stressed the transcendence and the immanence of God, but different traditions have placed the emphasis differently. Some traditions – known as the apophatic traditions or the *via negativa*, the negative way – emphasize the transcendence. God is the impassible, all-transcending wellspring of being, wholly other and unfathomable. The practical ways of prayer encouraged in this tradition bear a distant resemblance to Buddhist meditation. The desert fathers and mothers sought a perpetual watchfulness in which obsessive thoughts and narratives (*logismoi*) were left behind as the one praying sought a direct and naked encounter with God beyond all concepts. Martin Laird (2006, Chapter 4) describes this in terms of 'three doorways into the present moment.' In the first door, physical and mental distractions are overcome. In the second, the one praying becomes one with their prayer word 'the way a weaver is with the loom, or a dancer with the dance,' (p.

60). And in the third, there is a state of 'vigilant waiting in the silence of just being,' (p. 65). Meadow and others have argued (2007) that the writings of the Spanish Carmelite mystic St. John of the Cross can be harmonized with *vipassanā* to form a liberating pattern of Christian meditation.

But other traditions – including many very popular today – emphasize the personal side of God. God is a Father who loves and provides for his children, sometimes gets angry with them, and grieves and suffers when they sin. He is 'the great companion… the fellow traveler who understands,' (Whitehead, 1985, p. 351). According to many modern theologians, God does not suffer for us only in the body of Christ. Christ shows us what God is eternally like, eternally suffering; our sins actually do God harm. In such traditions mediation and contemplation seldom figure; the point of prayer is to talk to God and call upon his providence in petition for oneself and intercession for others.

What might a Buddhist make of these traditions? Well there are aspects he might see as a hyperbolic, mythological way of describing Mind. When we are conscious of hurt, Mind is conscious of it; Mind is a vessel of perfect and literal compassion. And to say God creates beings could be regarded as another way of saying that Mind thinks beings. And if we wanted to affirm the material reality of beings and the way they obey physical laws (something that some traditions of Buddhism do affirm, though not the main Mahayana schools) this could be interpreted in terms of the regularity and order Mind imposes when Mind thinks beings into being. The 18th century Anglican philosopher George Berkeley regarded beings in the same way, as ideas in the mind of God possessed of various regular and predictable features which God's mind imposed on them.

But there are two elements of the personal understanding of God which no Buddhist could accept. One is that there is a personal providence, whereby God might organize the universe to benefit individuals. This idea of providence only encourages us to see events from an egocentric or ethnocentric perspective. The God 'Who smote the firstborn of Egypt, for his mercy endures for ever' (Psalm 136.10) looks rather less than providential from an Egyptian perspective! The other unacceptable element is the idea that God might actually suffer harm as the result of our sin.

From the point of view of this book and the question of responding to hurt, I think the Buddhists need to be listened to here. For the healing of harms, it is important that we do not think of the world as organized by God to protect our own egos; and that we do not think we could in any way 'damage' God and provoke pathological responses – whether of rage or retribution or deep sorrow – from God. Put bluntly, the transcendent God, or the detached compassionate Mind, can heal us, but the providential suffering God is a 'caretaker' in disguise, and as such will end up perpetuating our harm.

Donald Kalsched, following Edinger and Jung, sees Job in his sufferings as the one who 'faces down' the caretaker God and liberates the transcendent God who restores him. Job's false comforters argue that Job's suffering is a form of punishment that is an aspect Yahweh God's personal providential care of Job. Such a view only plunges Job more deeply into his torment. However, Job has the courage to step out of this framework of vicious caretaking.

> In confronting Yahweh's cruelty, Job neither retaliates… nor does he collapse in defeat and humiliation. He stays astride his humanity, suffering God as God is unable to suffer himself. He expresses his anger, but also his humility in the face of Yahweh's power, and he never loses sight of Yahweh's potential goodness. (1996, p. 98)

God's own answer to Job from the wild tornado makes it clear that what Job has suffered from is the terrible but beautiful chaos in his creation, personified in the awesome Leviathan (Job 41.1–42.3). Job learns to bless this chaotic aspect of destruction and creation. Those who have been hurt – all of us, that is – need to make this move of Job, ceasing to see God as an ordering caretaker who both protects us and punishes us. God does neither. Our sufferings are the sufferings of the one who thought up the Leviathanesque shark and the girl the shark devours, the canker and the rose. If we can refuse shame and blame as we suffer, and stay astride our humanity, this truth can begin to rise in us creatively and forgivingly. As Blake put it, 'The cut worm forgives the plough,' (*Proverbs of Hell,* in 1971, p. 151).

Kalsched describes how his patients, as they are healed, often make the same move from a providential world that revolves around their need to a space that is tougher and more real.

> When… patients get better, even as their outer lives become more animated with their true selves, they go through a mournful period of dreaded loss of their inner worlds — or so it feels to them — a kind of agonizing sacrifice of what feels like their 'childhoods.' They do not want to give up 'God's world'… Yet life in the outer world is beginning to be more real and authentic. (1996, p. 164)

Therapists have to show tough love to help their patients through such a process. Tough impartiality and tender unconditionality are aspects of the same healing love. They are what lead the inner child out of her protected covenant with the 'caretaker' and enable her to get real. The marks of the real are danger, and safety. The real world is dangerous because in it the liberated child has to learn to live with the indifference of God, without magic protection from the consequences of her actions. But it is safe because there is no divine caretaker to turn on her in punitive wrath, but only a God who cannot do other than love her.

If there is a God who survives the loss of our magical childhood world, it will be the God who survived for Job: we might say, reversing Pascal, not the personal, caretaking God of Abraham, Isaac and Jacob, but the austere God of the philosophers and apophatic mystics. If we want to keep the caretaking God, we have to carry the psychic furniture of our nurseries with us all our lives.

But can we really imagine a God who is both indifferent and loving? Theologian Belden Lane asks the same question regarding his experience of God in the 'fierce landscapes' of Mount Sinai.

> Why am I drawn to desert and mountain fierceness? What impels me to its unmitigated honesty, its dreadful capacity to strip bare, its long, compelling silence? It's the frail hope that in finding myself brought to the edge – to the macabre, stone-silent edge of death itself – I may hear a word whispered in its loneliness. The word is 'love'... How, then, is desert terror dissolved into desert love? At what point does the mountain's immovable indifference make possible the deepest caring? In what way do wry, disturbing images of fierce landscapes – carrying us beyond language, into the unintelligible mystery of God – occasion for us an intimacy we might never have dreamed? (1998, p. 61)

Part of Lane's answer is that it is when we are stripped naked of consolations – including the consolations provided by our ideas of God – that we encounter the nakedness of God. For St. John of the Cross that is the essence of the journey up the mountain whose slopes are covered with the word *'nada, nada'* – nothing, nothing – which is where God is. As I put it, it is when the ego drowns that the ocean is embraced, and we know the Buddhist

Emptiness that overflows with compassion.

But Lane also relates a strange passage in 2 Esdras 10.

> A woman whose child has died goes out into the dark night to a remote field and pours out her grief, determined to stay there until she dies. The prophet Esdras speaks to her in the depth of her pain, telling her to 'ask the earth' what pain is all about. No mother grieves like that mother, says Esdras. The earth weeps for every creature to whom she's given birth, for every creature who returns again to her in death. (p. 156)

Discussions of the suffering of God too often confuse hurt and harm. On the one hand the traditionalists argue as if any kind of hurt constituted damage, so that if God suffers at all he is reduced to something less than the almighty God. On the other hand, some argue that if God does not really undergo harm and even destruction on the cross, he cannot be compassionate, or even be our equal in vulnerability. We cannot discuss this whole question now, but from the point of view of this book, if God is to heal our hurts, she must feel them as the hurts they are and yet also offer us the way not to be harmed by them. She must be something like Mother Earth: the sorrow of every death is her own sorrow, yet she is not harmed by the deaths; she continues to be, fully herself.

The resurrection story shows us such a God: *hurt* and wounded by the cross, but not *harmed* by the pain he suffers, nor damaged by the death he dies, but still as much there for us as he ever was, despite the real pain and death. The God who can heal is One not hurt or angered by our deviations, or embarrassed by our shameful acts. (Jesus is described as having most emotions, but shame and embarrassment are not in his repertoire.) Such a God loves not because we are good but simply because (in the words of the Anglican Prayer which traditionally precedes Holy Communion) it is her 'nature... always to have mercy.' Is that God different from the Emptiness that overflows with compassion?

Can Mindfulness be Global?

I cannot answer that question here – I make some attempt to do so in *Buddhist Christianity* (2010, Chapter 8). But the important thing now is to touch on the idea that we can pool our hurts into some kind of broader and deeper ocean that is all sorrow (and joy and other experience). That is what the woman was doing when she let Mother Earth's grief embrace her own. It seems to be what is involved in the practice of 'touching the earth' at Thich Nhat Hanh's Plum Village Community:

> The practice of Touching the Earth is to return to the Earth, to our roots, to our ancestors, and to recognize that we are not alone but connected to a whole stream of spiritual and blood ancestors. We are their continuation and with them will continue into the future generations. We touch the earth to let go of the idea that we are separate and to remind us that we are the Earth and part of Life.
> (Monks and Nuns at Plum Village, 2003)

This suggests a kind of mindfulness that is bigger than individual awareness, tending toward the global. 'Global mindfulness' was the very thing that Chapter 3 envisaged as the opposite of all our attempts to disclaim pain. But at that stage of the argument it was not clear whether it was really possible. We can now begin to see that it might be.

Global mindfulness would involve laying down the burden of the self, and taking up the burden of the earth, and finding it, paradoxically, a lighter burden. For a burden shared with other beings who have taken it up too is a burden that brings us new energy for social action, just as the burden of the self sapped all energy for action for others. (Of course nothing could be more burdensome than carrying both: carrying the earth as 'my' burden, being full of 'my' solutions to the world's problems, or importing my rage and blame into my struggle for the earth. But this is often attempted.) It is the burden taken up by the Bodhisattva of Mahayana Buddhism, who renounces enlightenment in order to save all sentient beings through his merits. It is surely the light and easy yoke and burden which that great Bodhisattva, Jesus, urged his followers to share with him (Matt. 11.30).

The five elements that would take us toward a global mindfulness have already been mentioned. There is, first, practice like *vipassanā* that strips away the narratives of the ego and enables us to experience experience as experience. Of course, the experience focused on is very small – as small as the intake and exhalation of breath. That sounds far from global. But at least, in that small point, I am making contact with the real. I touch and taste the ocean, if only in a drop. The analogy of a pinhole camera springs to mind. The smaller the aperture whereby I let in the light (so long as there is a hole) the sharper the world outside comes into focus on the film. The smaller the aperture whereby I let experience in as I meditate, the sharper the whole world will come into focus in my life.

The second element is an informed knowledge of the world. I need to know what is going on right now as I meditate. That is not to say I should meditate with one eye on the newspaper, or even encourage thoughts and images from the paper to come to my mind as I do so. But I should meditate as one who does know and care. That means not just reading headlines and accounts, but considering reflections on events from different points of view, so that I can develop a broad understanding of what is really causing changes in the world.

The third element consists of practices that bring the wider world into mindful living. As I eat, I should be mindful of the whole process that has brought that food to my table: the ecosystems, the fields or oceans where the food grew, the people who farmed or hunted or fished for it, those who traded it, and so forth. If there is anything unwholesome or exploitative going on in any of these stages, I should be aware of it and if possible change to food that is more 'wholesome' in every sense. Likewise as I go to work I should be mindful of the systems and processes through which I walk – the air, the noises around me, the transport systems. Hanh writes (2007, Appendix A) about mindful eating, walking, smiling, relaxing, telephone answering... innumerable ways in which a kind of global mindfulness can blossom in day to day living

The fourth element is that which transforms knowledge into concern, into something I care about. The practice of intercession belongs here. Rightly understood I do not think intercession is a matter of bending the ear and will of a divine being to make him change what he does in the world. In the churches I attend it is more a simple matter of laying the sufferings of the world before God, letting the big sufferings and my small sufferings touch the global suffering of God, and so piecing together in the community something of God's mind and will for the Earth. A Buddhist would not use 'God' language here, but something very similar is surely going on when Buddhists practice *metta* – 'loving-kindness' – by voicing good wishes towards various categories of being, until finally the loving-kindness reaches out to touch all sorrows and causes of sorrow in the universe. And Buddhist practice always begins or ends with a prayer that the fruits of the practice may benefit not only myself but all beings.

And the fifth element consists in the fact that the practices of meditation and intercession take place in a community that stretches worldwide. Buddhists speak of the Sangha, which is the community of monks and nuns but often interpreted as the community of all those committed to the path to enlightenment. Christians likewise speaks of the Church as both an institution and as the invisible body of all those committed to the way to salvation. In either case there is a community that is spoken of strongly as a single body in which the experiences of those all over the world come together in a single 'mind.' When we meditate or pray we do so as part of that mind, as well as part of universal Mind.

So though the point at which I contact reality is as small as my breath passing through my nostrils, that point of contact can become the focus of a worldwide range of sorrowful and joyful experiences which I have made an effort to learn about; which I have joined up through mindful daily living, prayer and loving-kindness into a single whole; and which is present in those who meditate with me as part of the committed community to which I belong. If so, when I meditate it will not be an individual me meditating, but a Mind that embraces all the joys and sorrows of the world meditating through the focus of my practice. As Christians affirm, we pray truly when it is the Spirit of God praying in us.

If I touch even a little of that, 'I' may still be hurt, but there will be no harm.

Summary

1. We have explored the tragicomic world view that sets harm and responsibility in a creative context, and looked at the interpersonal dynamics of remorse and forgiveness through which the wounds we have dealt each other may be healed. But how do we become the kind of people that can respond in such positive ways to hurt?
2. Much of the time we are somewhere in between psychopaths and saints, seeing one another through the mists of our own desire, rage and delusion. Modern culture exacerbates this by championing the self. It divides us into the 'right,' for which the enemy of the responsible self is irresponsible animality, and the 'left' for which it is

oppressive systems. What both ignore is what Buddhist and Christian traditions see: that the self is its own worst enemy. The problem is how to stop the self-deceiving itself.

3. In therapy and counseling the client is listened to with a non-judgmental empathy that enables her to loosen the grip of others' judgments. But in the end the self may be left to live with its own myths intact.
4. Buddhist insight meditation has ancient techniques for disengaging from automatic reactions and achieving mindfulness about what is actually there in our experience now. But that in itself does not open up a sense of the other's experience.
5. In Mahayana Buddhism, however, it is not the personal ego that experiences, but Mind. Through meditation the ego is dissolved and there is just Mind experiencing. In Christianity, God experiences all as it truly is, and in intercession and contemplation we begin to acquire the Mind of God. Both traditions suggest the possibility of a mindfulness that is not individual but global.
6. But there would be a great danger of simply smuggling our own egocentric need for honor, protection and even vengeance back in under the name of the God who provides for us. We need to distinguish the ego-fulfilling God of providence – 'the God of Abraham, Isaac and Jacob' – from the more austere yet liberating God of the philosophers and mystics.
7. Christian traditions of intercession and contemplation might blend with Buddhist traditions of insight meditation and mindfulness to generate a 'global mindfulness.' In such mindfulness might lie the secret of a positive response to hurt: the 'wounded wisdom' of the title.

Chapter 9

Birthpangs of Light: An End to Harm?

Dies irae

Love is boundless; therefore love denied
owes back blood to the infinite.

Whoever hears a near child yell
and pretends that all is well,
let her scream unheard in hell.

Whoever sees rape on DVD
and makes out it isn't he
relishing the pain, let him ravaged be.

May she who sees her lover's eyes
in envy hurt, and twists desire like wire
into ego's wreath, writhe in fire.

The subtle one who sees the art
and the glory, but is too cold at heart
to praise and bless, accursed depart.

May she who's quiet when a colleague's thwarted
by blame wrongly apportioned
know the greater silence, falling, falling…

May leaders, who know the hurts that blight
those they send away, and don't give a shite,
be dismissed into endless night.

May he who buys fruit of unfair trade,
so blights the tree and lets a people fade
from history, likewise be unmade.

Dies amoris

But love asks, what good would that do me
– the end of the one who would not love me –
when all I love is that beloved should be?

The one who hears the close child cry
I scream to her from infinity
to open the ears of love.

For the man who ravages in fiction
my broken body is in real affliction
till he be vulnerable to love.

She who enjoys her lover's jealousy
my eyes covet, watching restlessly
till closed eyes repose in love.

The clever man who cannot see
his way to worship, is adored by me
when he grows wise enough to love.

The office girl with her blind eye
will never depart from my keen sight
until she stands by what she sees.

Indignant official, who turned away:
I will just stay, and have my quiet say
each day, pending love's remembrance.

To those who take the unjust fruit

I give the leaf, the branch and shoot
of knowledge, till fairness bloom across the sea.

Dies illa
Love is boundless, therefore love denied
draws the blood of the infinite.

We say betrayal must burn in hell,
but there love singed – the scriptures tell –
the wings of his divinity
to enjoy our treacherous company.

May love's eternal labor pain
not prove fruitless or in vain
to lift us fools from endless shame:
let hurts be birthpangs of the light.
Eschaton – based on the 'Dies Irae'

Sometimes when asked for forgiveness people utter a remarkably beautiful phrase: 'It's water under the bridge.' The sense is that the hurt has passed away like water flowing away under the bridge where we are. The phrase allows the past to be past – with quite a Buddhist sense of impermanence and flux – so that 'on the bridge' so to speak a 'new we' may be crystallized. This does not mean literally forgetting the sin, but it does mean letting it go, and no longer calling it to mind.

But for many, forgetting evil done and suffered involves a kind of 'cheating,' offensive to those who have suffered it and dishonest for those who have caused it. In response to the Holocaust many framed the slogan 'Never forget, never forgive!' while others, as noted, are prepared to 'forgive but never forget.' The continuing importance of Remembrance Day nearly a century after the deaths it was designed to commemorate bears witness to the value we attach to remembering past sufferings. It is almost as if the remembering bestows eternal life on the departed: 'Age shall not weary them, not the years condemn. From the rising of the sun to its setting we will remember them.' This corporate remembrance seems to be becoming even more important at the time when very few can be alive who now personally remember those who died in the First World War.

For some, past evils can be forgiven and redeemed, but not by forgetting; rather by remembering in a different light, in which what seemed negative becomes part of our story. To forget such misfortunes would seem to be to repress and disown part of who we are.

So there are voices saying we must remember for the victims' sake, and others saying we must remember for our own integrity. Between them these voices would seem to carry the consensus: that we should never forget past hurts and harms.

But there are contrary voices, not least that of the Hebrew God:

> I, I am he who blots out your transgressions for my own sake, and I will not remember your sins. (Isaiah 43.25)
> I have swept away your transgressions like a cloud, and your sins like mist; return to me, for I have redeemed you.
> (Isaiah 44.21)
> They shall all know me, from the least of them to the greatest, says the Lord, for I will forgive their iniquity, and remember their sin no more.
> (Jeremiah 31.34, echoed in Hebrews 8.12)

In these and similar passages God declares not that he will forget sins (which would rather negate the divine omniscience!) but that God will no longer remember them or call them to mind. God will 'blot them out' – as if erasing a debt from the account book. The sin will no longer be a debt owed, or stand in the way of the relationship. This is surely what we mean when we talk about water under the bridge.

So despite all the need to remember, should we hope in the end to 'let the waters flow under the bridge' till there are no longer any hurts or memories of harm? Or should we rather hope for the flow of the waters of harm's recompense, praying in the words of Amos (5.24), 'let justice roll down like waters, and righteousness like an ever-flowing stream'? There are two radically opposed hopes for our final future, which my opening poem expresses in terms of two voices. A human voice cries out for the duplication of harms in retributive justice, while a divine voice persists gently in unconditional love until people repent and are healed of their harmful desires. Of course what the latter voice wants is justice too: but a healing, rather than retributive justice.

An End to Harm and 'Evil'?

Behind these deep issues lies a broader one: whether harms are somehow necessary to our existence, or coterminous with humanity, or whether we should envisage and strive for a time when harm is no more. Again, this seems to be the hope held out by the Bible:

> God will wipe every tear from their eyes.
> Death will be no more;
> mourning and crying and pain will be no more,
> for the first things have passed away. (Rev. 21.4)

This is not the same as to hope for a time without hurt as defined in the introduction. (That, too, may be envisaged in this passage, though only after the terrible series of harms described in Revelation.) From what we know about biology, history and the other sciences it would seem inevitable that people will go on getting hurt: by natural disasters, by accidents, by the sheer clash of different personalities, by the 'thousand natural shocks that flesh is heir to,' (*Hamlet* Act 3, scene 1). But the tenor of the preceding three chapters has been that hurts need not harm us, that hurts to our bodies and minds do not need to cause us damage. We can hold hurts still in a tragicomic perspective that attaches no deep blame. We can feel remorse for hurt done and forgiveness for hurt received, and so restore one another from harms once done. And we can allow ourselves to hurt without jumping onto the narratives that escalate us into blame, shame and disclaim. In these ways, though we may still hurt, we may bring harm to an end in us.

Whether or not we can do these things depends not on the intensity of the hurt so much as on the state of the self and society and the narratives we tell about our hurts. Maybe we can envisage a state of affairs where hurts no longer harm us, and that would mean too that they never generate the tough complexes of harm we call evil. And though it would be naively utopian to think that one day people will never hurt each other at all, maybe they will never do 'evil,' never do deliberate harm, because they are freed from the narratives that incite them to do so.

That would be a state of affairs where waters are allowed to flow under the bridge; where hurts are felt as *ultimately* fleeting affairs. This would not necessarily mean that hurts never lasted a long time, or that the consequences of hurt never needed to be wrestled with for perhaps a considerable duration. But it would imply a horizon beyond which we let all harm finally sail beyond our ken. And since calling harm to mind is a kind of persistence of harm in us, an end to all harm would have to include the end of the calling of harm to mind, as just discussed.

This chapter will explore how harms often do come to an end, through the natural process of healing. Then it will touch upon the issue of whether we need to deal with serious harm by harming (punishing) the harmers. For if we do need to do that, harm will generate further harm and cannot be brought to an end. In this connection the chapter will investigate the bold and seldom really considered Christian claim that God in Christ has brought the law and its punishment to an end, and then look at communities in which criminal justice has been brought to an end and replaced by a model that has healing rather than retribution at its heart. Finally it will return to the wider issue of whether our ultimate hope can realistically be an end to harm and the memory of hurt.

An End to Wounds? Healing

We say 'time heals all wounds,' but time itself heals nothing. It is the process of healing that makes wounds disappear, and those processes take time. And they are not automatic. We cannot accelerate them, but we can retard or even stop them. And some wounds cannot be healed: they cause death.

Of course, we would like to accelerate the healing process. As doom encroaches, Macbeth cries out to his doctor for some healing potion that will instantly dissolve the bitterness of his remorse:

> Canst thou not minister to a heart diseas'd,
> Pluck from the memory a rooted sorrow,
> Raze out the written troubles of the brain,
> And with some sweet oblivious antidote
> Cleanse the stuff'd bosom of that perilous stuff
> Which weights upon the heart? (Act 5, scene 3, line 37f.)

But the doctor replies with calm rationality: 'Therein the patient must minister to himself.' Macbeth was calling for a magic cure, but the doctor just tells him that if he wants to be rid of the pain, he must work to heal his own wounds. Like Macbeth, our contemporary world increasingly looks for instant cures. And our doctors – more expert but less wise – are often only too ready to prescribe 'oblivious antidotes' to pains deriving from bereavement, remorse, inner crisis and the like, which we might do better to feel and minister real healing to ourselves.

As you would expect in a book about hurt and harm, every chapter except (significantly perhaps) the two on 'evil' has referred to 'healing.' But what is healing? Chapter 5 quoted Augustine as offering the wound as a case of the privation of good. The wound is a 'negation' of healthy flesh, and wounds cannot exist without flesh that is at least alive. However, one sign of life is that wounds are healing. They represent a profound case of entelechy, the power of matter to order itself. Wounds represent a negation of a negation, for they are not the harm itself but the conversion of the harm to good.

So does the healing of wounds hold the secret of a world beyond all harm? To see, let us explore how bodily wounds heal. There are three medical stages.

1. **Inflammation**. The wound hurts intensely. The body may go into shock, withdrawing vital blood from the wound. Later, blood may flow in and congeal into a scab protecting the wound from infection. The wound may become inflamed as it swells with fluids protecting the body from infection. The emphasis is on isolating the dangers the wound poses and protecting the organism.
2. **Repair**. A constructive phase begins. Collagens move in to rebuild strength and bind the wound together. Blood vessels and other structures regenerate. By the same wonderful way in which a body knows how to grow what structures where, it knows how to repair thewound.
3. **Remodeling**. A much more gradual process that may take months or years. The initial 'emergency structures' that were put in place at stage 2 are slowly replaced by softer, stronger and more pliant tissues. Slowly the wound disappears, sometimes as if it had never been there, but in more serious

cases leaving a scar.

Wounds in the psyche caused by bereavement or deliberate attack heal in the same sort of way, though often taking longer.

1. **Denial and Rage.** The person may go into shock, unable to accept what has happened. This may give way to rage, an urge to hit back, as if this would undo the damage. These are the quick, natural reactions whereby the person defends himself and pushes the hurt as far away as possible.
2. **Grief**. The person may enter a long time of depression. Outwardly he may seem to be doing very little, unable to face the ordinary tasks of life. This is because the mysterious energies of the soul are at work repairing the inner damage.
3. **Regeneration**. The person accepts the loss or hurt and moves on, building a new life. Though an indelible scar of sorrow may remain, it does not impede the new life.

Physical healing can be helped by appropriate actions – applying antiseptic or antibiotics and putting on a plaster to help stage 1; stitches and vitamins to help the binding together at stage 2. Neglect can delay the healing or even stop it and cause death. In the same way we can help mental healing – expressing rage in appropriate ways that do not cause further damage at stage 1; talking to friends and perhaps counselors, and being kind to ourselves and not rushing to get on with life at stage 2 (or in some cases the apparent opposite, getting on with life to engage our superficial attention so that the inner work can go on at a deeper level).

But are there mental wounds that cannot heal? Harms so grievous that we can never emerge into regeneration? Certainly the healing process can slow down to a halt; and people do sometimes die of grief at loss of a loved one. Nevertheless

Buddhism and Christianity would unite in saying, finally, 'No.' Both faiths hold out the hope that all will come to a state in which there are no more wounds, no more suffering, even if that is not in this life. We shall return to those hopes at the end of the chapter.

But there are some who say that some wounds are wrongs that cry out, not for healing, but for 'righting'.

Retribution and Its Drawbacks

> Listen; your brother's blood is crying out to me from the ground! And now you are cursed from the ground, which has opened its mouth to receive your brother's blood from your hand. (Gen. 4.10–11)

In this significant story, already introduced in Chapter 1, God speaks to Cain following Cain's murder of his brother Abel. The blood he has shed cries out for vengeance. But whereas elsewhere the command to avenge death by death seems to come from God (e.g. Gen. 9.6), here the cry comes as a curse from the lowest place, from the ground that has itself just been cursed because of Adam's sin (Gen. 3.17), the ground along which the snake of temptation has been condemned to slide (3.14). Though elsewhere retribution seems to be a duty of God, here it seems to belong to a lowly, corrupt state of affairs, while God actually protects Cain from retribution.

Where does our need to punish come from – from the divine, or from a low place? Many reasons for punishing wrongdoers been put forward, but the main ones would seem to be:

- **Retribution**: to give justice to the victim by paying the criminal back for what he has done.
- **Restoration**: to make the criminal pay back, so far as he can, what he has taken or the harm he has done. Restorative justice has strong advocates today.

- **Just Distribution:** to restore the equality the criminal has destroyed by exploiting the victim. (This is a radicalization of restoration, which might, in the interests of equality, punish the over-wealthy in order to redistribute to the poor.)
- **Expression** of society's abhorrence of a crime, or of society's valuing of the victim.
- **Deterrence:** making the criminal a negative example for other people who might otherwise be tempted to commit a crime.
- **Detention**: confining to a safe place someone likely to cause harm if released.
- **Reform** of the criminal.
- **Healing** of the broken relationship the crime has created between criminal and victim, by creating he conditions for reconciliation.
- **Reconciliation** itself.

This is not the place to enter into a discussion of the strengths and weaknesses of these aims, which is a major unresolved issue in ethics. It is worth noting that the aims are not for the most part incompatible. A good theory of justice and punishment might well embrace several of them.

But our immediate subject is retribution. It is a strong instinct, when hurt, to want to 'get even,' seek to make people 'pay for their crimes,' and to 'get our own back.' What is this 'own' that has been taken from us? Perhaps it refers simply to something we rightfully own which the criminal has stolen from us. Or perhaps, more subtly, it refers to the fact that our 'own' self is diminished and our sense of self worth is reduced by crimes committed against us. Or both. When we speak of 'getting even' with the one who has hurt us the same framework of understanding is implied. The offender has treated us as inferior, a means to his ends. Through retribution – ideally – we seek to recreate the equality in which we can relate to one another as fellow human beings, neither of whom should be subordinated to the other's ends. In that sense retribution may be seen as serving restoration, and even just distribution and healing. 'Ideally' – but of course in practice retribution often seeks to humiliate the offender, and seldom achieves equality. It more often ends in mutual denigration than mutual respect.

So part of the desire to get our own back is quite logical. If a boy who already has an apple steals his sister's apple he creates an injustice: he now has two apples and his sister has none. It is reasonable to make him give her apple back. But what if the sister has been given two apples by the parents, while he has been given none? Some would say he has still stolen an apple and should give it back, others that he was rectifying an injustice and created a fairer situation that should remain. Restitution and just distribution begin to part company.

And what if the boy, instead of taking his sister's apple, cuts off her hand, or kills her? How can she be recompensed? How can she get her own – hand or life – back? Should the boy's hand be cut off; should he be killed? That is what the Old Testament *lex talionis* says: 'show no pity: life for life, eye for eye, tooth for tooth, hand for hand, foot for foot,' (Deut. 19.21, compare Exod. 21.24, Lev. 24.20). At the time of writing, in Saudi Arabia a gruesome example of this law has emerged, amounting to 'a spine for a spine.' A man attacked another with a cleaver and damaged his spine, crippling him. In retaliation the judge has been asking hospitals if they could damage the assailant's spine, crippling him in the same way. (*Guardian*, 19 August 2010.)

The *lex talionis* is often affirmed as the basis of law and punishment, and not only in Hebrew and Sharia law. A less literalistic principle of retribution underlies much of Western law. For the philosopher Immanuel Kant, for example, an injustice creates a kind of metaphysical 'imbalance' which the retributive punishment restores. Kant was drawing, of course, on the ancient symbol of the scales of justice.

However, at this point retribution begins to look odd. The metaphysics of balance and the symbol of justice correspond with no practical reality. Retribution does not *really* give people back their 'own' – the living reality they have lost and grieve. From the point of view of the sister, the severing of her bother's hand would not give hers back. His execution would not restore her to life. From the point of view of the parents, the punishment only increases injustice. Rather than one maimed or killed children, they now have two. In the same way continuing tit-for-tat vendettas like those between Israelis and Palestinians undoubtedly have the effect of reducing justice as a whole for Israelis and Palestinians alike. All have to live in a fear, and a lack of development, they do not deserve.

So though retribution appears to many to be the essence of justice, in practice it can perpetuate and deepen injustice for everyone concerned. I often marvel when, after a long campaign to see justice done, and a sentence is delivered on the person who murdered their child, people rejoice. Do they not realize, I wonder, that this will not give them back the child they lost? Retribution works with apples because it is really restitution that is achieved. But there are severe limits to what the search for retributive justice can do for the tortured or abused, whose lives may be marred forever and impossible to restore. In some cases hunger for justice may actually impede healing, imprisoning people at the first stage cited above – rage.

Some argue that retributive punishment is a way of expressing society's concern for the victim. It is true that people often feel let down or undervalued when a punishment seems insufficient relative to the harm they have undergone. But it is a strange thing to express value for one person by harming another. Much better, surely, to do so by helping the person to recover from the crime; in which case the purpose of justice has moved decisively from retribution towards restoration and healing.

If we then ask why such an unsatisfactory idea as retributive justice should have such a hold – underlying the widespread code of vendetta as well as formalized criminal justice – part of the explanation may lie in the need for a scapegoat as explored at the end of Chapter 1. The cry for vengeance comes from a low place.

An End to Punishment and Shame? Atonement

> You have heard that it was said, 'An eye for an eye and a tooth for a tooth.' But I say to you, do not resist an evildoer. But if anyone strikes you on the right cheek, turn the other also... (Matt. 5.38–9)

So Jesus with his usual bluntness overturns the *lex talionis,* and teaches us to live beyond the punishments of the law, in non-violent generosity and grace. And in his Passion he exemplifies what he taught. There Jesus neither fights his interrogators, nor submits masochistically to abuse. Like Job, he stands astride his humanity, allowing neither violence nor mockery nor criminal sentence to shame or anger him. As noted, the gospels carefully refrain from making him a warrior hero or a sacrificial scapegoat. They show him in tragicomic stillness, enduring in the awesome nakedness of God, even in death; then walking free into the new world of the resurrection.

It was no doubt the vulnerable yet powerful way in which Jesus had dealt with his mockers, torturers and judicial murderers, and the way his strength-in-weakness was proven, by the experience of resurrection, to be stronger than death, that led the disciples to a profound sense of the old order of law and punishment coming to an end in Jesus. On the one hand that order had shown its evil face in putting its supposed guarantor – God – to death in the person of Christ. On the other, the punishment had not succeeded in either shaming or permanently annihilating this Jesus.

In the earliest writings of the Church, we find many attempts to conceptualize this sense of the old law coming to an end, and something radically new beginning, in the death and triumph of the non-violent Jesus. We have already explored the tragicomic understanding expressed in Mark's Gospel. But for a more explicit understanding we need to turn to Paul. Paul regarded the law and its sacrifices and punishments as a temporary expedient, being 'our disciplinarian until Christ came.' However, 'Christ redeemed us from the curse of the law by becoming a curse for us' (Gal. 3.13), so 'now we are discharged from the law, dead to that which held us captive,' (Rom. 7.6). Christ is 'the end of the law' (Rom. 10.4), for 'he has abolished the law with its commandments and ordinances, so that he might create in himself one new humanity,' (Eph. 2.15). The 'curse' of the law is punishment by suffering and ultimately death. But in Christ, God was not the one who apportioned these punishments, but the one who received them. That turned the whole notion of God and punishment upside down

Or at least, it should have. In fact it was only for the first three centuries that the Church showed a commitment to non-violence. After the empire became Christian with Constantine, Christians reconciled themselves to at least some kinds of war. And they wholeheartedly supported the state in laws which included interrogation by torture, mutilation and capital punishment. How did this happen so easily?

In the words of an anonymous 18th century Italian hymn,

Abel's blood for vengeance
cried unto the skies,
But the blood of Jesus
For our pardon cries.

We have noted how Abel's blood cried out for retribution, but from a low, cursed place. Jesus' non-violent and forgiving death cried out from high up on the cross, 'Father, forgive them, for they know not what they do,' (Luke 23.34). Even the most heinous crime, the judicial murder of an innocent man, is seen – by the one Christians follow as divine – as a matter of ignorance rather than evil intent, and as such forgivable. But there is an unresolved question here, a gap in understanding which allows for the reintroduction of a vindictive God and vindictive punishment.

The question is: to whom does Jesus' blood cry out? The early Church had not answered this clearly. One main understanding was that Satan the Accuser had humanity in his grip. Jesus cries out to the Accuser to accuse humanity no more. In return for receiving God's own Son, Satan does let humanity go. But the Son, being divine, escapes by rising again from the dead, leaving Satan defeated, his prison empty of folk. There is something charming about the way, in this tale, God becomes the trickster, while Satan is the legalist, stern and inflexible but therefore easily outwitted! But many Christians felt uneasy about such wily dealing on the part of God.

In the 11th century, Archbishop Anselm of Canterbury proposed a view that made God more respectable. According to this, the cry for pardon was made to God the Father. God's non-negotiable honor demanded a stern retribution for the sins of humanity. To be sure, God the Father loved humankind, but love alone was not enough to enable him to waive his demand for punishment. So the Father sent his own Son to be a perfect satisfaction for his honor, so that he could forgive the rest of humanity. Satan dropped out of the equations. Anselm's account never prevailed among the Eastern Orthodox, but became normative for Roman Catholics. And in the variation called 'penal substitution' – for which Jesus accepts the death penalty God ought by the demands of justice to have imposed on us, so we can go free – it became a required belief in many Protestant churches.

To most Buddhists, and many Christians today, this seems an even stranger tale than the tricking of Satan. Either God the Father does not quite share the forgiveness and non-violence of his Son's teaching, but has an inflexible, punitive streak; or the Father does share those qualities of his Son, but is subject to a punitive law that transcends even the Father's power to alter. In the one case the Son ceases to be a full revelation of the nature of God, and becomes a kind of manifestation of God's gentler, more forgiving side. A hidden, punitive side of God remains in the Father, to be unleashed in terrifying violence on his own Son. In the other case, God is indeed altogether Christlike, but weak, being unable to bend the inexorable laws that demand retribution. For some reason, God has to appease them, just in the same way we have to, through sacrifice and punishment.

Both scenarios have heretical implications. In the one case, Father and Son do not wholly share the same nature; God is split into a retributive Father and a loving Son. In the other, retribution represents a Law above God, in the face of which the latter is less than Almighty. Yet it seems to me that one or other of these scenarios has tended to float half-acknowledged in the imagination of Western Christianity and in what theologian Timothy Gorringe (1996) has termed its 'structure of affect,' predisposing people towards a retributive approach to justice. The law and its punishments were now written, either into the mind of God, or into something greater to which even God must submit. The cross carries the message of forgiveness – but also tells us how colossal was the punishment we should have rightly borne ourselves!

Those who by their words or actions reject the cross of Christ should therefore, logically, bear the full weight of that punishment. So, according to Gorringe and others, a logic and an emotional climate was generated that justified retributive punishment including capital punishment. It is highly significant, I note, that retribution began to replace restoration as the basis of justice with the Norman Invasion in the later 11th century, including the period when Anselm was Archbishop of Canterbury. I suspect the relation here is not a simple cause and effect; rather, Anselm was reflecting a changed concept of justice in a theology that then led support to those changes.

Ironically, the advocates of these strange and violent theories see themselves as being faithful to the understanding of Jesus and St. Paul. Yet they have the effect of reversing both the non-violence of Jesus, and Paul's sense of Jesus' death creating a new order beyond the retributive law. While for Paul the cross meant an end to the deep need (discerned by Girard) for scapegoats and sacrifice, satisfaction and substitution atonement theories elevated this human need into a divine – or meta-divine – law (c.f. Heim, 2006).

What is to be done? Should we return, as Denny Weaver suggests (2001), to the older model of crafty victory over Satan? It seems to me that if we take 'Satan' to be a folklore character symbolizing a universal human malaise, this makes sense.

'Satan' – as noted in Chapter 1 – means 'the Accuser.' Originally Satan was a member of the heavenly court. He was, as it were, the Counsel for the Prosecution, whose task was to present to God as he sat in Judgment all the case against a person. He therefore had an important role in sifting people for the truth. In the Book of Job he is allowed to put Job to the test of suffering to see if Job's loyalty to God will be sustained. Only later did Satan degenerate from being the Prosecutor to being the thoroughly evil Slanderer – *Diabolos,* the Devil – who told lies about us, and grew horns and a tail and a fork to torture people forever! There is a place in every society for bringing the case for prosecution, and calling people to account for the harms they have done. But it is not a divinely sanctioned ultimate place.

As Chapter 1 suggested, we have in many ways become a

society in which accusation and blame rule, and accountability and recompense reign as ends in themselves. In short, we are a 'Satanic' society. The notes of comfort, affirmation, transformation and reconciliation are seldom sounded in the press, and seem to have no public role in our law courts and institutions. So many public figures move – in the typical tragic, scapegoat mode – from glory and idolization to scandal and disgrace, and thereafter no more is heard. But God's desire is not to condemn but to bring people to redemption and to friendship with Godself. That is why, whereas the Satan is a subordinate being, the Counsel for the Defense – the Advocate – is the Holy Spirit who in Christian tradition belongs to the Holy Trinity and shares in the very essence of God.

But faced with our human tendency to prefer accusation to comfort, what is God to do? Could he simply intervene and sweep aside these tendencies and establish a new order by force? If he did, how could we, from where we stand steeped in violence, make that new order our own? But imagine a judge who is hearing a murder case, and the jury found the case for the prosecution convincing, and gave its verdict of guilty. But the judge, instead of pronouncing sentence, swaps places with the defendant. The defendant puts on the judge's wig and pronounces the death sentence on the judge, who is led away to execution. The judge would be honoring the legal process with its demands for retributive justice. But only in a formal way. The law would have followed its normal course, and been respected, but for a change of personnel that calls the whole process into question. The result would be a peculiarly disturbing farce, yet also a tragedy as the judge goes on his way to death.

In the same way it seems to me that in the cross God in Christ gives 'Satan' – our human tendency to accuse and scapegoat – his due, but in a way that dethrones those tendencies and calls into question our retributive systems of justice. Instead of establishing a new non-violent order by force (which would be rather a contradiction!) God places himself, not under a law that stands eternal in the heavens, but under the demands of our half-rational, half-crazy penal law. He has allowed himself to be sentenced to death in our place, so telling a tragicomic joke that challenges us to build the new non-violent order ourselves.

Buddhists, of course, would find such ruses strange. Not having believed in a retributive God, there is no need for him to be overturned in this way. Buddhists are already committed in principle to the non-violent order.

An End to Criminal Justice? Healing Justice

Are we up to the challenge? Could a society be built without retributive punishment? This is an immense issue on which many have written, advocating one or more of the alternatives understandings of justice noted above. There is a huge literature today advocating that restoration should replace retribution as the primary focus of our legal systems (e.g. Zehr, 1990 and 2002; Wright, 1991; Hadley, 2001; Braithwaite, 2002; and from a Buddhist perspective Loy, 2001). According to its advocates, restoration was the basis of law in places as diverse as ancient Sumeria, Israel, Babylon and early Rome, the aboriginal first nations in Canada, the Maoris in New Zealand, in Tibet, in early Ireland and Germany, and in England prior to the Norman invasion. Modern systems of criminal justice, it is argued, regard crimes as offenses against the state, for which the state must exact retribution, or put a deterrent in place, or whatever. But this cuts the victim of the crime out of the picture. Justice should focus once more on the victim, restoring her sense of value, which the criminal has trampled down, enabling the criminal to realize the harm he has done, and ensuring that as far as possible he recompenses her for that harm. According to the website www.restorativejustice.org.uk restorative approaches have reduced re-offending rates by some 27%. All of this argument is in harmony with the centrality of remorse and forgiveness argued for in this book.

But recently Jarem Sawatsky has argued (2009, Chapter 2) that this broadening of focus does not go far enough. It still focuses on dealing with specific crimes, committed by individuals against other individuals. It deals mainly with cases referred to it by the state legal system, by means of care offered to victims and harmers, rather than identifying deep social causes of crime and promoting conditions in which harms and crimes will be less likely to occur. In all these respects it contrasts with aboriginal traditions of justice which offer what he calls 'healing justice.' However, healing justice seems to represent a deepening and intensification of the main thrust of restorative justice, rather than a new departure, and that is how I shall treat it.

Sawatsky documents in detail how healing justice has functioned in three geographically and spiritually distinct communities, with dramatic reductions in rates of crime and re-offence, and improvements in the general wellbeing of the societies themselves. At Hollow Water in Canada, aboriginal peoples who had suffered from huge rates of crime and alcohol addiction, including an 80% incidence of child abuse, began to build a new society based on their indigenous spiritual resources, resulting in a huge restoration of self-respect, a dramatic reduction in crime, and in particular, a remarkably low 2% rate of re-offending by sexual harmers. (In our society it is 10 to 20 times higher.) The Iona Community in Scotland had achieved similar results with its Christian traditions in a community that contained many gathered from 'sink estates' in Glasgow and elsewhere, while Plum Village in the South of France (founded by Thich Nhat Hanh) succeeded in gathering individuals traumatized by the Vietnam War into a peaceable community based on Buddhist principles of mindfulness and non-harm.

Only in the first case has the community worked (with the

co-operation of the police) in a way that actually replaces the usual legal system of the state. In the other cases the emphasis is on creating the conditions for healing justice rather than responding to specific crimes. However, the Truth and Reconciliation process in South Africa does represent a statewide and state-sanctioned process in which the priority is given to healing and restoration of society from the wounds of the past, by means of honest confession of wrongs followed by forgiveness and amnesty. The process has been criticized, as we have seen, by those who feel the amnesty denies victims their right to (retributive) justice. For all that, theologian John De Gruchy argues (2002) that South Africa has achieved a degree of healing and unity that is remarkable given the terrible injustices and state-imposed divisions of the past. This is premised on a trust in total honesty, a sense that people will give a full and truthful account of their crimes. And that of course is premised on the fact that honesty will not be punished, because there will be no retributive element.

Meanwhile in Tibet before the Chinese invasion, law scholar Rebecca French argues that a Buddhist perspective led to a similar focus on justice as healing.

> The goal of a legal proceeding was to calm the minds and relieve the anger of the disputants and then – through catharsis, expiation, restitution, and appeasement – to rebalance the natural order. (1995, p. 74)

Now in his novel *The Brothers Karamazov*, Dostoyevsky illustrates how even criminal justice can be turned to healing effect. Dmitri Karamazov is sentenced to exile in Siberia for a murder he did not commit. But he accepts his sentence, not because he is guilty but because all are guilty, as he puts it, of all crimes, all of us being bound together in the hurts that often lead to crimes. In a sense those who are actually sentenced are scapegoats, punished for the chains of sin that turn through all. But the scapegoat can enable redemption. Visited by his brother Alyosha in prison, Dmitri explains.

> Even there, in the mines, underground, I may find a human heart in another convict and murderer by my side, and I may make friends with him, for even there one may live and love and suffer. One may thaw and revive a frozen heart in that convict, one may wait upon him for years, and at last bring up from the dark depths a lofty soul, a feeling, suffering creature; one may bring forth an angel, create a hero! There are so many of them, hundreds of them, and we are to blame for them.
> (Book 9, Chapter 4)

Dmitri here uses very significant language in three respects.

A. 'Another convict and murderer by my side.' Though not actually a murderer, Dmitri accepts the murderer as his equal side by side. Rather than heaping shame on him, he sees him and works with him as one not fundamentally different from himself.
B. 'One may bring forth an angel... a feeling, suffering creature.' Dmitri sees the fellow convict as one that already has a good heart that can be thawed and revived, and has high hopes for the future liberation of this 'lofty soul.' The language suggests his Christian faith as the basis of this hope.
C. 'We are to blame for them.' Dmitri sees the causes of harm as going deeper than the individuals who commit it. All society colludes in and helps cause the sins of its members.

These features, which Dmitri invoked in a criminal justice setting that was essentially at odds with them, become the main focus in the communities embodying healing justice as described by Sawatsky.

A. As Chapter 2 argued, remorse is hard to achieve from a place of shame. Healing justice therefore does not heap guilt and shame on the harmer (p. 232). It works on the basis of profound respect and acceptance for both harmed and harmer (for which reason these terms replace the more judgmental 'perpetrator' or 'criminal' and 'victim.' For this reason both meet with representatives of the community in a circle to evaluate what to do about the harm done (p. 225) rather than in the strict hierarchy suggested by the layout of a law court. If the harm is serious the harmer may be sentenced, but not to punishment; rather to a community where they may undergo a healing remorse. Such communities are envisaged as being more like retreat centers than prisons (p. 227) places of quiet reflectiveness and times of silence rather than brutal clamor, overcrowding and violence.

B. Rather than merely responding to harm, the communities in question administer justice in the context of a broad vision of the human goal of restoration to joy and abundance of life. This vision incorporates traditions of loving one's enemies as a brother or sister, responding to harm with compassion not violence, and giving people space to find their own identity (p. 264–5).

C. The central model is not that of the individual standing before the judgment throne of the state and its laws, held to account for specific harms, but that of a community corporately implicated in the harms its members do to and suffer from one another. The time frame for considering harms is expanded deep into the past and the future (p. 117) Instead of considering a specific crime in isolation, one community typically looks back for seven generations into the causes of

> the harm, as well as looking forward towards the restoration to wholeness just described.

As noted in Chapter 5, Christians and Buddhists would want to go even further back and forward, ideally to the whole history of humanity. For we are all socially formed in original sin, or carry the seed of bad karma 'from beginningless time.' Theologian Alistair McFayden shows that cases of extreme sin like child abuse and the Nazi Holocaust demand an understanding that takes us beyond individual wrongdoing to take in historical and trans-generational causes. He argues that sin is essentially broken relationship that denies the way in which we are all bound together in being 'both dependent on and responsible for the joy of all others.'

> If in the very heart of my 'self,' I am born into radical and intrinsic relationality, *for* God and others, then one person's sin would be sufficient to disrupt the entire ecology of joy on which my very 'self' depends... If one sins, we are all inextricably involved in the very depths of our being.
> (2000, p. 248)

Healing justice is precisely about overcoming harm, not by harming the harmers, but by nurturing the whole 'ecology of joy'.

An End to the Violent Contract? The Stages of Social Healing

Now it has to be admitted that the examples cited by Sawatsky are communities in which all (including criminals and victims) are united in their commitment to a faith system (indigenous Amerindian, Christian and Buddhist respectively) that provides rituals and practices for the healing of harms. In a secular society those practices do not exist, and in a multicultural society many faith practices exist each with their own subscribers, as well as many who subscribe to none of them. Harmer and victim will very often come from different communities, and be unable to undergo a shared process of healing as described by Sawatsky. It may be questioned whether in such post-traditional societies we are forced back to retributive and deterrent justice simply because they represent the lowest common denominator which everyone can accept.

But our present criminal justice system is a crude form of justice which has little to recommend it. Even economically, it demands expensive, long-term, secure accommodation for offenders. It perpetuates harm by simply incarcerating harmers in a society of other harmed and harming people; and then further ensuring that a criminal record makes re-entry into society beyond this damaged fringe all but impossible. The only advantage of this system is this one decisive factor: that the majority in society accept it.

In the 17th century, the philosopher Thomas Hobbes pioneered the 'social contract' model that has become the norm in modern times. According to this, society's members agree (at some ill-defined point in an ill-defined way) to be policed by the absolute power of the state. They subject themselves to the possibility of punitive violence because, in a world assumed to be inherently violent, that is the only way of safeguarding their own person and property. In a post-traditional and multi-traditional world, it has become hard to imagine a workable alternative.

Whether healing justice might work as a state-wide model depends on whether the resources of different faith and non-faith communities might be drawn on to create a process of healing justice that would be manifestly more attractive than this kind of contracted violence. That would not mean the blending of all faith practices, of course, but a pooling of the wisdoms of all faiths into a shared approach to the difficult processes of social healing. But clearly the problems of constructing a model of healing justice in multicultural state are immense. Achievement, if not impossible, is a very, very long way off.

But this is one reason why inter-faith dialogue is not just an option for faith-dilettantes, but a practical imperative. Only through dialogue will those of different faiths, and those with none, come to realize where the shared ground lies on matters of justice, repentance, forgiveness, restoration and healing. Only then will we be able to provide a sharable ritual structure to enable those processes in our multi-cultural world. These are the necessary first steps towards providing real healing for society's wounds and harms. I sense that Christian-Buddhist dialogue is especially crucial here, because these seem to me to be the two faiths most committed (at least in theory) to a move beyond retributive and violent models of justice.

The advocates of healing justice are clearly using 'healing' as a basic metaphor, but I have yet to see this metaphor explored in depth. It occurs to me that the process physical and personal healing offers a very good template for social healing, a template that just might provide a model that would integrate many faith resources (as well as secular resources) without bias towards any particular tradition; a template, moreover, that seems to draw all the other models of justice into that of healing justice.

So I offer this crude sketch of a template. The template obviously is not a program but a way of structuring our thoughts and helping people to develop practical programs. It is probably naïve in some areas, but as a whole, I suggest, it combines toughness with love in the way required for healing.

1. **Isolation**. As the body and mind must first protect themselves by isolating wounds, so there is a place, in responding to harms, for isolating and detaining the harmer, putting him in a place where he cannot do further

harm. Retributive rage, detention, deterrence, and the expression of abhorrence, all have a place (perhaps a place that idealistic approaches underrate). But only as initial responses. The problem with our present penal justice is that this first stage gets perpetuated because we lack the spiritual resources of wisdom and courage needed for the later ones.

2. **Repair**. Just as the body introduces emergency structures, imperfect but workable, so there will need to be a process initiating restoration for the victim and reform for the harmer. These may not be perfectly achieved, but they need to be attempted and begun. In severe cases this may involve continued detention, so that the harmer may be held to account and not permitted to escape his responsibilities to the person and community he has harmed, and so that the momentum of remorse and inner change may not be dissipated or destroyed by exposure to the social contexts that have made him harm. But the ethos of the place of detention will be focused on change for the future rather than stigma and punishment for the past. There is no room for the elements of prisons that make them harm producing contexts themselves. And the process will certainly involve care and affirmation for the victim, ensuring she is in a safe place for the difficult processes involved.
3. **Restoration**. Just as very gradually the wound is reassimilated into the body and disappears as a wound, so there needs to be a process continuing long after the above and after any detention that may be needed, in which the harms of the past and the harms that still exist in the victim and harmer are dissolved, and if possible, reconciliation and forgiveness take place. Not all wounds heal perfectly; often they leave scars and disabilities, but we should aim for the body to come as close as possible to being 'good as new.' In the same way not all criminal harm heals; the process

> depends on a lot of goodwill, courage and commitment from both harmer and harmed. But our aim should be a state where the traces of the harm are dissolved and all is 'good as new.'

All of that, of course, concerns responding to harms. There is a whole area of health, which healing justice (more than restorative justice) focuses on, which concerns keeping the social body healthy and free from sickness and damage in the first place. It is this that our society does so badly. Our present penal system, which merely reacts to crises – specific crimes – by incarcerating people and so fixing them at stage 1, could be compared to a body full of running sores and badly plastered over, inflamed and festering wounds, which we do not know or care about enough to try to heal. The wounds are simply repressed, shut away out of sight, as in trauma as outlined at the start of Chapter 2. Thus oblivious and able to dissociate ourselves from social pain, we do not feel much need to prevent the conditions that will cause further wounds.

Thankfully, in communities like those mentioned, and in the Truth and Reconciliation process in South Africa, we see (however imperfectly) how a better approach might work in practice.

An End to the Memory of Hurt? Water under the Bridge

But should we all hope for a state that is 'good as new.' Mother Julian of Norwich tells us, 'all shall be well,' but will it? To return to our opening question, will we – should we – let all the waters of harm pass 'under the bridge'? Or should we thirst for the waters of divine retribution for all harm?

The poet Dante used the same image of a flow of water when he came to describe the forgetting of sin as the redeemed move from purgatory to paradise. He described the boundary between purgatory and paradise as bound by two rivers that spring from a single source, (c.f. Volf, p. 135ff):

> It issues from a pure and changeless fountain
> which by the will of God regains as much
> as, on two sides, it pours and it divides.
> On this side it descends with power to end
> One's memory of sin; on the other,
> it can restore recall of each good deed.
> To one side, it is Lethe; on the other,
> Eunoe; neither stream is efficacious
> unless the others' waters have been tasted:
> their savor is above all other sweetness.
> (*Purgatorio*, 1986, Canto 28, l.124–33)

In ancient Greek belief, Lethe was the river all the departed crossed on their way to Hades, the gloomy underworld. It involved the forgetting of all the life one had lived on earth. But in Dante it is only the bad of the past that is forgotten – and only after the evil effects of sin have been cleansed in purgatory by suffering and the tears of true remorse. Eunoe is Dante's own invention. After purging and then forgetting the evils of the past in this way, the redeemed souls drink in the remembrance of all they have done that was good and virtuous. Dante is suggesting in his allegorical way that the forgetting of evil is appropriate, but only in a strict context. First we must remember and acknowledge our sins in true repentance: this is what makes the difference between entering purgatory and consigning ourselves to hell, where sin is remembered but not acknowledged as sin. Second, we must have dealt with the effects of sin, in ourselves and (I suggest) on others, by true remorse and all the recompense to others we can achieve. Only in that context can it be right and honest to forget. And finally, the forgetting is *en route* to a glorious remembrance of the good of the self that can – in Christian terms – only be realized in the vision of the goodness of God.

Meanwhile in Buddhism too there is a great forgetting, but the logic and order is rather different. We forget every time we die and are reborn in another life. Except perhaps for the spiritually very advanced, there is no remembrance of past lives, yet we are responsible for what was done in those lives and bear the weight of the karma accrued in them. And in the Tibetan tradition, there is a kind of judgment. In the days after death we have successive possibilities of seeing ultimate reality and entering Nirvana, but the karma of past lives makes us afraid so that we recoil into the duller, heavier but safer light of worldly existence. The first such possibility arises on the first day after death, when

> the Wisdom of the *dharma-datu* [roughly, the true nature of things], blue in color, shining, transparent, glorious, dazzling... will shoot forth and strike against you with a light so radiant that you will scarcely be able to look at it. Along with it will also shine a dull white light from the *devas* [demigods], which will strike against you in your front. Thereupon, because of the power of bad karma, the glorious blue light... will produce in you fear and terror, and you will flee from it. You will beget a fondness for the dull white light of the *devas*.
>
> (*Tibetan Book of the Dead*, 1960, p. 106)

In Dante, then, we are first purified of bad 'karma' and then forget the evil of the past to enter the ultimate bliss. But in Tibetan Buddhism we first forget the past, and then we have the chance of entering bliss; but nearly always the bad karma of the past reasserts itself and we re-enter the ongoing purgatory that is this world. The 'demigods' represent the attraction of a state that is better, but still imprisoned in the cycle of delusion and desire. In Catholic Christianity the order is purgatory –

forgetting – bliss; in Tibetan Buddhism it is forgetting – bliss – purgatory.

The difference is immense. In Christianity we can only confess the sins we remember and acknowledge. In Buddhism *most* of the karma we are dealing with is forgotten in past lives; we acknowledge the existence of, and confess, sins we cannot possibly remember. But as we have seen, Theravada Buddhism gives us a way of dealing with the effect of past karma in the here and now, in *vipassanā* meditation where we deal with bodily effects whose causes we may or may not know. In Tibetan Buddhism, death itself gives us an opportunity to let go of murky karmic effects and embrace the ultimate light. And Zen urges that enlightenment may be instantaneous, cutting through the Gordian knot of karma in a stroke as we realize the enlightened Buddha nature that has always been there, unseen.

The goal of much therapy is to remember past hurts and discharge the long repressed feelings that relate to them. But in their different ways, Buddhism and Christianity both give forgetting a vital place. Life, after all, would surely not be livable without a lot of forgetting. In the night we forget the day. Our memories and thoughts slowly unravel into a confusion in which we dream. And in the morning we forget most of our dreams. From Friedrich Nietzsche through to Eckhart Tolle there has been a steady minority witnessing to the innocence that can only come to us through forgetting the past and inhabiting the now, extolling the animal and the child and the eternal present.

> The child is innocence and forgetting, a new beginning, a game, a self-propelled wheel, a first movement, a sacred 'Yes.' For the game of creation, my brothers, a sacred 'Yes' is needed.
>
> (Nietzsche, in Volf, p. 164)

Certainly, the desire to forget the past and achieve untroubled innocence in the now can be escapist and pathological; this was certainly the case for Macbeth as quoted above. Obviously Macbeth was desiring a shortcut. He wanted to get back to a state where he had not committed the atrocities he had, avoiding all the pain of remorse and recompense by means of some medicinal potion. Neither Buddhism nor Christianity allows us to forget in such a painless, effortless, magic way.

But who is it that really wants evils to have a perpetual memorial? Most victims would like to forget their wounds. The last thing a victim of rape or abuse would desire would be a plaque commemorating the deed to be erected in their home town. Volf argues that it is impenitent evildoers who most strongly desire an eternal memory. Serial killers, and those who commit genocide and the other deeds that remain forever in our history books because of their enormity are often very hungry for a fame they cannot acquire by mere good deeds. For their huge egos, it is better to be remembered for evil than forgotten. And so, if there is a heaven and a hell, would hell for such people not be a price worth paying if their monument will stand in the eternal memory of heaven?

> Would there not in the eternal memory of wrongs suffered resound a hellish laughter of the seemingly defeated and yet strangely triumphant underworld. Triumphant because it has succeeded in casting eternally its dark shadow over the world to come. To be fully overcome, evildoing must be consigned its proper place – nothingness. (Volf, p. 214)

And nothingness means no memory, and no lingering trace of the evil done.

But that cannot happen by a mere effort of repression. In Christian terms it is only the fullness of God that shows up the nothingness of evil. In any other context, to believe evil is nothing involves a kind of repression or deception. Dante's two rivers, the forgetting of evil and the remembrance of goodness in God, flow from the same divine source. It is as we are gathered in God – whose fullness involves our remembrance of all that was good – that the nothingness is forgotten.

> Forgetting is not a flight from the defective or the unbearable. It is a byproduct of the attachment to the perfectly Good... The forgetting of evil is in the service of remembering the good, and remembering the good is the consequence of being engrossed in God. (Volf, p. 141)

In Tibetan Buddhist terms it is the light of ultimate wisdom that draws us into the eternal present of Nirvana; and it is the karmic momentum of past hurt and harm that makes us recoil from that dazzling fullness in fear, back into the shadowy heaviness of rebirth (albeit without memory).

Not too soon – or as a way of avoiding the need for action and protest, or remorse and forgiveness – but ultimately, we need to move via the forgetting of past wrongs as 'water under the bridge' towards innocence of life in the transient present, as Buddhism teaches. In the fullness of what Christian call God, the nothingness of evil must return to nothing.

The birth of new life is a painful process, but in the new life the pain is forgotten.

> When a woman is in labor, she has pain, because her hour has come. But when her child is born, she no longer remembers the anguish because of the joy of having brought a human being into the world. So you have pain now; but I will see you again, and your hearts will rejoice, and no one will take your joy from you. (John 16.21–2)

Hurts are real, sometimes terribly real and harmful. But if our pains are to be remembered, it is as the labor pains of abundant life and light. Sometimes they just are that; and sometimes it is up to us to make them so.

Summary

1. The phrase 'water under the bridge' suggests that past harm done to us can be forgotten, but others urge that even if we forgive such harm, we should never forget. Should we hope for a time when all harm is forgotten?
2. The effects of hurt, in the form of wounds, generally come to an end in the natural process of healing. But how far can healing prove an analogy for the way in which other harms might come to an end? Are there 'wounds not healed by time' that require not healing but retribution?
3. Many reasons have been put for retributive punishment. But there are deep flaws in the logic of retribution.
4. Jesus preached against retribution, and Christians claim that by his cross and resurrection the law of retribution has been superseded. But theological distortions of this notion have enabled Christian states to continue to operate a retributive model of justice. Does authentic Christianity provide an agenda for a world without punishment?
5. That may seem utopian and impractical, but examples exist where a healing rather than retributive model of justice has operated with remarkable though not undiluted success. This model responds to harm not by harming the harmers in return, but by healing the broken 'ecology of joy' for which we are all responsible.
6. However, these are all communities united by a strongly shared traditional belief system, which provides a clear and powerful pathway for the healing of harms to which all are committed. A secular, multicultural society will always rely on violence, unless diverse faith communities can pool their faith resources in a shared process of healing justice. The analogy of the healing of wounds may provide a template

for such a shared process.

7. If 'evil' is ultimately nothing it must return to nothing. Christian and Buddhist traditions alike are committed to an ultimate forgetting of harm.

Chapter 10

Responding to Evil: A Buddhist-Christian Ninefold Way

Fetuses of eternity
we are:
            in life's womb and we do not see the One
in whom we live and move, and kick and sleep, and have all
our being. We cannot speak her
(or any) true tongue, and prayer is
most true when it is a listening to
her heartbeat, the deep inexorable pulse
that is all the life we have.

            But now breaks
Something new, merciless. Terrible
contractions crush and push down, inexorably down
towards loins that are the smothering of all our world.
Death throes
us out, finally – into light
unbearable. We shriek
For the first time a taking in lungful of spirit. Things
we never knew we had – called eyes –
dry, unmist and focus on
the blessed face.

            The one we lived all our life
on the inside of, we see from the outside now,
whole, weeping and laughing over us.
In joyous eyes, a love we had lived by
but not known, quite exhausted, triumphs,

and mouth tenderness. Responding, we realize
we have lips and speech,
and faces too.
Death considered as Birth

How are our hurts to become birth pangs of light? That is what this book has been about. I propose to sum up and carry forward the main themes of this book by offering nine precepts distilled from Christian, Buddhist and other perspectives. They are all ways of ensuring that our hurts give birth not to what is harmful and life-destroying, but to what is wholesome and life-giving.

Very roughly speaking, the first two precepts concern finding a richer and more realistic response than blame. They draw on the tragic and comic perspectives on the human condition discussed in Chapter 6, which derive ultimately from pagan Greece (though they have been carried forward in the Christian tradition and are quite harmonious with certain Buddhist perspectives, notably Zen and other traditions influenced by Taoism.) The next two concern how we overcome shame through the processes of remorse, repentance and forgiveness discussed in Chapter 7 – a central but by no means unique concern of Christianity. The next two concern the overcoming of our temptation to disclaim and disown hurt through the practices of meditation and mindfulness, leading to global mindfulness, as discussed in Chapter 8. These are central concerns of Buddhism, though Christian prayer is also highly relevant. The final three precepts turn to the (often distant seeming) hopes for an end to harm and the creation of a healing rather than retributive justice, as explored in Chapter 9. All the precepts model ways of living with harm with the kind of 'wily innocence' advanced in the Introduction to Part 2. The innocence prevents past harm from propagating itself in soul and society, but the wiliness protects both, so far as possible, from future harm.

In relation to the hurt, harm and evil you have suffered, done or participated in, the precepts urge:

1. **Lament**. Do not paint a silver lining onto every cloud; some are unremittingly dark. But not irredeemably. Let sorrows become a song of sacrifice ('tragedy') in which they are taken up and 're-membered' in the whole beautiful story. That way lies innocence and a tough vulnerability.
2. **Laugh** too if you can. Without disclaiming the immensity of many harms, see the absurdity of 'evil.' Laugh at yourself and relate to sinners as a fellow sinner, allowing for the foolish *bombu* nature of all that is human. That, paradoxically, is one way to the innocence of the child.
3. **Take care**. In the risky business of seeking and offering forgiveness, like a gentle dove avoid harming others. But also, like the wily snake, avoid getting walked over and harmed yourself. Look after the precious piece of the universe you are.
4. Give **time** for remorse and forgiveness to do their work. Do not let harm draw or impel you quickly into action or repression. It takes time fully to realize the harm you have done. It takes time to move from shame to blame, and from blame to forgiveness, and from forgiving to forgetting. Let time be the womb in which pain can gestate and finally create.
5. Give it a **space** of loving yet detached regard in which hurt can be understood and felt for what it is. Do not fight it or flee from it, but in the stillness of meditation and the empathy of listening, rest with it.
6. **Face** it, live without shame or disclaimer, and so learn to live face to face with the defaced face of the earth, your fellow human, and what Christians call God. Let the dark things and the light coalesce into the one mosaic of life, in which we see the face that is scarred but blessed.

7. **Seek healing justice** as described in the previous chapter. Never look for revenge. In all demands for justice make sure you are seeking it for the sake of the harmer as well as yourself. Be honest and remorseful but not repressive or self-obsessed about injustices you may have done.
8. **Believe**. Do not justify evil as inevitable, or simplify it into the actions of individuals you can blame. Though accountability has an important place, it cannot heal society of its harms. If we desire, hope and believe that good can be the last word, it will be; if not, it won't be. It is in that sense that faith, hope and love can save us.
9. **Take one step at a time**. The overcoming of harm is no easy matter, and healing justice takes longer than other forms. 'Ready meals' are rarely nutritious. Be suspicious of instant solutions, and be concerned not only for good and just goals, but the wholesomeness and fairness of the processes that leads to them.

These precepts are not intended to be stages in an infallible process of responding well to hurt, but as aspects of a single many sided and varied ethos. In what follows I link them to the blessings described in Matthew's version of Jesus' beatitudes (Matt. 5.1–8). These, likewise, are not set out as alternative pathways to holiness but aspects of one and the same blessedness. Many scholars would view the simpler and starker beatitudes in Luke 6.20–21 as closer to the words of Jesus, but Matthew's version has inspired a long Christian tradition that provides an illuminating parallel to the thought of this book; except that I have felt the need to expand it with an extra beatitude. I link them also to one of the nine fruits of the spirit (Gal. 5.22–3), and to the Buddhist eightfold way. Again I have had to add an extra item to the Buddhist eight to make nine. (Each of the 'fruits' also relates to one of the virtues listed in **Table 1**, though this relationship is suggested rather than explored.)

Lament

Blessed are those who mourn, for they will be comforted.

Is it the case that 'all's well that ends well' in the divine comedy? I would say, yes, in the way suggested at the end of Chapter 9, but not in a way that precludes tragedy, or casts out the need for lament. We probably all know of times in our lives when we have done ourselves or others great harm, and yet, looking back, we can see those times also as enabling ourselves or others to grow. Maybe we regret, now, bitter things said in adolescence to parents, or to a former spouse before divorce; yet we do not regret having grown up through that pain. The weaving of bad events into good stories is part of what we mean by redemption, and Christians see it most clearly in the way the horrible torture and judicial murder of a Galilean was re-woven by the resurrection into a story of forgiveness, hope and new life. That is why the Easter liturgy is not altogether mistaken to sing of the lucky fault of Adam, that brought about Christ the Redeemer (see Chapter 5).

But we can also see that had we been wiser, and perhaps clearer about what we were wanting, some of the pain could have been avoided. We can regret 'the expense of spirit in a waste of shame,' (Shakespeare, Sonnet 129) Growth could not have come about without cost and trauma, but it could have been achieved with less.

So Carla (whom we met in Chapters 2 and 7) comments:

> I could have saved myself a lot of pain if I'd known before I started on my adult life journey what would work and what wouldn't. I might not have felt the need to become a nun, only to leave after my twenties were gone. I might not have become a prostitute and experienced the bitterness of loveless sex and the self-betrayal in subterfuge. I might have found my way home straightaway and not played the game of emotional snakes and ladders. But who can live beyond

their evolution? And what would have happened to this story? (2006, p.434)

In the end we have to accept our evolution including our own and others' faults. But not without the need for remorse and lament over the unnecessary pain. Christians can only sing of the happy fault of humanity, that brought about the great redemption in Christ, if they also at the same time lament the tragic and wasteful fault of humanity, that necessitated so costly and painful a redemption; such that according to Christians Christ had to come not only as the glorious fulfillment he was always destined to be, but also as the crucified.

There is a long Christian tradition stemming from the desert fathers and mothers that speaks of the 'gift of tears': the ability to weep over the hurts in our soul, especially those that arise from our hurting of others, but also the general hurtness that is the condition of the world. Whether or not the Greek tragedies originated in laments over the goat of sacrifice, they are certainly full of the sound of the chorus' lament. Ancient cultures resound with the plaintive music of lament, which is familiar in our own rich repertoire of ballads. The word 'ballad' comes from the same word as 'ballet' – ballads were originally dance songs. Ballads and laments turn our grief into dance. Rather than blaming someone for grief, or complaining about it, or putting on a brave face, laments allow the grief to shine in its own stark beauty. But this is not a glorifying of sacrifice. Many a modern protest song (to those of my age, those of Bob Dylan, Pete Seeger and Joan Baez immediately come to mind) plaintively laments a deep injustice, not to glorify it or urge resignation, but to inspire action. Chapter 6 noted Kathleen Sands' remark that tragedy does not generate meaning or beauty but the desire for those things; but we might add that that desire is itself beautiful and meaningful.

Though there is plenty of lament in such protest songs, and

also in blues, spirituals and many love songs, lament is an undercurrent, not the main tide of our culture. Funerals are coming more and more to resemble weddings, with eulogy outshining the sorrow of loss. And though there is a deep Jewish and Christian tradition of lament going back to the psalms, modern day Christian worship seems to avoid any note of sorrow: triumphant hymns and happy choruses dominate the day. On the whole, rather than sing of our griefs until they become woven into our corporate being, we isolate them in the private individual where we bury them under the ground.

But the first requirement for responding well to hurt and harm is that we attend to them and hear them. So often we cram our sorrows into a private space of shame, or we moan about and resent them, or we self-indulge and obsess about them. In these ways we make our hurt ugly and cramped: either smaller or bigger than it really is, or both. The cadences of lament and – as we have seen – the performance of tragic drama can enable us to hold our sorrows in a larger space. We have already suggested how crucial that larger space for psychic maneuver is if we are to respond to hurt with creative action; this will form the basis of our fourth 'precept.' So let us relearn the art of lamenting well. If we have no singing voice or no one to sing with, at least we can sing in our hearts of the hurts we have received, and lament too the hurts we have caused.

In this way our characters will be suffused by the spiritual fruit of longsuffering (*makrothumia* – great heartedness) or 'patience,' that word with the same root as 'passion,' whose inner meaning is to suffer, to feel deeply, to undergo experience and be changed, which involves a spiritual kind of courage. In the Buddhist tradition there is little emphasis on lament as such, but endurance and longsuffering are involved in the path of right effort on the eightfold way.

Laugh

Blessed are those who laugh, for they have one foot in God's Kingdom now.

I had to invent a beatitude here. Though there is plenty of humor and irony in Jesus' teaching, the laughter has tended to get stifled by the solemnity to which religious traditions are so often tempted. The man of sorrows has swallowed up the man of feasts and friendship, wine and great laughter. It often takes us by surprise when we at last meet people we have long known to be great spiritual leaders (I think especially of the Dalai Lama) and have built up an expectation of being overawed by a lofty presence, when we find how much such people often laugh, in a manner generally unpredicted by the traditions they represent!

Chapter 6 made clear how humor and comedy can have a profound spiritual role. They create transcendence – enabling us to be 'beside ourselves' with laughter, seeing our sorrows in perspective – and they affirm the earthy, *bombu*-foolish nature of ourselves and those who have hurt us. Like the child who laughs at the naked emperor while everyone else assumes he has dignity and clothes, laughter restores an innocent perspective that cuts through human pretenses. It enables us to stand with one foot in God's Kingdom, and the other firmly planted on the earth; it is the tension between the sublime and the ridiculous than gets discharged in that strange shaking of the lungs!

Of course, laughter alone might make for a naïvely optimistic viewpoint, trivializing sorrow and always irritatingly 'looking on the bright side of life.' It is never an aim of good counseling to try to get someone to laugh at their sorrows. But such laughter is often the result of good counseling that enables us to see our pain in a wider context. Laughter can coexist with real sorrow and tears, which is why this precept belongs with the first. Though Greek tragedy is often unremittingly painful, Shakespeare and others learned the art of combining it with comedy and foolery, so deepening it as well as making it bearable.

To lament deeply and laugh deeply too is to open the way for the deep healing of our sorrows and the birth of true joy, *chara*. This term is closely related to *charis*, grace, something freely given, unexpected and underserved. Joyous laughter is from the gods; it can never be contrived. The word is present too in *Eucharist*, the central Christian act of 'thanksgiving.' For it is an essential ingredient of all right worship, or right rejoicing, which I suggest might make a valuable addition to the eightfold path.

Take Care

Blessed are those who are persecuted for the sake of justice, for theirs is the kingdom of heaven.

Despite the suggestion of this, the final beatitude, Jesus' non-violence does not masochistically welcome persecution or instill a 'doormat' mentality, letting ourselves be walked over and enjoying it! As Walter Wink has pointed out (1992, p. 179–84), when Jesus urged his followers to 'go the second mile' with those who forced them to walk one, he was speaking in the context of a Roman rule that allowed solders to commandeer civilians to carry their baggage for just one mile. The second mile was illegal. So the apparently generous offer turned the command of the oppressor against itself. The soldier would have an uncomfortable choice between capitulating to the Jewish upstart he had been bullying, and disobeying his own authorities. In the same way, Wink argues (p. 177–9), in a society where it was usual to wear just a coat and an undergarment, taking two garments from a person would leave them naked. So if when one garment is stolen, the other is offered too; the bully either has to back down or create a very embarrassing situation for himself!

It is often possible for non-violent protesters to succeed in their aims simply by exposing their exploiters to this kind of embarrassment, in which their power interests could no longer hide under the mask of benevolent rule. In this way Gandhi and his followers were able – not without great cost – to expose the brutal side of the British Raj, and as it were shame the British into granting independence. The process is rather like those forms of self-defense deriving from Buddhist and Taoist traditions of non-violence – tae-kwon-do and ju-jitsu for example – in which the violence of the attacker is not resisted, but diverted to cause his own downfall.

So when persecuted and attacked, it is important that we 'do not resist an evildoer' (Matt. 5.39 – the context of the sayings Wink discusses) but do not simply succumb to him and get hurt either. Peacemaking is a risky process, which can spark a painful rejection or cynical exploitation. James Alison describes the 'wily innocence' required in the offer of genuine forgiveness and non-violence.

> You forgive them by living with them with the twin attitudes of the serpent, knowing very exactly how to slither away to avoid being trampled on when danger is around, but the innocence of doves, who do not think ill of those whom they are seeking to forgive, nor are in any sort of rivalry with, but are able to give themselves... to the addicts [of violence]. (2003, p. 43)

The Theravada Buddhist practice of *metta* or loving-kindness includes the wish that you, your loved ones, your community and all sentient beings in all directions of the universe may 'take care of themselves easily.' The wish expresses the Theravada understanding that good things can come to beings only through their own actions – not through divine providence or as a direct result of others' prayers.

A Christian might want to place more emphasis on divine grace, but it seems to me that God can only take care of us if we ourselves exercise some concern and stewardship for this little bit of the universe we are. A joke relates how a woman in church persistently prayed to win the lottery. One day an exasperated God stormed down through the roof of the church, imploring her at least to do her bit and buy a lottery ticket! But seriously, because non-violent peacemaking and healing justice eschew the outward defenses of aggression and retaliation, it is very important that those who practice them take proper care of themselves inwardly.

In this proper care, the spiritual gift called *enkrateia* is essential. Literally meaning 'having one's ruler within,' it is variously translated as moderation, autonomy, self-control or self-mastery. It means not letting yourself be ruled by reactions to others' attacks, or even by mechanisms within yourself that you are not really choosing. When a person attacks with a humiliating remark, to retaliate in kind is to be ruled by them. Likewise to crumple into abject apology. The person with self-mastery will note these impulses of the self, and the associated feelings, allowing them time to disperse. And having thus taken control of themselves, they will respond with something that expresses their true being.

Such mastery is especially important when it comes to speech. It is unfashionable these days to be too bothered about swearing, gossip, backbiting and rude, hurtful language. But the letter of James sees all kinds of loss of control as resulting from an unbridled tongue. In the eightfold way, right speech seems to be the virtue relevant here. Before we can actually be violent to people we need to violate them by our public speech, or by that inner speech whereby we feed aversion with narratives describing them as inferior. If we wish to speak peaceably and safeguard ourselves, it is vital to take great care with how things are expressed.

Give Time

Blessed are the peacemakers, for they will be called children of God.

The process of remorse and forgiveness described in Chapter 7 cannot be rushed. It takes time – in some cases more than a lifetime – to move from forgetfulness to remembrance, to anger or distress, to remorse, to forgiveness, to full repentance, to restitution and perhaps ultimately to forgetting. In the process the immediate harm has to be acknowledged, and the wider story needs to be told and heard, as we move from 'you versus me' to the 'new we.' The same is true of the corporate processes of healing justice described in Chapter 9, which require that we look back and forward for seven generations.

This is bad news in a culture that emphasizes that because we have only one life, we must make the most of it and get what fulfillment we can within its limits. If this life is all we have, we may well jettison long-term programs of reconciliation in the interest of a quick fix. In the same spirit we find it hard to do things that previous generations took for granted, like planting trees and laying hedges that will take generations to mature. We much prefer the 'instant garden,' moving in expensive full-grown shrubs like so many pieces of furniture. In the same way we look for a government that will – in its five-year term – mend our broken society, and restore justice to the poor without any cost to ourselves. In all this rush there takes place a great deferral of all issues that take time to resolve, including true reconciliation. It is in such a context that there arise ever more strident demands for quick-fix justice, so that whenever anything goes wrong the thing to do is blame and punish.

Buddhism and Christianity, in their different ways, give us much more time than this one life. That might seem to deflate all sense of urgency. But the reverse is true. In both traditions, all time hinges on this present moment now. How I live now, in Christianity, determines my eternal destiny. And in Buddhism there is really no time but now. So while the secular view of this life as all there is leads to a great deferral of issues like forgiveness and reconciliation, the Christian and Buddhist understanding of vast time hinging on this moment make it absolutely urgent to be a peacemaker right here and now, even if peacemaking will take a very long time to achieve its goal.

As for the spiritual fruit that nourishes and results from the long processes of peace, it is surely *chrestotes*, the kind of attractive kindness, sweetness, courtesy and charm we love in a good host or hostess, which is quite close to the playfulness we love in children. We see it in Jesus as he hosts his scandalous feasts with sinners, slowly and subtly building peace between them and their God. It goes with Buddhist right understanding or vision, for it involves seeing reality non-judgmentally with a generous acceptance of how it actually is.

Give Space

Blessed are the merciful, for they will receive mercy.

Chapter 8 explored the importance of giving our hurts the kind of spiritual space or room for maneuver that mindfulness and meditation bring.

> We can go home to ourselves. We can use the energy of mindfulness to recognize the pain inside and hold it tenderly, like a mother holding her baby. Mindfulness is the mother. Your pain, your sorrow, your despair, is your baby... When a mother hears her baby crying, she puts aside what she is doing, goes immediately to pick up the baby, and holds the baby tenderly. She may not know what is wrong with the baby at first, but the fact that she's holding him tenderly like this already brings relief. (Hanh, 2007, p. 50–51)

In the place where I meditate, when I open my eyes the first thing I see in the center of my vision is a Russian icon of Mary, Mother of Tenderness. It is very dark, brown and earthy, but on it Mary is holding her baby Jesus to her cheek with the same kind of attitude I need to have to my feelings. The Hebrew Bible calls it *hesedh,* the steadfast loving-kindness of the Lord which persists whatever we do, and which is compared with the love of a mother for her child (Isaiah 6.13).

We might add that a good mother will not immediately rush to stuff a crying baby with a milk bottle, but will wait and attend to the baby until it becomes clear what its needs actually are. Nor, when mindful, do we 'feed' our feelings with thoughts that explain or justify them, or lead into a narrative of what we must immediately do. A good mother does not hide her baby away where she cannot be disturbed by it. In the same way, a mindful person will not repress disturbing thoughts. Rather we give the pain space to tell its own story, and ourselves the space to respond to it intelligently rather than reactively. Hanh describes this spaciousness to move and grow as being like sunlight.

> Imagine a flower in the morning. The flower is not yet open. The sunshine embraces the flower, and the sunshine begins to penetrate the flower. The sun does not just go around the flower. The light naturally penetrates the flower, and an hour later the flower has to open itself to the sun. The sun is our mindfulness, embracing the flower of our feelings. (p. 51)

The spiritual fruit involved here is *agathosuné* – goodness or virtue of a persistent, robust, active kind, the steadfast loving-kindness which like the sun cannot avoid shining on good and bad alike (Matt. 5.45), whether in ourselves or in others. It relates closely to justice and impartiality. The 'mercy' described in the beatitude is this same loving-kindness, spacious, strong and liberating. As explored in Chapter 8 it is the root and fruit of right mindfulness.

Face

Blessed are the pure in heart, for they shall see God.

Throughout, but especially in Chapters 3 and 8, this book has stressed the importance of facing the hurt and harm we suffer, cause or participate in. The concept of 'facing' and the 'face' is profoundly important in connection with our theme. Theologian David Ford (1999) has built a whole theology around the theme of the face, and the following both develops his thought in relation to our concerns, and adds some thought of my own.

Faces can be beautiful, frightening, peaceful, angry, frightened, dreamy... Though emotions have their effect on the body (adrenalin, pace of heart and breath, sweat...) it is in the face that we primarily read them. It is that on the 'outside' of a person from which we can tell what is going on 'inside.' When we are ashamed of what we are aware of in ourselves, we hide our faces. When we depict evil, or holiness, how we draw or paint the face has a special significance. What depiction of evil is more haunting, more likely to give you nightmares, than the faces in Bosch's paintings of the mocked Christ (discussed in Chapter 4)? In the Orthodox icons, when a figure is depicted, like Judas or Satan, whose presence in the image is not desired, he is painted in profile so that his face will not be seen, whereas Christ and the saints are depicted face on. If we hate or despise someone we 'despise their image' (Psalm 73.20) and we may even 'deface' a picture or sculpture of them. The face, not the whole statue, was the main target of the puritan iconoclasts. There is something demeaning about depicting the body without the face or with the bodily parts rather than the face as the focus of attention, as in pornography. True erotic art, by contrast, subordinates the naked body to the desiring and desirable expressiveness of the face.

The Bible speaks of 'the face of the earth,' and creation itself happens by the moving of God's breath or wind over the 'face of the deep' and the 'face of the waters' (Gen 1.1). Even before anything had any *being* at all, it is as if there was a *facing*, a primordial encounter from which all being sprang. This encounter before creation is perhaps is one of the things the Christian doctrine of the Trinity is trying to express. The doctrine suggests to me that it was out of the primordial analogy of faces – the breath and word and perhaps the kiss of the mouth, the responsiveness of primordial ears, the sight of the first light – that all beings came to be. This cannot literally be the case, since faces and so forth are part of creation. But maybe this is how, as children face to face with mother, awareness of a real world around us first begins.

One of the dramatic things that has happened since space travel began is that it has become possible to see the whole 'face of the earth' in the image of the blue and white wonder that is now so familiar. As we have come to envision the possibility that the earth is a unified and self-regulating 'body' – Lovelock's 'Gaia' – the face of Gaia has begun to enter our deep imagination. Ecological invasions and exploitation of the earth can be seen as 'defacing' the earth. These ways of imagining and feeling the earth seem to me very important. I do not think they involve a pantheistic 'divinization' of the earth, or a pagan worship of the earth. When I delight in the faces of those I love, and desire not to see them defaced, nobody suggests I am worshipping them or treating them as gods!

But some ways of depicting the face do suggest an idolatrous divinization. In totalitarian regimes the face of the leader is characteristically displayed on every street corner and in every shop and office, filling the place left by the faces of the gods in pagan societies and Jesus and his sacred heart in many Catholic countries. The face is generally benevolent and kindly, like the Jesus of the sacred heart tradition, rather than penetrating and heart-searching as in the Jesus of the Orthodox icon. Nevertheless the message is that 'big brother is watching.' The benevolence is conditional on obedience to the state and its laws, and has its converse, guilt-inducing, conformity-enforcing side.

God is often presented as the ultimate 'leader' of this kind, his benevolence sheathing a terrible wrath. On the other hand, the Hebrew God, when giving the law to Moses, *hid* his face, allowing only his back to be seen (Exod. 33.12–23). Was it perhaps that the vision of the divine face in the context of the giving of the divine law would be overpowering and crushing? Was the face-to-face contact avoided in order to save the people from feeling shamed and condemned in their failure to keep the law, so that the keeping of the law could remain free and not totalitarian? Certainly in one Hebrew tradition it was thought impossible to see God face to face and live.

On the other hand a major aspiration in the Psalms is to see God's face. We read, 'Do not hide Your face from me in the day of my distress,' (Psalm 102.2, sung as a plaintive refrain throughout Orthodox Lent) and, 'As for me, I shall behold Your face in righteousness; I will be satisfied with Your likeness when I awake,' (Psalm 17.15). The goal of the Jewish and Christian mystics was the Beatific Vision in which God was seen face to face. As the beatitude cited above suggests, this was understood to require purity of heart. Generally it was thought impossible without the ultimate purification of death: 'when I awake' was understood to mean the ultimate awakening of death itself.

In line with these suggestions, my opening poem compares the experience of birth – when having been inside mother for nine months we actually see her face – with that of death, in which we see face to face the One in whom we have lived and moved and had our being all our life long. But this dying and birthing could be seen as a move we are called to make in every moment, from a dimly aware inhabiting towards clarity, in which we face both the hurts we have nursed within us and the love that has sustained us through them.

That is the facing that this book advocates. We need to 'face' evil. This does not mean confronting it aggressively. But it does mean refusing to turn our faces away and ignoring it, looking elsewhere in order to disclaim its reality. It means not holding our faces down in shame, unable to look evil in the face, so that it creeps up on us stealthily through our bodies and our actions. But it also means *giving* evil a human face. Or rather, giving back to the person who does evil their human face, in place of the alien and monstrous faces we imagine when we scapegoat people. For evil has no face of its own. It exists only as a distorting or a defacing or a sheer absence of the good that resides in the face. If we stand face to face with evil, neither fighting nor fleeing, it is forced to assume a more human face. It ceases to chill us with anonymous dread.

I have suggested that this is what Hallowe'en is about (2008, p.159–60). When children put on masks that are caricatures of evil monsters and demons, they give evil a quasi-human face they can play with and laugh at. The vague spiritual chill we all feel at the frosty days, the long dark evenings and the dying of summer's life and light, gives way to a carnival in which we laugh at evil and dance with death, because the evil is focused in a face we can face.

I remember once seeing God depicted in a cartoon as a splendidly robed figure on a throne, but where the facial features should have been there was nothing. I felt at the time that this figure – so full of faceless power but lacking in any human feeling – was a depiction of evil. To worship such a figure would be to worship faceless power, to worship evil.

By contrast, one way of overcoming evil is to welcome it into face to face communion. I once heard of a nun who was attacked in a subway by a man who tried to rape her. But she persisted in talking to him as an ordinary person, and eventually succeeded in inviting him home for breakfast! Her humanity broke into the faceless obsessions that had taken hold on him, until he could no longer continue in his fantasy world but had to succumb to the human world. She refused to be the body he wanted to invade, and insisted on remaining a person 'astride her humanity,' neither fighting nor fleeing, which were the responses his perversion depended on. The subhuman mechanism in him was subverted by her determination to address the whole person he was.

To do this required exceptional spiritual strength and self-possession. It is not the way most people would be able to deal with rapist attacks. Just as it is only the pure in heart who can see God, so it takes great purity of heart to face those who attack us and to see and address the divine image in them. It is not always possible to overcome evil by greeting it face to face, thus personalizing and humanizing it. But it is only ever possible to overcome it by these means.

This happens when those demonized as terrorists are welcomed to the conference table. Often this strategy is rejected as it is thought to imply making concessions, but the primary agenda is not to concede but simply to meet others as fellow human beings, and overcome stereotypes. Part of the reason why Mo Mowlem was so successful in laying the foundations for peace in Northern Ireland was surely her contagious earthy humanity and humor, her tough refusal to play the pious power games of the various factions, and her gradual build-up of shared human warmth across the divide.

To look evil in the face is to force it out of being evil. A face has a mouth, ears and eyes. When we give the terrorist or rapist or murderer these features, we allow him to have a voice to speak with, ears to hear the cries of those he has hurt, and eyes to have a vision which may be wholly alien to ours, but which can be shared and built on.

A terrorist, like a rapist, has become locked in deeply negative and destructive ways of responding to harm. But that does not mean he has no true perceptions, and has nothing to say to us, especially about the ways in which we ourselves have been negative and destructive. To those in power, who have responsibility for maintaining order, it is easy to disclaim the harm done in our name as the necessary price of fulfilling this responsibility. The violence of the terrorist is more naked, obvious and shocking, but not always actually more intensive and relentless than the routine violence of those in power. Compare, for example, the death toll resulting from Palestinian 'terrorist' aggression with the deaths caused by Israeli bombs and military operations in the name of 'protecting' its citizens. (The Wikipedia article *Israeli-Palestinian Conflict* estimates 1540 Israelis killed compared with 7506 Palestinians between 1987 and 2010.)

Nor is it the case that if we refuse to listen to the terrorist's voice and perspective, he will begin to see how wrong his response has been. Quite the reverse, as Thich Nhat Hanh urges:

> My experience with several wars in Vietnam has led me to the firm belief that terrorism cannot be removed by force and that deep listening is more powerful than bombs. Terrorism is born from wrong perceptions... If we know how [terrorists] think, we can help them remove these wrong perceptions. (2007, p. 162)

It is by giving the terrorist a voice and a face that each of us may begin to discern what we need to hear from the other, both negatively in terms of wrong perception and positively in terms of vision, so that some idea of a *common* good may begin to present itself.

But the same applies to the 'terrorists' in us, the parts of us that have become evil through festering without a face or a name. When in *vipassanā* meditation we attend to an unnamed pain in our bodies or emotions, we do not think about that pain or reflect on it or ask where it comes from or what it means; we let it have its own 'face' and its own 'voice' so as to welcome it back into the parliament of the soul.

The spiritual fruit that accompanies this kind of facing is love (*agapé*). In Buddhist and Christian terms this is more than our natural love of those who love us. It is *agapé,* love of enemies, of the unloving and the unlovable: loving the other into showing a loving and lovable human face. Such love is certainly advocated and practiced in Buddhism (though generally expressed more cautiously as *ahimsa,* non-harm) and it is at the core of right action in the eightfold path.

Seek Healing Justice

Blessed are those who hunger and thirst for justice, for they will be filled.

We move from the interpersonal issues of peacemaking and reconciliation to those of establishing justice in society at large, and urge that there can be no real justice that is not healing justice as discussed in Chapter 9, built out of reconciliation and directed towards it. The beatitude urges us to yearn for this and depend on it as we yearn for and depend on food and drink: we need to be addicted to justice. But it also promises – against all who tell us to the contrary – that this dependency, this need, will be met. Justice will come, and there will be fullness, abundance.

A great many of Jesus' parables are about this kind of justice. From the parables themselves we can deduce that the mysterious term 'Domain (or Reign or Kingdom) of God (or Heaven)' is shorthand for a society where healing justice reigns. Many parables detail the radical forgiveness and reconciliation it requires. And in the parable of the vineyard workers (Matt. 20.1–16) we hear that the justice involved is not a meritocracy in which each gets what she 'deserves' from what she has contributed to society, but each receives the same generous amount. There is enough for all.

It is a utopian vision, perhaps, but one worth hungering for. And it is not impossible to practice that vision ourselves. At the heart of Buddhism, as of Christianity, lies the ideal of a non-discriminating generosity like that of the sun. We have seen how in meditation we are bidden to shine with the equitable sun of mindfulness on all our experiences and actions. In that sense justice in society is like a corporate mindfulness, in which harmed and harmers are heard, valued and loved into the whole. Of course that gradual process will not exclude but require acts of restoration and restitution to restore the balance the harmer has overruled. Jesus does not tell us that there are no debts, but he does urge us to cancel the debts owed to us, because the huge debt we owe God for life and being has itself been cancelled. Life as such is a free lunch, so we should not count the cost of our own hospitality!

The spiritual fruit involved creating and flowing from such justice is peace, *eirené,* which generally means a joining of that which was divided. The Hebrew term, *shalom,* has richer overtones of a shared abundance of life in which there is no need for conflict. Peace is emphasized in Buddhism too, of course, but with a different aspect: the inner peace that comes from right concentration or meditation. We have seen how vital meditation was in the Plum Village approach to healing justice, and healing justice can probably not be found without some form of spiritual focusing; all three communities discussed in Chapter 9 employed some form of this.

Believe – in the Impossible

Blessed are the poor in spirit, for theirs is the kingdom of heaven.

For many the world seems not abundant, but scarce and dwindling in resources, so that humans are bound to compete. The next precept involves *believing* that that is not the case; that shalom is a possibility. In reality scarcity is not a feature of the world as such. Enough is grown and produced to enable everyone to have a good life, free from the extremes of suffering. Scarcity is a self-perpetuating human myth: once people believe there is a shortage, they will hoard resources and fight for them, and the resulting inequalities and wars will mean many do suffer extremes of want.

So the crucial thing is to believe in what the evidence of the earth suggests, rather than what human history suggests: there is enough to go round. Believe that exploitation and inequality are not inevitable. Cut through and expose the narratives that suggest it is. Believe that though it is not possible for everyone on earth to consume as much food and energy as the average American or British person, a modest utopia is possible. With careful international co-operation, we could provide a reasonable home and education, enough energy to meet moderate demands, wholesome work and good food for everyone. So Colin Tudge (2004) urges us all to be eco-friendly gourmets.

David Mitchell's acclaimed novel *Cloud Atlas* (2004) consists of a series of stories nested inside each other. In most of them a hero manages, in situations of rather ghastly and sometimes petty oppression, to change the things just a little for the better. The story with which the novel begins and ends deals with the eradication of the Moriori people at the hands of the more powerful Maoris. The hero of this story, Adam Ewing, is slowly poisoned by a Dr. Goose, who pretends to be administering medicine. He is saved in the end by the last of the Moriori people, Autua. After he is saved, and taken to a hospital on Hawaii, Ewing reflects on the orphans he sees playing after school:

> After their studies are done, the children conduct their play in a beguiling babel. Sometimes, the more daring of their number brave the nuns' displeasure by scaling the wall & conduct a grand-tour above the hospice garden by means of the candlenut's obliging branches. If the 'coast is clear,' the pioneers beckon their more timid playmates on to this human aviary & white faces, brown faces, kanáka faces,

> Chinese faces, mulatto faces appear in the arboreal overworld… The orphans grin down at me, imitate monkeys, poke out their tongues, or try to drop *kukui* nuts into the mouths of snoring convalescents & do not let me stay mournful for very long. They beg me for a cent or two. I toss up a coin for dexterous fingers to pluck, unerringly, from the air. (p. 527)

A perfect picture of wily innocence! Ewing is prompted to reflect on what hope there is for these children, his son Jackson, and the world.

> If we *believe* that humanity may transcend tooth & claw, if we *believe* divers races & creeds can share this world as peaceably as the orphans share their candlenut tree, if we *believe* leaders must be just, violence muzzled, power accountable & the riches of the Earth & its Oceans shared equitably, such a world will come to pass. I am not deceived. It is the hardest of worlds to make real. Tortuous advances won over generations can be lost by a single stroke of a myopic president's pen or a vainglorious general's sword. A life spent shaping the world I *want* Jackson to inherit, not the one I *fear* Jackson will inherit, this strikes me as a life worth the living. (p. 528)

These words at the end of the long novel distil the core message that if we believe in peace and justice, they will come about; but if we lose that faith, they will not. Protestant Christianity teaches that we are 'justified' – made just – by faith; and indeed it seems to be our faith that justice will prevail that can make us just ourselves.

But such belief requires something akin to Frankl's 'tragic optimism.' It requires that the many injustices and hurts of this world have not made us cynical. Is this perhaps what that obscure phrase 'poor in spirit' means: the retention of a basic innocence; a refusal of negative despair, but also of the naïve optimism that cannot acknowledge patent injustice? Poverty of spirit requires us to remain empty and hungry until the kingdom of healing justice prevails. That involves the spiritual fruit of *faith* or trust: the ability to *believe* (stressed three times by Ewing) what many deem impossible. Buddhists describe this as right intention, the very beginning of the eightfold way. We have first to believe, and want, that all-pervasive suffering is not the end of the story.

Drops – to Fill the Ocean

Blessed are the gentle, for they will inherit the earth.

In *Cloud Atlas,* Ewing's father-in-law responds cynically:

> Sail to the Old World, tell 'em their imperial slaves' rights are as inalienable as the Queen of Belgium's! Oh, you'll grow hoarse, poor & grey in caucuses! You'll be spat on, shot at, lynched, pacified with medals, spurned by backwoodsmen! Crucified! Naïve, dreaming Adam. He who would do battle with the many-headed hydra of human nature must pay a world of pain & his family must pay it along with him! & only as you gasp your dying breath shall you understand, your life amounted to no more than one drop in a limitless ocean!
> (p. 528–9)

But in the final sentence of the book, Ewing reflects:

> What is any ocean but a multitude of drops?

The previous precept enjoined a bold and sweeping ideal; the present one shifts from the largest to the smallest of scales, and requires us to hold that vision in mind in the minutest detail of our lives. We must not be 'absent-minded' – professing lofty ideals that make no practical difference to our lives – but mindful of the goal in each and every moment. Only through a peaceful present can a peaceful future come about. In the oft-quoted words of peace activist A.J. Muste: 'There is no way to peace; peace must be the way.'

Jesus tells us to 'take... no thought for the morrow... Sufficient unto the day is the evil thereof,' (Matt. 6.34, Authorized Version). In the Lord's Prayer we move straight from the utopian – 'your kingdom come, your will be done on earth as it is in heaven' – to the ordinary day to day: 'give us this day our daily bread.' We are engaged in filling an ocean by moment-by-moment mindful drops. And there is time enough for that. Each act I do is small, but springs from a vast array of causes from the beginning of time, and extends to a vast array of consequences till the end of time. Buddhists call that array of causes and consequences karma, but Christians know too that in each moment the Kingdom may arrive, or be pushed away, by what I do.

To know this is to bear the spiritual fruit that is variously translated gentleness, meekness or *humility*, and which features in our beatitude. This concerns developing what Buddhists call 'right livelihood.' We might prefer the broader and trendier word, 'lifestyle,' which describes our ultimate beliefs as they work themselves out in the warp and weave of daily life. A humble and unpretentious lifestyle, and wholesome routines, form the royal road to the Kingdom. T.S. Eliot wrote that 'humility is endless' (*East Coker*, Part 2). If we never cease encountering hurt with drops of healing, the advance of goodness cannot be ended. The earth will become full of divine knowledge 'as the waters cover the sea' (Habakkuk 2.14).

* * *

I offer these 'precepts' and this book as another drop in that ocean so many long for. I hope it may make the world a fraction of a degree less anxious, cold, critical and wary; a fraction more gracious, graceful, generous and warm. In its woundedness, I pray that it may find wisdom.

Bibliography

Introduction

Ross Thompson, 2010, *Buddhist Christianity: A Passionate Openness*, Winchester: O Books

Don Cupitt, 2010, *Theology's Strange Return*, London: SCM. Quotation from extract in Church Times, 2 July 2010

Chapter 1

Joseph Butler, 1987, *Upon Resentment and Upon Forgiveness of Injuries* in W.E. Gladstone, ed., *The Works of Joseph Butler, Vol.2: Sermons*, Oxford: Clarendon Press

Terence Centner, 2008, *America's Blame Culture: Pointing Fingers and Shunning Restitution*, Carolina: Carolina Academic Press

René Girard, 2005, *Violence and the Sacred*, London: Continuum

G.S. Kirk, J.E. Raven and M. Schofield, 1983, *The Presocratic Philosophers*, Cambridge: Cambridge University Press

Lawrence Kohlberg, 1984, *The Psychology of Moral Development*, New York: Joanna Cotler Books

Alistair McFayden, 2000, *Bound to Sin: Abuse, Holocaust and the Christian Doctrine of Sin*, Cambridge: Cambridge University Press

Michael Pearn, Chris Mulrooney and Tim Payne, 1998, *Ending the Blame Culture*, Aldershot: Gower Publishing

Miroslav Volf, 2008, *The End of Memory: Remembering Rightly in a Violent World*, Grand Rapids: Eerdmans

Slavoj Žižek, 2008, *Violence*, London: Profile Books

Chapter 2

James Alison, 1998, *The Joy of Being Wrong: Original Sin Through Easter Eyes*, New York: Crossroad Herder

Marcella Althaus-Reid, 2004, *From Feminist Theology to Indecent Theology*, London: SCM

Morris Berman, 1989, *Coming to our Senses: Body and Spirit in the Hidden History of the West,* London, Sydney, Wellington: Unwin

Peter Brown, 1990, *The Body and Society: Men, Women and Sexual Renunciation in Early Christianity,* London: Faber and Columbia: Columbia University Press

J.M. Coetzee, 1999, *Disgrace,* London: Secker and Warburg

Joseph Conrad, 1994, *Lord Jim,* Harmondsworth: Penguin

E.R. Dodds, 1951, *The Greeks and the Irrational,* Berkeley: University of California Press

Mary Douglas, 2002, *Purity and Danger: An Analysis of Concepts of Pollution and Taboo,* London: Routledge

D. Finkelhor, 1994, *Current Information on the Scope and Nature of Child Sexual Abuse,* in *The Future of Children* 4 (2), p. 31–53

James Gilligan, 2001, *Preventing Violence,* New York: Thames and Hudson

Paul Goodliff, 2005, *With Unveiled Face: A Pastoral and Theological Exploration of Shame,* London: DLT

Donald Kalsched, 1996, *The Inner World of Trauma,* Hove and New York: Brunner-Routledge

Alistair McFayden, 2000, *Bound to Sin: Abuse, Holocaust and the Christian Doctrine of Sin,* Cambridge: Cambridge University Press

Martha Nussbaum, 2004, *Hiding from Humanity: Disgust, Shame and the Law,* Princeton and Oxford: Princeton University Press

Stephen Pattison, 2000, *Shame: Theory, Therapy, Theology,* Cambridge: Cambridge University Press

Marcus Pound, 2007, *Psychology, Psychoanalysis and Trauma,* London: SCM

Carla Van Raay, 2006, *God's Callgirl,* London: Ebury

Julia Whealin, 2007, *Child Sexual Abuse,* National Center for Post Traumatic Stress Disorder, US Department of Veterans Affairs

Rowan Williams, 2000, *Lost Icons*, London and New York: Continuum

Jeremy Young, 2007, *The Violence of God and the War on Terror*, London: DLT

Chapter 3

Sidney Dekker, 2007, *Just Culture: Balancing Safety and Accountability*, Aldershot: Ashgate

Terry Eagleton, 2010, *On Evil*, New Haven: Yale University Press

Heather Eliott, 2010, *Peering under the Hood: Be Friends with Children*, in *Church Times*, 5 January

Mary Midgley, 1984, *Wickedness*, London and New York: Routledge

Andrew Shanks, 2008, *Against Innocence: An Introduction to Gillian Rose*, London: SCM

D.P. Strachan, 1989, *Hay Fever, Hygiene, and Household Size*, British Medicine Journal 299 (6710), p. 1259–60

Angela West, 1996, *Deadly Innocence: Feminism and the Mythology of Sin*, London: Continuum

Rowan Williams, 2000, *Lost Icons*, London and New York: Continuum

Chapter 4

Hannah Arendt, 1994, *Eichmann in Jerusalem*, Harmondsworth: Penguin

William Blake, 1971, *Complete Writings*, Oxford: Oxford University Press

William Blake, 1970, *Songs of Innocence and Experience*, Oxford: Oxford University Press

Christopher Booker, 2004, *The Seven Basic Plots: Why We Tell Stories*, London and New York: Continuum

Terry Cooper and Cindy Epperson, 2008, *Evil: Satan, Sin and Psychology*, Mahwah: Paulist Press

James Gleick, 1988, *Chaos: Making a New Science*,

Harmondsworth: Penguin
William Golding, 2002, *Lord of the Flies*, London: Faber
Chaim Kaplan, 1999, *The Scroll of Agony: The Warsaw Diary of Chaim A. Kaplan*, Indiana: Indiana University Press
John Kekes, 1990, *Facing Evil*, Princeton, NJ: Princeton University Press
Aurel Kolnai, 2008, *Ethics, Value and Reality: Selected Papers*, New Brunswick: Transaction Publishers
David Mitchell, 2001, *number9dream*, London: Hodder and Stoughton
Mary Midgley, 1984, *Wickedness*, London and New York: Routledge
Adam Morton, 2004, *On Evil*, London and New York: Routledge
Arthur Schopenhauer, trans. E.F.J. Payne, 1969, *The World as Will and Representation*, New York: Dover
Angela West, 1996, *Deadly Innocence: Feminism and the Mythology of Sin*, London: Continuum
Elie Wiesel, 2008, *Night*, Harmondsworth: Penguin
Walter Wink, 1992, *Engaging the Powers: Discernment and Resistance in a World of Domination*, Minneapolis: Fortress Press

Chapter 5

James Alison, 1998, *The Joy of Being Wrong: Original Sin Through Easter Eyes*, New York: Crossroad Herder
Marilyn McCord Adams, 2006, *Christ and Horrors: The Coherence of Christology*, Cambridge: Cambridge University Press
Hannah Arendt, 1994, *Eichmann in Jerusalem*, Harmondsworth: Penguin
Karl Barth, trans. G.W. Bromiley and T.F. Torrance, 2004, *Church Dogmatics*, Edinburgh: T & T Clark
Terry Eagleton, 2010, *On Evil*, New Haven: Yale University Press
Matthew Fox, 1983, *Original Blessing*, Santa Fe: Bear & Co
Viktor Frankl, 2004, *Man's Search for Meaning*, London: Rider

Raimond Gaita, 2004, *Good and Evil: An Absolute Conception*, London and New York: Routledge
John Hick, 1968, *Evil and the God of Love*, London: Fontana
Claudia Koonz, 1987, *Mothers in the Fatherland: Women, the Family and Nazi Politics*, London: Cape
Vladimir Lossky, 1973, *The Mystical Theology of the Eastern Church*, Cambridge and London: James Clarke
Eric Osborn, 2005, *Irenaeus of Lyons*, Cambridge: Cambridge University Press
Philip Pullman, 1995–2000, *His Dark Materials* (Trilogy), London: Scholastic Press
Paul Ricoeur, trans. J. Bowden, 2007, *Evil: a Challenge to Philosophy and Theology*, London: Continuum
Pierre Teilhard de Chardin, 1975, *The Phenomenon of Man*, New York: Harper
Klaus Theweleit, 1989, *Male Fantasies Vol 2: Male Bodies: Psychoanalyzing the White Terror*, Cambridge: Polity Press
Arne Johan Vetlesen, 2005, *Evil and Human Agency: Understanding Collective Evildoing*, Cambridge: Cambridge University Press
Simone Weil, 2002, *Gravity and Grace*, London and New York: Routledge
Angela West, 1996, *Deadly Innocence: Feminism and the Mythology of Sin*, London: Continuum
Elie Wiesel, 2008, *Night*, Harmondsworth: Penguin
Slavoj Žižek and John Milbank, 2009, *The Monstrosity of Christ: Paradox or Dialectic?*, Cambridge, Mass and London: MIT

Chapter 6

Marilyn McCord Adams, 2006, *Christ and Horrors: The Coherence of Christology*, Cambridge: Cambridge University Press
Christopher Booker, 2004, *The Seven Basic Plots: Why We Tell Stories*, London and New York: Continuum
Stanley Cavell, 1976, *Must We Mean What We Say?* Cambridge:

Cambridge University Press

Terry Eagleton, 2003, *Sweet Violence: The Idea of the Tragic*, Oxford: Blackwell

Rita Felski, ed., 2008, *Rethinking Tragedy*, Baltimore, Maryland: John Hopkins University Press

Viktor Frankl, 2004, *Man's Search for Meaning*, London: Rider

Paul Hammond, 2009, *The Strangeness of Tragedy*, Oxford: Oxford University Press

George Harris, 2006, *Reason's Grief: an Essay on Tragedy and Value*, Cambridge: Cambridge University Press

Tony Harrison, ed., 1985, *The Mysteries*, London: Faber

Donald Kalsched, 1996, *The Inner World of Trauma*, Hove and New York: Brunner-Routledge

Walter Kaufmann, 1969, *Tragedy and Philosophy*, New York: Doubleday Anchor

H.D.F. Kitto, 1966, *Greek Tragedy*, London: Methuen

Laurence Michel and Richard Sewall, eds., 1963, *Tragedy: Modern Essays in Criticism*, Englewood Cliffs, NJ: Prentice Hall

Martha Nussbaum, 1981, *The Fragility of Goodness: Luck and Ethics in Greek Tragedy and Philosophy*, Cambridge: Cambridge University Press

Rudolf Otto, 2004, *The Idea of the Holy*, Whitefish, Montana: Kessinger

Louis Ruprecht, 2008, *This Tragic Gospel: How John Corrupted the Heart of Christianity*, San Francisco: Jossey-Bass

Sophocles, trans. E.F. Watling, 1947, *The Theban Plays*, Harmondsworth: Penguin

George Steiner, 1980, *The Death of Tragedy*, New Haven: Yale University Press

J.L. Styan, 1968, *The Dark Comedy: The Development of Modern Comic Tragedy*, Cambridge: Cambridge University Press

Enid Welsford, 1968, *The Fool: His Social and Literary History*. London: Faber

Chapter 7

James Alison, 2003, *On Being Liked*, London: DLT

David Bromwich, 1989, *A Choice of Inheritance: Self and Community from Edmund Burke to Robert Frost*, Cambridge, MA: Harvard University Press

Anthony de Mello, 1982, *The Song of the Bird*, Anand, Gujerat: Gujarat Sahitya Prakash

Raimond Gaita, 2004, *Good and Evil: An Absolute Conception*, London and New York: Routledge

Julian of Norwich, ed. Robert Llewelyn, 1980, *Enfolded in Love: Daily Readings with Julian of Norwich*, London: DLT

David Loy, 2001, *Healing Justice: A Buddhist Perspective*, at www.zen-occidental.net/articles1/loy2.html

Peter Matthiessen, 1979, *The Snow Leopard*, London: Pan Books

Solomon Schimmel, 2002, *Wounds Not Healed by Time: The Power of Repentance and Forgiveness*, Oxford: Oxford University Press

Ross Thompson, 2010, *Buddhist Christianity: A Passionate Openness*, Winchester: O Books

Carla Van Raay, 2006, *God's Callgirl*, London: Ebury

Miroslav Volf, 2008, *The End of Memory: Remembering Rightly in a Violent World*, Grand Rapids: Eerdmans

Rowan Williams, 2000, *Lost Icons*, London and New York: Continuum

Walt Whitman, ed. Justin Kaplan, 1982, *Complete Poetry and Collected Prose*, New York: Library of America

Chapter 8

William Blake, 1971, *Complete Writings*, Oxford: Oxford University Press

John Cowan, 2004, *Taking Jesus Seriously: Buddhist Meditation for Christians*, Collegeville: Liturgical Press

Thich Nhat Hanh, 2002, *Be Free Where You Are*, Berkeley: Parallax Press

Thich Nhat Hanh, 2007, *The Art of Power*, New York: Harper

Christmas Humphreys, ed., 1960, *The Wisdom of Buddhism*, London: Rider; also 1995, London: Routledge

Martin Laird, 2006, *Into the Silent Land: The Practice of Contemplation*, London: DLT and New York: Oxford University Press

Belden Lane, 1998, *The Solace of Fierce Landscapes*, Oxford and New York: Oxford University Press

Mary Jo Meadow, Kevin Culligan and Daniel Chowning, 2007, *Christian Insight Meditation: Following in the Steps of St. John of the Cross*, Boston: Wisdom Publications

Monks and Nuns at Plum Village, 2003, *How to Enjoy Your Stay in Plum Village*, Berkeley: Parallax Press

Sayadaw U Pandita, 2002, *In This Very Life: Liberation Teachings of the Buddha*, Somerville, MA: Wisdom Publications

Paul Reps, ed., 1971, *Zen Flesh, Zen Bones*, Harmondsworth: Penguin

Carl Rogers, 1951, *Client-Centered Therapy: Its Current Practice, Implications and Theory*, London: Constable

Paul Scott, 1979, *The Birds of Paradise*, London: Granada

Angela West, 1996, *Deadly Innocence: Feminism and the Mythology of Sin*, London: Continuum

Alfred N. Whitehead, 1985, *Process and Reality*, New York: Free Press

Rowan Williams, 2000, *Lost Icons*, London and New York: Continuum

Chapter 9

Dante Alighieri, trans. Allen Mandelbaum, 1986, *The Divine Comedy: Purgatorio*, New York: Alfred A. Knopf

John Braithwaite, 2002, *Restorative Justice and Responsive Regulation*, Oxford: Oxford University Press

John de Gruchy, 2002, *Reconciliation: Restoring Justice*, London: SCM

W. Y. Evans-Wentz, trans., 1960, *The Tibetan Book of the Dead*,

Oxford: Oxford University Press

Rebecca French, 1995, *The Golden Yoke: The Legal Cosmology of Buddhist Tibet*, Ithaca, NY: Cornell University Press

Timothy Gorringe, 1996, *God's Just Vengeance: Crime, Violence and the Rhetoric of Salvation*, Cambridge: Cambridge University Press

M.L. Hadley, ed., 2001, *The Spiritual Roots of Restorative Justice*, New York: Albany University of New York Press

Mark Heim, 2006, *Saved from Sacrifice: A Theology of the Cross*, Abingdon

David Loy, 2001, *Healing Justice: A Buddhist Perspective*, in Hadley, see above; also at www.zen-occidental.net/articles1/loy2.html

Alistair McFayden, 2000, *Bound to Sin: Abuse, Holocaust and the Christian Doctrine of Sin*, Cambridge: Cambridge University Press

John Sanders, ed., 2006, *Atonement and Violence: A Theological Conversation*, New York: Abingdon

Jarem Sawatsky, 2009, *The Ethic of Traditional Communities and the Spirit of Healing Justice*, London: Jessica Kingsley

Jay Scott, 1983, *A Castro Cast-off Cut from Cardboard Scarface: The Scuzziest of Them All*, in *Globe and Mail*, Toronto, December 9

Miroslav Volf, 2008, *The End of Memory, Remembering Rightly in a Violent World*, Grand Rapids: Eerdmans

J. Denny Weaver, 2001, *The Nonviolent Atonement*, Grand Rapids: Eerdmans

Martin Wright, 1991, *Justice for Victims and Offenders*, Milton Keynes: Open University Press.

Howard Zehr, 1990, *Changing Lenses: A New Focus for Crime and Justice*, Scottdale, PA: Herald Press

Howard Zehr, 2002, *The Little Book of Restorative Justice*, Intercourse, PA: Good Books

Chapter 10

David Ford, 1999, *Self and Salvation: Being Transformed*, Cambridge: Cambridge University Press

David Mitchell, 2004, *Cloud Atlas*, London: Hodder and Stoughton

Ross Thompson, 2008, *Spirituality in Season*, Norwich: Canterbury Press

Colin Tudge, 2004, *So Shall We Reap: What's Gone Wrong with the World's Food – and How to Fix it*, Harmondsworth: Penguin

Walter Wink, 1992, *Engaging the Powers: Discernment and Resistance in a World of Domination*, Minneapolis: Fortress Press

Index

Only the main text is indexed, not the chapter summaries or bibliography.